FEDERICO FELLINI

Painting in Film, Painting on Film

Federico Fellini professed a desire to create "an entire film made of immobile pictures." In this study, Hava Aldouby uses this quotation as a launching point in her analysis of Fellini's films as sequences of "pictures" that draw extensively on fine art, and particularly painting, as a reservoir of visual imagery. Aldouby employs an innovative approach that allows her to uncover a wealth of connections and conclusions overlooked by Fellini scholars over the years.

Federico Fellini: Painting in Film, Painting on Film examines the links between Fellini's films and the works of various artists, from Velázquez to Francis Bacon, by identifying references to specific paintings in his films. Using new archival evidence from Fellini's private library, Aldouby sheds light on Fellini's in-depth knowledge of art history and his systematic use of art-historical allusions.

HAVA ALDOUBY lectures in the School of the Arts in the Faculty of Humanities at the Hebrew University of Jerusalem.

Federico Fellini

Painting in Film, Painting on Film

HAVA ALDOUBY

UNIVERSITY OF TORONTO PRESS
Toronto Buffalo London

© University of Toronto Press 2013
Toronto Buffalo London
www.utppublishing.com

ISBN 978-1-4426-4516-5 (cloth)
ISBN 978-1-4426-1327-0 (paper)

Publication cataloguing information is available from Library and Archives Canada

This book was published with the support of the Israel Science Foundation, the Research Committee at the Faculty of Humanities, Hebrew University of Jerusalem, the Robert H. and Clarice Smith Center for Art History at the Hebrew University, and the Fund for Promotion of Publication of Books of the VP for Research, Bar-Ilan University.

University of Toronto Press acknowledges the financial assistance to its publishing program of the Canada Council for the Arts and the Ontario Arts Council.

 Canada Council for the Arts   Conseil des Arts du Canada

University of Toronto Press acknowledges the financial support of the Government of Canada through the Canada Book Fund for its publishing activities.

In loving memory of my parents
Naftali and Shulamit (Ibby) Gellis

Contents

List of Illustrations ix

Acknowledgments xi

Preface xv

1 Fellini, Painting on Film 3

2 *Giulietta degli spiriti*: Symbolist Virgins Meet Decadent *Femmes Fatales* in Art Nouveau Interiors 22

3 *Toby Dammit*: Rembrandt Meets Velázquez on Screen 52

4 *Fellini Satyricon*: Bruegel Meets Klimt in the Sewers of Imperial Rome 85

5 *Fellini's Casanova*: Casanova Meets de Chirico on Böcklin's Isle of the Dead 111

Conclusion
"A New Hypothesis of the Truth": Painting as Vehicle of the Real in Fellini's Films, 1960s–1970s 131

Notes 135

Bibliography 163

Index 179

List of Illustrations

2.1 *Giulietta degli spiriti*. Laura's drowned body appears in Giulietta's hallucination.
2.2 Gaetano Previati, *The Funeral of a Virgin*, 1895.
2.3 John Everett Millais, *Ophelia*, 1852.
2.4 Federico Faruffini, *Sacrifice of a Virgin to the Nile*, 1865.
2.5 Enrico Guazzoni, *La Sposa del Nilo*, 1911.
2.6 *Giulietta degli spiriti*. Red-haired *femme fatale*.
2.7 Aubrey Beardsley, *The Dancer's Reward*.
2.8 *Giulietta degli spiriti*. Giulietta in the claustrophobic room.
2.9 Max Ernst, *The Master's Bedroom*, 1920.
3.1 *Toby Dammit*. "Butchered meat" shot.
3.2 Rembrandt van Rijn, *Slaughtered Ox*, 1655.
3.3 Francis Bacon, *Three Studies for a Crucifixion*, March 1962 (detail).
3.4 *Fellini's Roma*. A butcher shop window.
3.5 *Toby Dammit. Bambina diavolo*.
3.6 Diego Velázquez, *Las Meninas*, 1656 (detail).
3.7 Pier Paolo Pasolini, *Che cosa sono le nuvole*.
4.1 *Block-notes di un regista*. Contemporary Roman butchers and imperial Roman busts.
4.2 *Fellini Satyricon*. "The unfortunate hero of the battle at Quadragesimo."
4.3 *Fellini Satyricon*. A Bruegelian cripple featured in the Hermaphrodite scene.
4.4 *Fellini Satyricon, insula felicles*.
4.5 *Fellini Satyricon*. Trifena.
4.6 Gustav Klimt, *Judith*, 1901.
4.7 *Fellini Satyricon*. Minotaur.

4.8 Pablo Picasso, *Minotaur*, 1933.
4.9 *Fellini Satyricon*. High-angle shot of the labyrinth.
4.10 Fabrizio Clerici, *Pomeriggio à Cnosso (Afternoon in Knossos)*, 1967.
5.1 *Fellini's Casanova*. Shot of Casanova's bedpost.
5.2 Giorgio de Chirico, *The Enigma of the Oracle*, 1909–10.
5.3 *Fellini's Casanova*. Casanova in the company of mannequins.
5.4 *Fellini's Casanova*. A mysterious boat approaches the Isoletta di San Bartolo.
5.5 Fabrizio Clerici, *Latitudine Böcklin (Böcklin Latitude)*, ca. 1979

Acknowledgments

This book arises from my long-term engagement with Fellini's oeuvre. Along the way I have benefited from the advice and support of several people, to whom I feel indebted and immensely grateful.

My first academic encounter with Fellini's films took place at a Hebrew University seminar taught by Yehuda Moraly, later to become coadvisor on my PhD. My thanks go to him for igniting my scholarly interest in the infinitely rich body of work which is Fellini's oeuvre. I am grateful for having had the opportunity to share thoughts and insights with him over many years, first as a student and then as a colleague. His tutoring, enhanced by constant support and encouragement, was invaluable to the evolution of my work.

My research and writing have gained immensely from the close critical reading, extensive remarks, and academic guidance offered by Haim Finkelstein of Ben-Gurion University. A senior art historian, and coadvisor on my PhD, his suggestions were crucially important, always opening up new directions for thought. His contribution was decisively important for the formation of my work, brought to fruition in this book.

At the Hebrew University I wish to thank Edwin Seroussi for several discussions, which afforded a chance to evolve thoughts and ideas in an intellectually stimulating environment. His support, as chair of the School of the Arts at the Faculty of Humanities, made possible the realization in 2011 of an international symposium, "Fellini – Between Life and Fantasy," with distinguished keynote speakers Ingrid Rossellini and Peter Bondanella. It is a pleasure to thank Manuela Consonni of the Department of Romance and Latin American Studies for her major role in organizing and coordinating this symposium.

I feel extremely privileged to have received critical input from two major North American scholars of Italian film, Peter Bondanella and Millicent Marcus. Peter Bondanella, definitely the senior expert on Italian cinema, and specifically on the cinema of Federico Fellini, kindly agreed to meet a junior scholar who came to Bloomington to mine the collection of Fellini manuscripts which he had obtained for the Lily Library of Rare Books at Indiana University. Since then he has been extremely generous in providing helpful information, critical feedback, and friendly advice. First and foremost, my work has benefited from his reading of my texts at various stages of their formation. I am profoundly grateful for his firm support, which has helped this book come into being.

I am greatly indebted to Millicent Marcus, of Yale University, for her detailed critical remarks, resulting from close reading of my text at various points of its evolution. Her contribution to the evolution and realization of this book is immense. I deeply value her ongoing interest in my work, and support thereof. I have gained a lot from the occasions when I could share my research interests with her in person. My profound thanks go to her for her enlightening remarks, her encouragement, and her friendship.

In Italy I have been assisted by Gianfranco Angelucci, Fellini's scriptwriter and collaborator, and head of the Fellini Foundation in Rimini at its initial phase. Thanks to his cooperation I was granted access to the huge corpus of Fellini's private library, yet uncatalogued at the time. Always ready to answer my every question, he provided invaluable information and important contacts, which enabled me to interview key figures of Fellini's career. The research presented in this book owes significantly to his assistance.

I consider myself fortunate to have had the opportunity to interview Tullio Kezich, Fellini's biographer and lifetime friend, who is not with us anymore. The late Rinaldo Geleng, painter, collaborator, and close friend of Fellini's, generously shared his knowledge of Fellini's creative process and art-historical interests with me. Set and costume designer Piero Tosi kindly granted me an interview, and at the Fellini Foundation I was assisted at a later stage by Giuseppe Ricci, who granted me permission to examine part of the content of Fellini's library when it was not easily accessible.

At a very early phase of my work I decided to follow in Fellini's steps and visit Carl Gustav Jung's Tower on Lake Zurich. I am grateful to my host on that visit, Jung's grandson Niklaus Baumann, who guided me through the place and shared some valuable information regarding Fellini's contacts with the Jung family.

I thank Avi Bauman and Yael Bauman, of the Israel Institute of Jungian Psychology, for reading and commenting on an earlier essay in which I offer a Jungian reading of Fellini's imagery. Part of this essay has been incorporated into this book.

Milly Heyd, of the Hebrew University, supervised my PhD at its initial stages, as well as earlier work on Fellini's drawings. I am indebted to her critical insights and important suggestions during the early phase of my work.

My research owes a lot to the efficient and friendly assistance of Wendy Ben-Haim, theatre and media librarian at the Hebrew University, who obliged my every wish for media materials, whether electronic or printed, before I even had a chance to name them.

At University of Toronto Press, Ron Schoeffel kindly and professionally guided me through the production of my first book. I deeply regret that he is not with us any more to see it brought to fruition in print. I thank David Zielonka for the thorough editing of my manuscript, and Ani Deyirmenjian for taking professional care of the images.

Research at the Fellini Foundation in Rimini, and the Lily Library of Rare Books at Indiana University, Bloomington, was made possible thanks to travel grants awarded by the Robert H. and Clarice Smith Center for Art History at the Hebrew University.

The publication of this book is made possible with the help of publication grants awarded by the Israel Science Foundation, the Research Committee at the Faculty of Humanities, Hebrew University of Jerusalem, the Robert H. and Clarice Smith Center for Art History at the Hebrew University, and the Fund for Promotion of Publication of Books of the VP for Research, Bar-Ilan University.

Last but not least, my thanks go to my family. I thank my children for their patience at all times, and Yanir, my lifetime companion, for his love and support. This book could not have been completed if not for his untiring encouragement and assistance. This book is dedicated to my beloved parents, Naftali and Shulamit (Ibby) Gellis, holocaust survivors, who contributed to the establishment of the state of Israel, a safe haven for their offspring. Their profound commitment to life and achievement has been my inspiration.

Preface

"A film made of fixed, immobile pictures," is how Fellini envisioned his *Satyricon* in *Fare un film*, his eclectic collection of notes and reflections.[1] In Fellini's idiom, "pictures" are primarily paintings, as further reading in *Fare un film* makes clear. *Fellini Satyricon*, as conceived by Fellini, is "a contamination of the Pompeian with the Psychedelic, of Byzantine with Pop art, of Mondrian and Klee with barbaric art."[2] These lines cannot be read as anything but a formulation of what for Fellini was the quintessential film – a series of "pictures" evoking an eclectic array of art-historical intertexts.

In his writings, Fellini relies time and again on art-historical reference, particularly when the need arises to describe childhood impressions, or generally convey the atmosphere of a scene. "When I think of Gambettola," he writes, reminiscing about the grotesque population of his grandmother's village, "Hieronimus Bosch always comes to mind."[3] And elsewhere in *Fare un film* Fellini invokes "the pig-castrators, with the sharp knives hung around their belly, as in Bruegel's paintings."[4]

And yet, when I set out to chart the network of art-historical evocations in Fellini's films, all of my interviewees – and the list includes the late Rinaldo Geleng, Fellini's long-time personal friend and associate, and a highly acknowledged portraitist, as well as Fellini's biographer, the late Tullio Kezich, Gideon Bachmann, a journalist who had been close to Fellini during the late 1960s, and Piero Tosi, Fellini's set and costume designer in a couple of 1960s films – all of these prominent authorities on Fellini's cinematic practice insistently rejected the idea that his idiom might involve an underlying, art-historically informed matrix.

It was designer Piero Tosi, however, who incidentally provided me with a most significant clue, or indication of the extent to which the visual arts were indeed involved in the evolution of Fellini's cinematic text(ure). One night during the filming of *Toby Dammit*, Tosi recalled, he received a late night call from Fellini. The sleep-deprived designer was required to prepare for the next morning's shoot a number of paper-bag hoods which, Fellini required, should be "in the style of Saul Steinberg," an American graphic artist active in Italy during the late 1930s.[5]

It had taken me years of interviewing to come by this tiny bit of information, presented fleetingly while talking about the maestro's tyrannical habits. Significantly, however, the overt reference to Steinberg means more than it discloses at first sight. Fellini's private library, now preserved in Rimini by the Fondazione Federico Fellini,[6] holds no less than four graphic novels by Saul Steinberg: *Il Labirinto* (published in Milan, 1961), *The Catalogue* (1962), *The New World* (1965), and *The Inspector* (1973), as well as two Steinberg catalogues dating from 1971 and 1987. Fellini's copy of *The New World* bears a dedication in Steinberg's handwriting, dated October 1965, indicating the two artists' personal acquaintance. The friendship between Fellini and Steinberg appears to have dated back to the end of 1938, when Steinberg, fleeing anti-Semitic persecution in his native Rumania, arrived in Italy and began to work as a caricaturist for the magazine *Bertoldo*, owned by the same publisher as *Marc'Aurelio*, the magazine at which Fellini was employed at the time. According to the recollection of Rinaldo Geleng, Fellini made Steinberg's acquaintance on one of the latter's visits to the offices of *Marc'Aurelio*.[7] Among Fellini's drawings one finds a considerable group of distinctly Steinbergian line drawings, which indicate an involvement with Steinberg's graphic oeuvre that outreaches mere personal friendship. The idea of having his characters wear Steinbergian paper bags, then, indicates an extensive knowledge of Steinberg's work, and what seems like a long-time preoccupation with it on Fellini's part.[8]

Tosi's offhand mention of the maestro's phone call, albeit seemingly a minor anecdote, sheds light on Fellini's deep engagement with the visual arts. In fact, close scanning of his private library reveals a recurrent pattern of acquaintance growing into close friendship with a number of prominent visual artists, among which one may count Hans Richter, Balthus, Leonor Fini, Roland Topor, and Fabrizio Clerici. I regard it as even more significant that although he did not have any formal education, academic or other, in art history (nor in any other academic field for that matter), Fellini's private library indicates extensive erudition in this field. In fact, a considerable number of volumes in this huge library address the visual arts, spanning Byzantine mosaics to surrealist painting via eighteenth-century Venetian painting, Goya, and the Douanier Rousseau. Even a brief look at this library, catalogued in 2007 by the Fondazione Federico Fellini in Rimini, suffices to render beyond doubt his serious interest in, and knowledge of, the vast cultural reservoir which constitutes art history.[9]

It is thus that Fellini's growing emphasis on visuality toward the mid- and late 1960s calls for a thorough understanding of precisely how painting is transmedialized – that is, incorporated into the texture of his films – and in what way it is made to participate in the cinematic experience.[10] What W.J.T. Mitchell has referred to as the "pictorial turn,"[11] occurring in critical thinking on the arts, has apparently not been fully implemented in the study of Fellini's films, or in cinema studies in general. Underlying the present study is thus a wish to introduce a "pictorial bias" into Fellini studies, by turning critical attention toward his extensive reliance on painting as a vehicle of visual communication.

"If a pictorial turn is indeed occurring in the human sciences," W.J.T. Mitchell asserts in *Picture Theory*, then art history will be facing a "challenge to offer an account of its principal theoretical object – visual representation – that will be usable by other disciplines in the human sciences."[12] This being the case, Mitchell continues, "[t]ending to the masterpieces of Western painting will clearly not be enough. A broad, interdisciplinary critique will be required, one that takes into account parallel efforts such as the long struggle of film studies to come up with an adequate mediation of linguistic and imagistic models for cinema."[13] In the present study I take on Mitchell's challenging propositions, attempting to merge linguistic and imagistic models, freely crossing disciplinary boundaries between classical art history, film studies, and critical theory, whereby I opt for a fresh comprehension of Fellini's incorporation of painting into the cinematic text.

Beyond direct treatment of Fellini's films, however, this study bears wider implications that pertain to the growing interest in and scholarship of the interface between film and the visual arts. In the first chapter I review the extant body of theoretical writing on this subject, and highlight a conspicuous lacuna in its treatment, or rather lack of treatment, of Fellini's "painting on film." This lacuna, it will be argued, reflects a wider problematic in this relatively young field of study, which needs to relate to a wider range of cinematic idioms, including those that do not conform to the theoretical framework in its current shape. While it addresses Fellini most specifically, my hope is that this book will make its modest contribution to the evolving critical discourse on transmedialization and interart relations.

FEDERICO FELLINI

Painting in Film, Painting on Film

Chapter One

Fellini, Painting on Film

Cosa avrei voluto fare con questo film [*Il Casanova di Fellini*]? Arrivare una buona volta all'essenza ultima del cinema, a quello che secondo me è il film totale. Riuscire cioè a fare di una pellicola un quadro.[1]

Federico Fellini

"Transforming film into [a] painting" is Fellini's idea of the "total film," as expressed in the citation that opens this chapter. Are Fellini's films, then, to be approached as veritable "painting on celluloid"? To what extent did he involve art-historical referencing in his creative process? And, is there a single critical method, or a single disciplinary outlook that can account for the transmedial cinematic form which seems to reflect the aesthetic standpoint he expressed? In the present chapter I pose and enlarge on these questions, offering some theoretical assumptions alongside well-established research findings, which introduce the reader into the multilayered, heavily tangled network that forms the signifying body of Fellini's cinema. The chapter will begin by introducing some archival and circumstantial evidence for Fellini's deep engagement with the visual arts, painting in particular, and will subsequently lay out the theoretical concerns of the present study, and its place within the wider context of the extant literature on the film/painting interface.

Let us thus begin with certain items found in Fellini's library, which disclose evidence of his active engagement with particular art-historical intertexts. A couple of scribbled notes found between the pages of a 1952 monograph on *Las Meninas* by Velázquez constitute a noteworthy example. On page 24 of this book, Fellini made a pencil mark beside a paragraph describing the visual traits of the Infanta Margarita, the royal child portrayed at the centre of Velázquez's painting. On a separate sheet of paper, Fellini translated the same paragraph from the original Spanish into Italian. Also inserted into the book were two sheets of paper onto which other portraits of the Royal Infanta by Velázquez had been pasted. This intriguing hint of Fellini's involvement with the seventeenth-century masterpiece is discussed at length in chapter 2.[2]

How is it, then, that the prominent critical view of Fellini's work locates his visual sources exclusively in the popular culture of comic strips, and the world of the circus and *varietà*? As it appears, Fellini had the cooperation of his close circle in cultivating the persona of a slightly puerile genius, alien to all sort of highbrow culture and intellectual theorization. Thus, for instance, a 1965 monograph by Brunello Rondi makes recurrent use of the terms "uncultivated" and "barbaric" in reference to the director and his creative process. In fact, Rondi employs the term "barbaric" no less than three times in the space of a few paragraphs in the introduction, where Fellini is represented as a sort of natural philosopher, one who "had never even leafed through a philosophy book."[3]

Admittedly, Rondi does indeed mention Bruegel, Bosch, and Rembrandt as Fellini's favourite painters. He does so, however, only to stress that these painters are to be regarded as mere "pictorial nourishment, *without explicit reference*."[4] However, Rondi's assertion that Fellini's cinema "is alien ... to pictorial re-elaboration"[5] is certainly unconvincing with regard to *Giulietta degli spiriti* (1965), which is the last film discussed in his monograph. As I show in this chapter, *Giulietta degli spiriti* discloses a visible shift toward pronounced visual intertextuality, in that it involves a considerable number of art-historical evocations.

Rondi's text could not have been published without Fellini's approval, given that the two were working closely together in those years. Fellini had clearly been involved, if indirectly, in the generation of this persona of an untaught genius, emphasizing his indebtedness to popular comic strips such as *Little Nemo*, *Happy Hooligan*, *Arcibaldo*, and *Fortunello*, grouped together with popular *varietà* theatre and the circus into the acknowledged body of Fellini's cultural and visual sources. Fellini's early career as a cartoonist probably contributed to this widely circulating view.[6]

Fellini's conspicuous absence from contemporary critical studies of the cinema-painting interface is thus unsurprising. And yet it begs an explanation. What I will be asking is whether Fellini's unique mode of transmedialization is essentially incompatible with contemporary theory, and thus requires an altogether different theoretical framework. It is apparently more than just Fellini's astute tactics of disorientation that are responsible for this amazing failure on the part of cinema-painting theory to recognize the central place of art-historical referencing in Fellini's oeuvre.

A brief review of the extant literature on the film/painting interface reveals an overall engagement with power-relation systems, whether social, political, or cultural. The participation of painting in filmic texts is conceived in terms of aesthetic, cultural, social, or even sexual Otherness, as in Jill Ricketts's reading of Pasolini's *Decameron*.[7] During the 1980s, critical writings on cinema and painting tended to highlight what they regarded as an Oedipal power struggle, where film engages painting as its "senior," culturally sanctioned medium. Scholars writing in this vein have coined theoretical concepts that foregrounded the hybridity inherent in all forms of transmedialization. A case in point is the *plan-tableau* ("painting-like shot"), conceived by Pascal Bonitzer around 1985, and the *picto-film* and *toile-écran* ("canvas-screen"), coined by François Jost at the outset of the 1990s.[8] Jost places strong emphasis on the temporary arrest of the filmic flow in *picto-film*s. For Jost, the dialectic of movement and stillness is central to the *picto-film*'s production of meaning.[9] Highlighting dichotomies of stillness and motion, flatness and depth, artificiality and "realness," Pascal Bonitzer, François Jost, Jean-Louis Leutrat, Antonio Costa, Brigitte Peucker, Angela Dalle Vacche, and Susan Felleman all pivot on "how film figures static visual representation in its texts, how it engages it, how it seeks to undo it and how, in the process, it defines its own modalities."[10]

In light of their distinct conception of film and painting as alien systems of representation posited in permanent clash, it is only to be expected that the critical works under discussion assign the film-painting hybrid a metadiscursive function. "[W]henever other arts are foregrounded within a film," Fredric Jameson writes, "what is at stake is always some implicit formal proposition as to the superiority of film itself as a medium over these disparate competitors."[11]

The idea that a power struggle is inscribed into the cinema-painting relationship is further elaborated in writings on film and painting of the 1990s and 2000s, which assume a distinct social bent, pivoting on social and gender power relations. This is best expressed in Laura Sager Eidt's more recent study, *Writing and Filming the Painting: Ekphrasis in Literature and Film* (2008). Beyond its contribution to the body of work on film and painting with its suggestion of a new taxonomy based on the concept of ekphrasis, Eidt's work presents the sociological bias mentioned earlier. Eidt focalizes her discussion, first, on the way in which "the insertion of works of art into a film functions as a self-referential comment on the film as a 'moving image,'"[12] and, second, on "[how] art function[s] in films to convey social or economic positions."[13] Thus, if Jost, Bonitzer, and Jameson were concerned primarily with how film features painting as its aesthetic Other, Eidt has a proclaimed intention of going beyond "questions such as how the various sign systems are interrelated within one medium," to concern herself primarily with issues of gender and social power-relations, which she finds encoded in film's representation of painting.[14] In so doing, Eidt follows in the footsteps of Mitchell, whose essay on "Ekphrasis and the Other," although it does not engage filmic ekphrasis directly, manifests the same bias that prevails in contemporary thinking on interart transpositions. Concerned predominantly with the social tensions encoded in the basic binaries of ekphrasis, in this case the formal opposition of "temporal" versus "spatial," Mitchell believes that beneath these dichotomies lie "our anxieties about merging with others."[15]

Surprisingly enough, and not insignificantly, none of the studies just reviewed take up Fellini's cinema as subject for discussion. The assumptions and theoretical formulations underlying these studies, so it appears, draw on a body of films which self-pronouncedly foreground the alterity of painting. It is thus Godard, Pasolini, Hitchcock, and Greenaway whose films recur as quintessential examples of the cinema-painting dialogue. *Passion* by Godard; *La Ricotta, Il Decameron*, and *The Canterbury Tales* by Pasolini; and *The Draughtman's Contract* and *A Zed and Two Noughts* by Peter Greenaway are recurrently taken up as subjects for analysis. And these films indeed mobilize various strategies to foreground formal and conceptual clashes between the modalities of film and painting. With *tableau vivant* – which for Brigitte Peucker epitomizes "representational hybridity"[16] – as their key trope, these films are expressly committed to an intellectualizing, self-referential examination of cinematic representation. The technicalities of transposing painting onto film are exposed via explicit discussions on production, lighting, and camera movement, as in Godard's *Passion*, to name but one example. This strain of films has various ways of marking painting as Other. Sudden arrest of motion, abrupt cutting between "painterly" and "cinematic" shots, marked tensions between surface and depth, split screens, marked passages from illusionistic colour to artificial palette, and rapid transitions from mundane or natural soundtracks to classical ("sublime") music constitute a few of the recurrent devices in the foregoing body of films. Contemporary theory conceives of these alienating devices as quintessential to the transmedialization of painting into or, rather, onto film.

Fellini's idiom, however, does not fit neatly into this theoretical frame of thought, in that it refrains from foregrounding hybridity, and eschews the pronounced formal clashes that are the hallmark of the films on which contemporary theory draws. Rather, Fellini privileges a form of cinematic enunciation which I would like to think about in terms of Bakhtinian *heteroglossia* and *dialogism*. Fellini interweaves painting and film into a richly textured fabric where cinema is nourished by painting, rather than engaging in aggressive appropriation of its cultural and social aura.

Bakhtin's terms for dialogic writing, spanning *heteroglossia, polyphony,* and *double-voiced discourse*, best describe Fellini's incorporation of painting into the fabric of film. In Bakhtin, *heteroglossia* refers to a multiplicity of languages, or voices, that resist the "centripetal forces" which marginalize the Other in the text.[17] In the chapters that follow I implement the Bakhtinian idea that true *heteroglot* utterance employs *"concealed form"* for incorporating diverse languages into a single text. For Bakhtin, heteroglot utterance rejects "the *formal* markers usually accompanying such form."[18] As I show in the discussion of four of his films, Fellini markedly refrains from the formal or structural compartmentalization of painting one finds in Pasolini's *La Ricotta*, or Godard's *Passion*, to name but two of the many cinematic endeavours which pronouncedly mark painting as cinema's Other. Fellini's idiom radically departs from this mode of marked differentiation. It is essentially *heteroglot* in giving rise to "new combinations of signs ... into innovative discursive formations," to adopt Franco Ricci's phrasing in his discussion of Italo Calvino and the ekphrastic treatment of Giorgio de Chirico.[19]

In other words, and this will be my central argument, Fellini does not conceive of painting as cinema's Other, nor does he formally alienate it. In Fellini, painting is conceived as a lead, a conduit, to film's foundational origins, in that it enables the emergence of novel signifying formations which augment its instinctual level of communication with the spectator.

It is precisely this disparity between Fellini's transmedial formations and the paradigmatic, self-reflexive forms of Pasolini, Godard, and others that informs contemporary theory, which may explain the fact that, apart from a few lines in Costa's *Cinema e pittura* and a few pages in Campari's *Il fantasma del bello*, theoretical writing in this field practically ignores Fellini's work. Fellini's idiom is indeed fundamentally incompatible with the basic paradigms of otherness and hybridity in contemporary theory. In exposing the essential incompatibility of Fellini's "painting on film" with contemporary thinking on film and the visual arts, the present study draws attention to the diversity of modes in which film transmedializes painting. This pregnant interdisciplinary field may thus open up to a fresh consideration of the role of painting in film experience. A wider outlook may thus be afforded on the interface between painting and moving-image art.

In "Ekphrasis and the Other," mentioned earlier, Mitchell outlines a tripartite structure which, he maintains, underpins the discourse on ekphrasis. Although he does not bring up cinematic ekphrasis in any way, Mitchell offers some insights that pertain to the present discussion of Fellini's cinematic ekphrases, if they may be so called. Beginning with *ekphrastic indifference* as one aspect of the proposed triadic structure, Mitchell highlights an inherent "commonsense perception that ekphrasis is impossible ... articulated in all sort of familiar assumptions about the inherent, essential properties of the various media."[20] *Ekphrastic fear*, Mitchell's second category, is "the moment of resistance or counterdesire that occurs when we sense that the difference between the verbal and visual representation might collapse."[21] Imbued with suspicion about transmedial relations, "ekphrastic fear perceives this reciprocity as a dangerous promiscuity and tries to regulate the borders with firm distinctions between the senses, modes of representation, and the objects proper to each."[22] *Ekphrastic hope*, in turn, represents a utopian aspiration for mutual reinforcement, a hope for "overcoming of otherness."[23] Beyond apparent differences, Mitchell believes, these three modes of discourse reflect a set of social and ideological concepts inscribed with anxiety vis-à-vis the possibility of merging with the Other.[24]

I would like to attempt a take on Mitchell's idea of ekphrastic "hope" and "fear", respectively, without conforming, however, to his socially inclined reading of ekphrasis. I will thus be taking some liberty with Mitchell's theoretical construct, in that I employ his concepts elastically, uncommitted to the concerns presented in the essay I have been quoting.

To begin with, I would identify ekphrastic fear with the tendency (manifest in Pasolini, Godard, Greenaway, and others) to foreground difference and promote clashes between the "painterly" and the "cinematic." Ekphrastic fear, which for Mitchell connotes "an attempt to repress, or 'take dominion' over language's graphic Other,"[25] applies to the idea, quoted earlier, that film's encounter with painting inevitably invokes a power struggle, whether aesthetic, cultural, or social. Ekphrastic hope, on the other hand, would be helpful in describing Fellini's mode, where transposition of painting, unmarked and smoothly interwoven into the cinematic texture contributes to the emergence of new possibilities for visual suggestion.

In thinking about ekphrastic hope, and the way it becomes manifest in Fellini's idiom, I propose to draw on the concept of intertextuality as evolved in the writings of Julia Kristeva, Roland Barthes, and of course Mikhail Bakhtin. Relying primarily on Kristeva and her psychoanalytically oriented concept of intertextuality, my discussion veers away from the cultural/sociological bias of the current film-and-painting discourse.

Albeit exploited to the point of banality, intertextuality and its related concepts are still extremely useful in theorizing Fellini's art-historical references. At the core of the matter lie Bakhtin's notions of *dialogism* and *heteroglossia*, discussed earlier, and his pervasive idea of *carnivalism*. That Fellini's idiom qualifies as carnivalesque goes almost without saying. His figures and settings; unstructured narratives of chaotic disarray; his style of pronounced visual excess, often referred to as "baroque"; and, finally, the heightened intertextuality of his middle and late films all qualify as essentially carnivalesque. As noted earlier, *dialogism* and *heteroglossia*, which for Bakhtin are essential to the *menippean* text, are highly applicable to Fellini's incorporation of painting into the cinematic text.

In the middle to late 1960s, Julia Kristeva expanded the concept of *dialogism*, coming up with the now widely used term *intertextuality*.[26] At the core of Bakhtin's theory of language, Kristeva maintained, lay the idea that "any text is constructed as a mosaic of quotations," vertically layered with traces of "an anterior or synchronic literary corpus."[27] In her theory of intertextuality, Kristeva adopts a psychoanalytical outlook, conceiving of intertextuality as "abandonment of a former sign system, the passage to a second via an instinctual intermediary common to the two systems."[28] In the major interview she gave to Margaret Waller in 1985, Kristeva reiterates this idea, asserting that "analysis should not limit itself simply to identifying texts that participate in the final texts, or to identifying their sources, but should understand that what is being dealt with is a specific dynamic of the subject of the utterance."[29] Reinstating the "subject of the utterance," eliminated earlier in Barthes's "Death of the Author," Kristeva posits a kaleidoscopic "subject in process," reflected in the text's essential plurality and fragmentation. Speaking in a plurality of voices, this disjointed subjectivity manifests itself in "fragments of characters, or fragments of ideology, or fragments of representation."[30] Thus, where Roland Barthes postulates the death of the author,[31] Kristeva, as Megan Becker-Leckrone puts it, "binds the speaking subject ... inextricably to the textual processes she describes, and vice-versa."[32]

Kristeva's reinstitution of the subject of the utterance undergirds my analysis of Fellini's intertextuality.[33] I will thus be thinking of Fellini's intertextuality as a more or less conscious practice, in which the author is either a wholly conscious agent or operates in "a half-light of agency where influence and intertextuality may swim together."[34] In the following chapters I will be asking what it is that makes the particular "creative subjectivity," generally referenced as "Federico Fellini," respond to specific art-historical intertexts, and how art-historical references function in his construction of cinematic experience. In the spirit of Kristeva, I will be particularly interested in the non-verbal, presymbolic stratum of cinematic communication. It is there, I hope to show, that painting reaches the height of its function in Fellini's films, heightening the potential for immediate, non-verbal suggestion.

Trying to tackle aspects of non-verbal communication in cinematic experience, I return to Kristeva, and to the concept of the *sémiotique*, a chaotic stratum of language rooted in the preverbal stage of early infancy.[35] The *sémiotique*, as elaborated in Kristeva's writing, enables articulation of "a sort of corporeal memory ... a reminiscence of the play of energy and drives – both destructive and pleasurable – experienced in the body with great intensity before the achievement of real and symbolic separation from the mother, of subjectivity."[36] I find this concept highly useful for theorizing Fellini's recourse to painting in the middle period of his career. As I show in the chapters that follow, painting is Fellini's primary conduit for the *sémiotique*, potently conveying, in Kristeva's words, "what representative and communicative speech does not say."[37]

To complete the discussion, I propose to wed Kristeva's *sémiotique* with Maurice Merleau-Ponty's phenomenological meditations on painting, particularly in "Cézanne's Doubt" and "Eye and Mind."

What makes the phenomenological approach to painting particularly pertinent to Fellini's work is the emphasis on embodied experience. As

Vivian Sobchack puts it in her phenomenological theory of film experience, "[w]hatever its specific structure, capacities, and sensual discriminations, vision is only one modality of my lived body's access to the world and only one means of making the world of objects and others sensible – that is, meaningful – to me."[38] "Vision," Sobchack elaborates quite figuratively, "may be the sense most privileged in the culture and the cinema ... nonetheless, I do not leave my capacity to touch or to smell or to taste at the door, nor, once in the theater, do I devote these senses only to my popcorn."[39]

Evoking a primal and "nonhierarchical unity of the sensorium," traces of which survive in synaesthesia, Sobchack postulates a spectator that is a "cinesthetic [sic] subject ... able to commute seeing to touching and back again *without a thought*."[40] Sobchack's "cinesthetic subject," for whom, I believe, Fellini intends his evocations of painting, is endowed with "an embodied intelligence that opens our eyes far beyond their discrete capacity for vision, opens the film far beyond its visible containment by the screen, and opens language to a reflective knowledge of its carnal origins and limits. This is what, without a thought, my fingers know at the movies."[41]

Sobchack's assertion that "perception is a *primordial structure* of encounter and engagement of the lived body with and in the world"[42] is particularly helpful when theorizing the aesthetic experience of Fellini's "painting on celluloid." I thus propose to return one step backward, to Merleau-Ponty, whose writings constitute Sobchack's proclaimed theoretical premise. In "Eye and Mind" in particular, Merleau-Ponty ascribes considerable primacy to painting as a conduit for primal experience. "Now art," he writes, "especially painting, draws upon this fabric of brute meaning ... Indeed we cannot imagine how a *mind* could paint. It is by lending his body to the world that the artist changes the world into paintings."[43]

In this last essay he had written, which was published posthumously, Merleau-Ponty considers painting as the site where a perceiving artist, immersed in his subject matter, meets an addressee in whom the artist's embodied perception is reconstituted, or relived. In this vein of thought, painting conduces to a heightened experience of the real, in that "[q]uality, light, color, depth, which are there before us, are there only because they awaken an echo in our bodies and because the body welcomes them."[44] Significantly, however, it is not merely the tactility of the paint but rather the sensation of embodied experience transposed onto canvas that enables a similar experience in the viewer, as close to the real as the original experience that prompted it. "Things have an internal equivalent in me; they arouse in me a carnal formula of their presence," writes Merleau-Ponty. "Why shouldn't these correspondences in turn give rise to some tracing rendered visible again, in which the eyes of others could find an underlying motif to sustain their inspection of the world?"[45]

I propose to bring Merleau-Ponty's phenomenology of painting, together with Sobchack's theory of embodied film experience, to bear on the function of painting in Fellini's cinematic works, where painting has the function of a lead, or conduit, to that "insurpassable [sic] plenitude, which is for us the definition of the real."[46]

To my knowledge, Fellini had not read Merleau-Ponty, although it is tempting to note the historical coincidence between the publication of "Eye and Mind," in 1964, and Fellini's emergent recourse to painting, beginning in 1965 with *Giulietta degli spiriti*. Whether this coincidence is attributable to a general notion of *zeitgeist*, or to Fellini's instinctual understanding of the "real-ness" of painting, is beyond the capability of the present research to determine. It will be my project, however, to show that Fellini makes recourse to painting whenever the need arises to face up to the crisis of the real in postmodernity. In these anxious moments, Fellini attempts to bridge the abysmal split between art and the real, by producing an intense, non-verbal, and highly embodied experience of what Merleau-Ponty calls the "zone of the 'fundamental.'"[47]

Appropriating the heightened suggestiveness associated with painting, Fellini mobilizes its capacity to involve the viewer in a holistic experience of the *sémiotique*, whereby the real – long lost in postmodernity – is reinstated in the cinematic text. "Art," Merleau-Ponty writes in "Eye and Mind," "is not construction, artifice, the meticulous relationship to a space and a world existing outside. It is truly the 'inarticulate cry' ... And once it is present it awakens powers dormant in ordinary vision, a secret of preexistence."[48] It is this power to evoke the "secret of preexistence" and share it with the spectator that Fellini seeks in the intermedial moments where painting is woven into film.

I am here in complete disagreement with a certain vein in recent studies of Fellini's works. These are perhaps best represented by Christopher Sharrett's conception of Fellini's overt intertextuality as frustration with "the artist's (increasingly ineffectual) ability to manipulate."[49] In fact, as analysis of individual films and their embedded art-historical intertexts will show, what Fellini reaffirms time and again is precisely the artist's "ability to manipulate." In Fellini's work, particularly of the period specified earlier, painting fulfils a role of origin, a core of "real-ness" whence the experience of meaning originates. In a way, then, Fellini plays the postmodern trope of intertextuality against the grain, employing contemporary form in the service of an essentially romantic project, which he never tires of pursuing.

What remain to be considered at this stage are the basic units of Fellini's intertextual fabric. Here I find Roland Barthes's concept of the *lexia* extremely helpful, in that it provides a concise definition for the basic unit of the intertextual network. In Barthes, *lexiae* constitute the atomic unit "in which a group of connotations are discovered within the signifier."[50] Figuratively imagined as a "minor earthquake," the *lexia* occasions an "explosion and scattering of meaning"[51] whereby the essential plurality of the text is maintained, preventing the formation of a single definitive message. I will be employing this term in relation to individual frames and short frame sequences, where several intertexts occasion "minor earthquakes" of art-historical reference.

A thought-provoking convergence may be pointed out between the post-structuralist conception of the text as a web of interlinked *lexiae* and the emergence of *hypertext* as a central concept in information technology.[52] George Landow defines *hypertext* as a network of "individual blocks of text, or lexias [*sic*], and the electronic links that join them."[53] The essential paradigm underlying *hypertext*, then, is network construction, constituted via electronic links that open up the text, through embedded *hyperlinks*,[54] to an inexhaustible number of related materials. The basic units of *hypertext* "take on a life of their own as they become more self-contained, because they become less dependent on what comes before or after in a linear succession."[55]

Intertextuality and hypertext, two late 1960s concepts of the text as plural and complex, thus converge at several points. George Landow emphasizes the way the two systems share the network paradigm. By pointing out the recurrence of hypertext-related terms such as "link," "network," "web," and "interweaving," in the writings of Bakhtin, Barthes, Derrida, and Foucault,[56] Landow convincingly argues that intertextuality and hypertext share a rejection of "conceptual systems founded upon ideas of center, margin, hierarchy, and linearity," for which they substitute "multilinearity, nodes, links, and networks."[57] Following Landow's proposed association of *lexia* and *hyperlink*, I will use these two terms alternately to define and label Fellini's art-historical signifying units.

To be more specific, the present study privileges analysis of individual frames, or very short frame sequences, as autonomous signifying units. Using video-editing software, I have been able to approach each film as a sequence of pictures, returning, one might say, to the genetic origin of the "moving pictures" medium. Although film viewing and film studies are more conventionally predicated on the individual shot rather than the single image as the basic unit of film aesthetics, the approach adopted here proves particularly effective in relation to Fellini's use of atomic visual units, overdetermined with art-historical references. Roland Barthes's notion of the film still as bearer of a "third meaning" is pertinent in this regard. Barthes rejects traditional notions of the still, or single film frame, as "a pornographic extract ... a reduction of the work by the immobilization of what is taken to be the sacred essence of cinema – the movement of the images."[58] Rather, Barthes proposes, the individual image, extracted from the cinematic flow, is a potent conduit for an emergent "third meaning," which "begins only where language and metalanguage end."[59]

In a 1991 essay, "The Film Stilled," Raymond Bellour meets Barthes's call for a comprehensive theory of the still. In this essay Bellour conceptualizes the nonmoving film image as an "irrational, unnamable fragment that fascinates."[60] In Fellini's oeuvre, I will be arguing, one can chart a rich network of images charged with art-historical echoes, which participate in the film experience as "unnamable fragments that fascinate." Precisely how each of these units constructs and communicates meaning will constitute the focal concern of this book.[61] This study thus calls upon Fellini studies and art history alike to "think beyond disciplinary boundaries," to adopt a proposal made by Eidt in her recent discussion of cinematic ekphrasis.[62]

Before embarking on an analysis of specific art-historical hyperlinks, I wish to return briefly to the question of periodization arising from the present study. The chapters that follow look at the network of art-historical references that emerges in the middle period of Fellini's career, roughly between 1965 and 1980. At the focus of attention are *Giulietta degli spiriti* (1965), *Toby Dammit* (1968), *Fellini Satyricon* (1969), and *Il Casanova di Fellini* (1976), although reference is made as well to *Fellini Roma* (1972). The group of films created between the late 1960s and late 1970s manifests an emphasized painterly slant, which distinguishes it from the rest of Fellini's oeuvre. The films in this group present a dense network of mostly implicit (although at times quite explicit) references to painting(s), of a sort that is absent, or is much less conspicuous, in the films Fellini made before and after this period.

My study thus takes *Giulietta degli spiriti* (1965) as a turning point in Fellini's oeuvre, based on its introduction of colour and with it an enhanced presence of art-historical reference woven into the cinematic text. Fellini's treatment of painting(s) before *Giulietta degli spiriti* and after *Intervista* may therefore serve as a foil to his middle period. Although Fellini makes occasional recourse to painting and paintings throughout his oeuvre, a notable change occurs between *Otto e mezzo* (1963) and *Giulietta degli spiriti* (1965), and then roughly between *La città delle donne* (1980) and *E la nave va* (1983). Both *La dolce vita* and *Otto e mezzo* feature paintings in conventional settings, framed and hanging on the wall in a mode that Eidt would refer to as "attributive ekphrasis."[63] In *La dolce vita* it is the famous Morandi, to which Mauro Aprile Zanetti has dedicated an entire volume (2008).[64] Notwithstanding the heightened self-referentiality of this trope, on which Zanetti elaborates quite convincingly, Fellini's introduction of the painting into the film does not signal a significant departure from traditional cinematic narration. Neither do the paintings hanging in the corridor along which young Guido is dragged by the furious priest in *Otto e mezzo*. These framed paintings do not in any way convey the sensual excess, or "wild meaning," that explodes in the art-historical *lexiae* of Fellini's subsequent films, beginning with *Giulietta degli spiriti*. Similarly, in *E la nave va*, Fellini seems to return painting to its domesticated place within the frame, as elegantly framed paintings hanging in the bourgeois interiors of the ship replace the excessively suggestive shots, overdetermined with art-historical evocations, of *Fellini Satyricon* and *Il Casanova di Fellini*. With painting re-framed, Fellini's later films signal a shift backward, from the language of the *sémiotique* to the more intellectualized, much less embodied modality which Kristeva has named *le symbolique*. It is thus possible to delineate a distinct period of heightened reliance on painting in Fellini's oeuvre, where the films are characterized by visual excess, expressly privileging the *sémiotique*. The present study opts to offer a new key to the dating and periodization of Fellini's oeuvre, based on changes in his mode of intermedial transposition.

While it is hardly possible to provide a definitive explanation for the occurrence of these significant shifts in Fellini's idiom, some assumptions may be made with regard to what caused, or triggered, these profound changes. Let me begin by noting that the emergence of post-structuralist theory is tangential to the appearance of enhanced art-historical intertextuality in Fellini's works. Fellini's middle period thus coincides – and this is significant – with the period of political and intellectual upheaval that gave rise to theories of intertextuality and hypertext, revolutionizing traditional conceptions of the text, and bearing far-reaching social and cultural implications. The political and cultural turmoil of that era is clearly reflected in the post-structuralists' emphasis on plurality and complexity as forms of resistance. Intertextuality, which pluralizes and multivocalizes the text, represented for the post-structuralists a carnivalistic form of transgression vis-à-vis the hegemony of "good" structure.[65] Kristeva's view of intertextuality is thus imbued with strong opposition to "the linguistic, psychic, and social 'prohibition'" embodied in the monologic concepts of "God, Law, Definition."[66]

The post-structuralists' endorsement of complexity and intertextuality as vehicles of resistance might have struck a responsive chord in a Fellini who often expressed his aversion to authority, owing to his early experience of fascist oppression coupled with religious and parental coercion. Alberto Farassino makes an interesting point in his discussion of Fellini's provocative "doodles" as acts of resistance. The director's expressed aversion toward state power, Farassino notes, assumed the curious form of scribbling over formal certificates such as his driver's license.[67] Fellini would thus be responsive to the conception of intertextuality as sociopolitically subversive, notwithstanding his proclaimed anti-intellectual stance.

One question which inevitably comes up is whether the historical coincidence pointed out here implies that Fellini was fully aware of, or intentionally engaged in implementing avant-garde ideas and forms. In other words, is Fellini's middle period directly informed by post-structuralism?

While this question may not be answered definitively, Fellini's unpublished shooting script for *Toby Dammit* (1968) presents a reference to the writings of James Joyce which helps reveal if not thorough acquaintance with poststructuralist theory on Fellini's part then at least a clear awareness of its focal ideas. Notably, Joyce's *Ulysses* was conceived by Kristeva and other post-structuralists as the epitome of intertextuality in avant-garde literature. *Ulysses* is widely referenced by Kristeva and in some cases also by Umberto Eco in their discussions of intertextuality. As Becker-Leckrone points out, the *Tel Quel* group and the French intellectual milieu employed the name (and term) "Joyce" as "a signifier for intertextuality, for the revolutionary poetics of the avant-garde, for a writing without repression and without end ... an expression of verbal *jouissance* in the face of abjection."[68] I thus deem most significant the following passage from the unpublished shooting script for *Toby Dammit*, where explicit reference is made to Joyce, and to *Ulysses* in particular.

Fellini's machine-typed manuscript, currently preserved at the Lily Library of Rare Books in Bloomington, Indiana, includes a scene that eventually went unrealized in the film. Neither is this scene included in the published script.

The omitted scene evolves as follows. Having landed in Rome, Toby Dammit, a stage actor in acute mental crisis, walks through the airport halls and passages, immersed in an air of overwhelming anxiety.[69] Having completed this ghastly course, "Dammit stops near the counter where the customs-officers open the valises. They rudely rummage inside. They open also Dammit's valise: inside there is only a bottle of Whisky and a copy of Joyce's *Ulysses*."[70]

Fellini's eventual omission of this explicit reference to *Ulysses* notwithstanding, it is clear that the central character of his film was originally associated with the highly intertextual masterpiece by James Joyce. Curiously enough, no copy of *Ulysses* is to be found in Fellini's private library, at least as it is preserved to date. This absence may be accounted for by Fellini's own remark that one did not need to have read Joyce's *Ulysses* to be aware of its widespread influence,[71] which is sufficient indication of Fellini's awareness as regards the centrality of Joyce in contemporary thinking. As Becker-Leckrone points out, for Kristeva and her intellectual milieu, "Joyce belong[ed] to the radical group of writers who most self-consciously produce[d] texts riddled by ... complex transpositional 'concatenations.'"[72] Fellini's explicit reference to *Ulysses* may thus be taken as a significant indication of his acquaintance with the essentials of the group's theoretical writing.

Fellini's remark may further indicate an acquaintance with the ideas and writings of Umberto Eco, where Joyce's works are referred to as the epitome of the "open work." As Peter Bondanella points out in *Umberto Eco and the Open Text*, it was Eco who introduced Joyce and his revolutionary writing to Italian intellectual circles, particularly through the publication of *Opera aperta* (*The Open Work*), published in Italian in 1962.[73] In "The Poetics of the Open Work," later translated into English in *The Role of the Reader*, Eco refers to *Ulysses* as a "major example of an 'open' mode, since it deliberately seeks to offer an image of the ontological and existential situation of the contemporary world."[74] Highlighting the chaotic structure, polyvalence, and multi-interpretability of Joyce's texts, Eco shows that one sentence in *Finnegans Wake* may suggest as many as six historical intertexts.[75]

Eco's writings thus emerge as a critical text which very probably informed Fellini's conception of cinema during the 1960s and onward. The fact that he envisioned a copy of *Ulysses* as his protagonist's sole possession, aside from the inevitable bottle of whisky, clearly indicates an underlying concept of film as a Joycean network of intertextual links.

In *Toby Dammit* we also encounter the grotesque Padre Spagna, in whose "Catholic western" Toby is to participate, mentioning "il mio amico Roland Barthes" (my friend Roland Barthes). "[B]ut you know, you understand with your artist's sensibility ... that a certain cinema of, let us say, structure, may render this sublime poetry with hard, elementary images ... Simple, syntagmatic frames, as my friend Roland Barthes would say ... something between Dreyer and Pasolini with a pinch of Ford."[76] And Padre Spagna proceeds to remark that the film should bring together "Piero della Francesca and Fred Zinnemann."[77]

While Bondanella regards this paragraph as "Fellini's grotesque picture of the state of Italian cinema,"[78] an instance of "merciless satire,"[79] I believe that it reveals more than mere satire of Italian cinema. As I see it, this paragraph indicates a profound shift in Fellini's conception of the cinematic text, toward Barthes's "multi-dimensional space in which a variety of writings, none of them original, blend and clash."[80] The question remains, of course, why it is that the reference to Barthes is assigned to the Padre Spagna character, the most ridiculous figure in the film. In fact, what is being challenged and satirized in Padre Spagna's lines is the requirement for a "cinema of structure," as in Barthes's earlier, structuralist phase. What Padre Spagna is suggesting, in obvious parody of the time's intellectualizing talk, is a rigidly linear or "syntagmatic" narrative, which produces an authoritative, monological message. Padre Spagna is a parody of a stiff "structuralist," so to speak. His ideas are diametrically opposed to the liberatory principles of post-structuralist thinking, where the text is never "a line of words releasing a single 'theological' meaning (the 'message' of the Author-God)."[81]

Fellini is in fact quoted in Giovanni Grazzini's *Comments on Film*, as saying that structuralism and semiology are "inevitable things which keep you posted on artistic and cultural conditions but deprive you of that uproarious and disquieting atmosphere, that somewhat savage joy that linked the cinema to the circus."[82] Fellini was thus clearly aware of contemporary literary theory, and the particular distinction between structuralism and its more flexible and liberated successor, post-structuralism. *Toby Dammit* presents precisely the kind of "uproarious and disquieting" cinema which the ridiculous clergyman rejects. While Padre Spagna is assigned the role of inflexible structuralist, Toby Dammit, the undisciplined actor and doubtless an alter ego of Fellini, travels with Joyce's *Ulysses* in his otherwise empty valise. In the final cut, while on the soundtrack we hear Padre Spagna rave about his "syntagmatic" film, on-screen we are presented with a succession of Toby's drug-induced visions. Fellini's film all but conforms to the priest's requirements. Toby Dammit is incapable of any structured utterance whatsoever owing to his unstable and fragmented subjectivity, embodies post-structuralist notions of complexity.

The fact is that Joyce's *Ulysses*, the epitome of intertextuality in post-structuralist writing, was about to become one of the focal signifiers in Fellini's *Toby Dammit*. This can hardly be ignored when considering Fellini's acquaintance with contemporary theory. In fact, can his description of the "Catholic western" as an amalgam of "Dreyer and Pasolini with a pinch of Ford [...] Piero della Francesca with Fred Zinnemann"[83] be considered anything but a vision of film as an intertextual construct?[84]

I will thus be thinking about Fellini's middle period as informed to a great extent by avant-garde notions of complexity and mulitivocality. In the period delineated earlier – which appears to have exhausted itself around 1980 – Fellini's cinematic language was shifting toward multilayered, intertextual construction, in which art-historical *hyperlinks* played a pivotal role.

The question still remains, why it is painting in particular that occupies such a focal position in Fellini's intertextual matrix in these years, and what could have triggered this occurrence.

While this question is not easy to answer, I would like to risk an assumption based again on a historical coincidence. In or around 1960, Fellini became involved in a therapeutic and intellectual relationship with Ernst Bernhard, a disciple of C.G. Jung and a prominent Jungian analyst, then residing in Rome. Not only did Fellini undergo Jungian therapy with Bernhard, a fact which he never admitted,[85] but he was introduced to Jungian literature and its rich visual imagery by the same Bernhard.[86] Fellini's private library holds a considerable number of Jungian volumes. He began keeping detailed dream notebooks,[87] and is known to have made a pilgrimage to Jung's "tower" on the shore of Lake Zurich, where he would have seen the wall paintings in Jung's own hand.[88] Fellini was even admitted into the "secret room," which is allegedly painted all over and to which the entrance remains prohibited by the Jung family to this day.[89]

While the crucial role that Jungian psychology played in Fellini's shift to dream narratives has been widely acknowledged,[90] I propose to consider the particular role of the rich visual imagery in the Jungian literature in inducing Fellini's growing reliance on "pictures" as an effective mode of communication. I wish to refer in particular to one Jungian volume, *Man and His Symbols*, published in 1964. Fellini owned a copy of this illustrated volume, which was Jung's last project before he died and is essentially a popular account of Jungian psychology, realized in collaboration with three of his closest disciples.[91] The excessive illustration of *Man and His Symbols* reflects the primacy of visual imagery in C.G. Jung's writing and thinking. *Man and His Symbols* is practically stuffed with an eclectic choice of photographs and paintings, from Pompeian wall paintings to Paul Klee's watercolours, through Piero della Francesca, Rubens, and de Chirico, not to mention Navaho sand paintings.[92] An entire chapter of this book (out of a total of five) is dedicated to the subject of visual art. The unconscious, *Man and His Symbols* seems to say, speaks first and foremost through pictures. The visual arts, like dreams, are thus conceived as its vehicle of communication.

The fact that *Man and His Symbols* dedicates the same space to the visual arts as it does to dreams is indicative of an essential association between these two visual media, an idea to which Fellini would have been highly responsive given his deep engagement with dreams. Painting would thus emerge as the medium closest to dreams, particularly in light of the extensive attention it is accorded in *Man and His Symbols*.

Notably, it is in the height of Fellini's engagement with Jung that we encounter in his work a growing recourse to painting. This coincidence is thought-provoking, to say the least, although one must acknowledge that Fellini had an interest in the visual arts long before 1960. He was a practicing graphic artist since the age of eighteen, and his private library holds art-historical monographs that predate *Man and His Symbols* by a decade or so.[93] However, Fellini's early graphic work may distinctly be associated with comic strip aesthetics, and his films do not seem to engage masterpieces of painting significantly before *Giulietta degli spiriti*. Fellini's immersion in the visual wealth and conceptual framework of Jungian literature may have catalysed this important shift in his cinematic idiom.

In this study I do not purport to offer a reading of *all* art-historical hyperlinks embedded in Fellini's oeuvre, or even in a particular group of films. Fellini's art-historical intertexts constitute a huge and highly eclectic corpus. Resisting systematic cataloguing, they do not allow neat and easy thematic or stylistic arrangements. I therefore approach Fellini's intertextual network with due caution, turning focused attention to "particular signifying spaces," as Kristeva says.[94] In the chapters that follow I examine a number of "particular signifying spaces," which are overdetermined with art-historical evocations. I will be looking at four films from Fellini's middle period: *Giulietta degli spiriti* (1965), *Toby Dammit* (1969), *Fellini Satyricon* (1969), and *Il Casanova di Fellini* (1976). The art-historical hyperlinks embedded in these films span Rembrandt and Velázquez, Symbolism and art nouveau, metaphysical painting and Francis Bacon.

A brand of visual studies is currently emerging which regards the image as "a presentation, a source of power whose nature as an object endowed with being requires that its analysts pay careful attention to the way in which it works its magic on its viewer."[95] To be evoking "magic," as does Keith Moxey, within the critical discourse seems to me pretty daring, and highly liberatory. The moment has come for Fellini studies to return to the notion of "magic," so central to Fellini's world and to his aesthetic, and join in with the brand of critical visual studies which privileges notions of "presence" over "meaning," in the context of an "iconic turn" in the humanities. In his discussion of this significant turn in the study of visual art, Moxey posits, "[w]orks of art are objects now regarded as more appropriately encountered than interpreted."[96] With the advent of the iconic or pictorial turn, critical attention is increasingly directed toward "that which cannot be read, to that which exceeds the possibilities of a semiotic interpretation, to that which defies understanding on the basis of convention, and to that which we can never define."[97] Earlier in this introduction I mentioned Raymond Bellour and his conception of the individual film still as that "irrational, unnamable fragment that fascinates."[98] Approached as a complex network of "unnamable fragments that fascinate," Fellini's evocations, or rather invocations of painting on screen will be presented, charted, and analysed in the following chapters to the full extent and power of their magic.

Chapter Two

Giulietta degli spiriti: Symbolist Virgins Meet Decadent *Femmes Fatales* in Art Nouveau Interiors

Giulietta degli spiriti (*Juliet of the Spirits*)[1] was Fellini's first film shot in colour upon deliberate artistic choice.[2] Fellini's decision to confront the challenge of colour in *Giulietta* was induced by his growing interest in depth psychology and the role of the unconscious in the creative process. The changes in both narrative form and thematic interests that arose from Fellini's involvement with depth psychology entailed an analogous change in his visual language.

In dreams, Fellini writes in *Fare un film*, "color is idea, concept, feeling, as in truly great painting."[3] The explicit association of dream and painting via colour signals a shift in Fellini's idiom. Colour comes to be employed as "a most precious expressive means, if used pictorially."[4] In this passage from *Fare un film* Fellini conceptualizes colour in terms of pictoriality, and film in terms of "great painting." To make this even more explicit, he forges a direct analogy between the painter at his easel and the film director behind the camera, referring to film as a "picture," or *tableau*. The director is expected to control colour like a painter.[5]

However, Fellini's introduction of colour in *Giulietta* exceeds what Antonio Costa has termed *effetto pitturato*, or the "painterly" effect.[6] Rather, I will be arguing, the employment of colour in *Giulietta* indicates an emergent intertextual referencing of art history. Frank Burke regards *Giulietta degli spiriti* as "the beginning of a shift in Fellini's career toward an aesthetic of cultural reproduction, citation, imitation."[7] What is completely overlooked in Burke's discussion, however, is that this shift involves a network of art-historical evocations, which begs critical attention.

While Fellini's films are generally eclectic in their art-historical choices, *Giulietta degli spiriti* manifests a surprisingly systematic and coherent corpus of visual references. Harking back to late nineteenth-century culture, the film draws mainly on Symbolist painting, particularly Italian Symbolism. At the same time, the film takes a step further back, to the mid-nineteenth-century British school of the Pre-Raphaelites, recognized as the major visual source for Italian Symbolism. Art nouveau décors, often inhabited by red-haired *femmes fatales*, are ubiquitous in this film, and again seem to emerge from Symbolist painting, particularly of the Decadent brand.

Giulietta is a suburban housewife experiencing an unexpected irruption of unconscious materials – memories, anxieties, suppressed desires – that invade her waking life in grotesque apparitions. These become increasingly monstrous and aggressive toward the culmination of Giulietta's inner voyage in the film's concluding scenes. The scenes that feature the apparitions, or "spirits," constitute the loci for Fellini's newly conceived art-historical hyperlinking. The Symbolist idiom, I will further argue, constitutes the major visual paradigm underlying the film's moments of introverted vision, in those scenes where memory, fantasy, and hallucination prevail.

Like Peter Brunette writing on Antonioni, I am reluctant to force the "recalcitrant particulars" of Fellini's film into "overpowering master narratives that claim ... to control or subjugate them."[8] Nonetheless, the art-historical references embedded in *Giulietta degli spiriti* seem to crystallize around three foci, which I will discuss in the following order: (1) Giulietta's childhood memories, recording emotional oppression and sexual inhibition; (2) Suzy's realm, a world of primal instinct and unleashed sexuality; and (3) Giulietta's final confrontation with the "spirits" inside the claustrophobic room.

Symbolist Strands Embedded in Giulietta's Childhood Scenes

In one of the film's major scenes of childhood memories, little Giulietta is elected by the nuns running her grade school for the stage part of an early Christian martyr burned alive on the stake.[9] As per Bondanella, Giulietta continues to play the martyr throughout her adult life.[10] As an adult she wears nun-like outfits closed up to the neck in pronounced physical reserve, and accepts without protest her husband's patronizing and alienated attitude as she goes about her monotonous household chores. Indeed, this character fits Bram Dijkstra's typology of "the household nun," as it is formulated in *Idols of Perversity*.[11] In mid- and late nineteenth-century painting, Dijkstra points out, this type reflected the "ever-increasing enclosure of women within the ornate walls of the middle-class household."[12]

The protagonists of Giulietta's childhood are victimized by two social power systems, the first explicitly indicated in the film and the second only hinted at. The Church – brainwashing the young girls into identifying with the martyr who willingly burns alive to protect her faith, and probably her chastity – is explicitly indicted in the film for obstructing the girls' sexual development[13] and producing immature, unconfident, and anxious adults.

Fascism, on the other hand, is not referenced overtly in the film, as for example in *Fellini Amarcord* (1973). However, as the film's *soggetto*, or original story, indicates, earlier versions of the story explicitly linked fascist oppression with religious coercion, both of which are presented as the formative forces of Giulietta's childhood. To begin with, in both the *soggetto* and the published script Giulietta's father is a detestable fascist, sporting black boots, who imposes merciless discipline on his daughters.[14]

Let us have a look at the script's description of Giulietta's father. Dressed in black uniform, the father stands beside the red-bearded headmaster of the school – whose "barba rossa" shall be discussed in a moment – waving his hands with indignation at the rebellious grandfather eloping with a showgirl in a hot-air balloon. "Il Duce was also present," Giulietta remarks as she recounts this memory to her friends. Quoting her father as saying "that Il Duce was the father of us all," she remarks that as a child she indeed tended to confuse him with Il Duce. "He was a fanatic fascist ... I remember him only this way, wearing a black shirt and boots ... He made us exercise with the window open, even in the winter."[15] At this point in the script, Giulietta and her sisters are "seen performing gymnastics ... in front of a wide open window: outside everything is frozen. The father, in a black shirt and boots, orders them around."[16]

Although this scene, and with it the father character as a whole, have been eliminated from the final cut, the presence of a fascist father in the script and *soggetto* highlights Fellini's association of fascism with the *law-of-the-father*. Clearly, we are not dealing with a historic account of childhood under fascism. The film rather explores the fate of tender subjects like Giulietta and, by implication, the artist himself, as they are initiated into the law-of-the-father, which inevitably entails losing contact with the domain of the "spirits."

As noted, however, Fellini eliminates the fascist father from the film without leaving a trace. Or is this entirely the case? In fact, he leaves intact the grotesque headmaster, whose red beard, or "barba rossa," may refer the attentive viewer to *Operation Barbarossa*, the Nazi invasion of Russia in 1941 named after the medieval German emperor Friedrich Barbarossa.[17] Thus, while Fellini eschews all overt reference to fascism in this particular film, he certainly employs this subtle visual cue to hint at the role of fascism in moulding the young Italians of his generation into the submissive, mentally crippled creatures embodied in Giulietta's character.

But this is not all. The final cut, unlike the script, figures a black-bearded headmaster in the scenes of waking life, while the *barba rossa* becomes an exclusive attribute of hallucination. It appears whenever the headmaster is featured as one of Giulietta's demons, or "spirits." The early experience of mental oppression is thus associated with unconscious contents. What is at stake are the forces that inhibit mental growth, particularly in the creative artist.

One may be led to conclude that the female characters featured in Giulietta's childhood recollections are all but active, creative agents. This, however, is only partly true. Giulietta, in particular, appears to possess visionary faculties which in Fellini are often associated with the creative process. As the film makes quite clear, when Giulietta grows into a mature person she is the only adult around capable of seeing spirits. Generally, this character is highly receptive to various oneiric phenomena. Giulietta and the other female characters of the childhood memories are featured as simultaneously passive subjects and creative seers.

As the film progresses toward its ending, the appearance of little Giulietta and her friend Laura becomes increasingly pale, fuzzy, and immaterial. The school play sequence marks the introduction of the Laura character, portrayed as a pale-faced girl lost in melancholic reverie. In the foreground, relatively large surfaces of embroidered lace serve to flatten the image, transforming the living figure into a disembodied image framed by an articulate decorative pattern.

The entire sequence is dominated by *effetto pitturato*[18] as a key visual code. The stage is circumscribed by bare walls and semi-opaque screens, which obstruct the gaze and generate a painterly flatness. The walls and other elements of the décor are markedly painted. A colour scheme of muted ochres, white, and grey dominates. The clothes worn by Giulietta and her schoolmates are of a similar hue, to which a shade of yellowish white has been added. The artificiality and painterliness of the scene are underscored by the heavy makeup applied to the young visages. As the script clearly indicates, they are to look "cadaver-like."[19]

The figure is flattened to an even greater extent in the shot portraying the dead body of Laura (Figure 2.1). The girl, we are made to

Figure 2.1 *Giulietta degli spiriti*. Laura's drowned body appears in Giulietta's hallucination. DVD frame capture.

understand, has committed suicide by drowning. Still clothed in the white dress and wreath of the school play, the body floats in the stream among an abundance of waterweed, while the whispering voice-over of Laura invites Giulietta to join her "dreamless sleep." The lifeless figure underwater is extremely disembodied, as if transformed into a veritable "painting on film." Notably, the ripple of watery surface over the white dress suggests painted brushstrokes, adding the ultimate touch of *effetto pitturato* to this shot.[20]

Representations of Giulietta as a little girl manifest a similar increase in disembodiment and immateriality. In the visit to the circus, Giulietta is visible behind a gauzy screen, wearing the same yellowish-white dress as in the school play scene. The semi-transparent screen appears to serve no other purpose than to transform the little girl into a dematerialized silhouette. The following shot underscores the diminished sense of body by juxtaposing this figure with a group of muscular "primitives."[21]

In their coupling of pronounced painterlines and disembodied flatness, with a hint of otherworldly eeriness and a tinge of Christian spirituality, the pallid little girls featured in *Giulietta degli spiriti* strongly evoke the female types of Symbolist painting, particularly those of the spiritual brand. To be more particular, Fellini constructs his submissive virginal maidens on the template of Italian Divisionism, with its muted chromatic key, grainy texture, and pronounced rejection of deep space. I wish to draw particular attention to the works of Gaetano Previati (1852–1920), whose work seems to reverberate in Fellini's imagery. In addition, Fellini's art-historical hyperlinks seem to reach back to Pre-Raphaelite painting, to which Italian Symbolism is heavily indebted. As will be shown in the following pages, certain shots in *Giulietta degli spiriti* distinctly call to mind the frail and introverted young women in the paintings of the Pre-Raphaelites.

Fellini had images of Italian Symbolist painting at his immediate disposal in four richly illustrated monographs on nineteenth-century Italian painting found in his private library. These monographs had been published in close proximity to the making of *Giulietta*, and would thus be readily available during the conception and shooting of the film.[22] Moreover, given his deep interest in the visual arts, it is highly probable that Fellini would have been acquainted with the large collection of nineteenth-century Italian painting in the *Galleria nazionale d'arte moderna e contemporanea* (GNAM) in Rome, in which Italian Symbolists are and have been widely represented.

In the permanent exhibit at the GNAM, Fellini could have seen *I funerali di una vergine* (*The Funeral of a Virgin*, 1895), by the Divisionist painter Gaetano Previati, the painting having been on permanent exhibit since 1925 (Figure 2.2). This is probably the one painting most closely associable with the bloodless female types that prevail in the childhood scenes of *Giulietta degli spiriti*.

Figure 2.2 Gaetano Previati, *The Funeral of a Virgin*, 1895, triptych, oil on canvas, central panel 150 × 159 cm, side panels 156 × 220 cm each. Rome, Galleria nazionale d'arte moderna e contemporanea. Su concessione del Ministero per i Beni e le Attività Culturali. Photo G. Schiavinotto.

Previati's large triptych portrays a melancholic funereal procession of "sad figures of young women, accompanying in the endless prairies the corpse of their chaste companion towards final repose."[23] The left panel portrays two rows of young maidens holding lilies, and behind them a farther row of older women, their heads covered with shawls. The young women, crowned with wreaths, bend their heads in resignation. In its reiteration of identical figures the painting sacrifices individuality, privileging an image of mass devotion.

The central panel portrays the dead virgin, lying upon an elevated platform. At her side two groups of three girls each, their eyes lowered in chaste contemplation, carry wreaths. Another two rows of seemingly younger females are depicted in the right-hand panel, the only one in which male figures appear. While the girls carry flowers, like their peers in the left and central panels, the clergymen behind them carry a crucifix and an incense burner. The heads of the female figures gradually shift from a downward bend on the left to a pronounced upward tilt on the right, in the figures closest to the celestial source of light. The sky in the right-hand panel is rendered in light hues, which turn darker toward the left panel. The triptych as a whole signals a movement upward toward the celestial light, reflecting what for Aurora Scotti Tosini is Previati's focal interest, "reopening the way to the possibility of the sacred and the religious in art."[24]

Like *The Funeral of a Virgin*, Previati's *Maternità* (*Maternity*, 1890–1) is populated by a host of pious females rendered in his particular style. The painting features a group of feminine angels engaged in adoration of a breastfeeding mother. Like the virginal maidens in *The Funeral of a Virgin*, the angels of *Maternity* form a mass of identical figures, their individuality abolished in favour of a generalized portrayal of mystical adoration. In *Assunzione* (*The Assumption*, 1901–3), yet another Previati in the permanent collection of the GNAM which Fellini could have had direct acquaintance with, a mass of similarly modelled female angels surrounds the ascending virgin.

Returning to *Giulietta degli spiriti*, note that Fellini's host of submissive little girls, winged and dressed in yellowish white as in the schoolplay scene, speak to Previati's female types, particularly the submissive "brides of God" in *The Funeral of a Virgin* and *The Assumption*. It is not only the typology of the figures but also the colour scheme and expressed painterliness of the scenes under discussion that echo Previati's minimized palette and pronouncedly grainy texture. The ochres and greys of Previati's *Funeral* reverberate in *Giulietta degli spiriti*, in the yellowish white of the girls' dresses, the grey-washed walls, and the ochre gauze curtains, all of which recall the haziness and muted colouring of Previati's Divisionism.

But the childhood scenes in *Giulietta* constitute an intertextual crossroads that brings together more than one art-historical reference. A close look at the Laura character may further disentangle this art-historical mesh.

Laura, we understand, is one of Giulietta's pallid little schoolmates, the epitome of the "bride of God" discussed earlier. In the school play scene, she asks Giulietta to communicate with Him on her behalf on the occasion of her "ascension" toward a door in the theatre ceiling. Like the other figures in this scene, the Laura character draws on the pious and melancholy young women in Previati's *Funeral of a Virgin* and more generally on this brand of Symbolist types.

Furthermore, close reading of the script reveals that Laura is even more closely associable with Previati's *Funeral* than appears at first sight. In fact the script, as distinct from the film, has a funeral scene – the funeral of young Laura – and thus a veritable "funeral of a virgin." Although the scene was apparently filmed by Fellini, it was eliminated from the final cut.[25] And thus, while the film is extremely sparing in the information it provides about Laura, the published script offers a lot more detail, as does the typewritten shooting script preserved at the Lily Library of Rare Books at Indiana University.

These two versions of the script dedicate an entire scene to Laura's funeral. The scene begins with Giulietta, now a mature woman, driving desolately along a wayside canal. When a funeral procession goes by she notes the small coffin, fitted for a child. The view of the child's coffin triggers a flashback vision of the funeral of her friend Laura, who had taken her own life at a tender age. The spectator would have then seen a group of young girls, Laura's schoolmates, sadly following the coffin. Whether the mise en scène actually echoed Previati's funeral scene is an intriguing question which cannot be answered with currently available materials. However, the very existence of a funeral scene in the shooting script buttresses the association of Previati's *Funeral of a Virgin* with the imagery of *Giulietta degli spiriti*.

As revealed in the script, Fellini planned to make the circumstances of the girl's death more explicit than he eventually did in the final cut. The following scene of the funeral sequence, again eliminated in the final cut, was to present the drowned girl being pulled out of the stream, while a voice in the crowd would remark on "disappointed love." In the following third scene, Laura was to suddenly appear beside Giulietta, who would still be seated on the ground by the roadside canal. Laura was to look pale and soaked, and it would be Giulietta's turn to ask whether she had seen God in the otherworld. Laura's apathetic answer would be that she had had no revelation, except that everything was grey and lonely.[26] The *soggetto*, or story, which dates earlier in the evolution of the film, is even more explicit on this matter: "God? She never had the slightest hint of his real existence: no one in the other world ever talked about Him; no one ever received any message or had any notion ... No, God does not exist ... He does not exist."[27]

These three scenes unmistakably feature "the funeral of a virgin." The explicit reference to the existence of God and the suggestion of existential loneliness indicate the measure of detachment and irony with which Fellini approaches Symbolism. In fact, his representation of Laura and her little friends cannot be considered in terms other than an ironic twist on Previati's themes and subject matter. The pious submission and self-effacement of the naïve little girls acquire in Fellini the quality of mental disturbance, rather than high virtue – a psychic distortion effected by social and political power systems. In the school sequence, for instance, a row of faceless nuns in black distributes artificial wings to a succession of little girls. Previati's rows of virgins in yellowish white is met in Fellini's film by a row of black nuns, in an irony that verges on overt hatred.

Thus, while Previati's paintings convey religious mysticism altogether devoid of irony, in accordance with the Symbolist idiom, Fellini's cinematic rendering of his "brides of God" exposes inherent sociocultural biases. Modelling his characters as an ironic (in) version of Previati's bloodless virgins, Fellini appears to be interested primarily in exposing the power systems that subjugate the individual in society.

It must be noted, however, that there is more to Fellini's evocation of Symbolism than typical 1960s political concerns. In fact, I find that the irony of these scenes is mitigated by Fellini's distinct affirmation of the mysticism inherent in the Symbolist idiom. Laura and Giulietta possess uncanny visionary powers, and both display a strong desire to know that which is hidden behind the closed trap door in the ceiling. The film actually ends with another mysterious door, hiding an unknown space where Giulietta's spirits lurk. Like truly Symbolist figures, Laura and Giulietta are unusually receptive to otherworldly phenomena, or rather to their own unconscious. Endowed with distinct

Symbolist traits, these characters reflect Fellini's identification with the privileging of introspective as well as visionary faculties in the female figures of Symbolist painting.

Fellini is not ironic, then, when he references Symbolism as a signifier of receptivity to the irrational. Rather, his engagement with Symbolist painting is dialectical, in that it plays sociopolitical irony against an earnest fascination with the irrational and the mystical. This ambivalence is preserved in the film primarily through its imagery and visual strategies.

Further examination of embedded art-historical intertexts may shed light on this dialectic. As mentioned earlier, the shot that first introduces Laura is a medium close-up, featuring her as a melancholy figure whose flowing hair frames a vacant gaze. The shot under scrutiny evokes a contemplative female type recurrent in Symbolist painting. A painting by Belgian Symbolist Fernand Khnopff (1858–1921), *I Lock My Door upon Myself* (1891), comes to mind as a typical example, as do *La Donna della finestra* (1879) and *La Pia de' Tolomei* (1880), both by Pre-Raphaelite painter Dante Gabriel Rossetti (1828–82), to whose work I will refer shortly.

Although it cannot be established beyond doubt that Khnopff's painting was known to Fellini around 1964–5 or earlier, it best exemplifies the Symbolist type echoed in Fellini's rendering of Laura. Khnopff paints a young woman with an absent stare, as if retreating into unconscious or unnatural vision. The head of Hypnos, situated on a shelf behind the woman's back, underscores the suggestion of dream or hallucination. The Symbolist image of a woman gazing vacantly represented the epoch's pervasive concern with introspection. Notably, Khnopff draws heavily on the work of Dante Gabriel Rossetti, particularly the series of works that feature daydreaming young women. *La Pia de' Tolomei* (1868–81), *La Donna della Finestra* (1879), and *The Day Dream* (1880) are typical examples.

An avid reader of art history, Fellini was bound to be acquainted with the works of the Pre-Raphaelites, who in their turn have been widely acknowledged as a major influence on Symbolist painting. Judging from the 1960s literature on Italian Symbolism found on the shelves of his private library, Fellini was bound to have at least second-hand knowledge of the Pre-Raphaelite idiom. It would have been practically impossible for him to have read anything about Previati or Italian Symbolism without encountering some mention of Rossetti and Pre-Raphaelitism. It is thus fairly possible that Rossetti's work was directly known to Fellini in those years, judging by his deep interest in art history, nineteenth-century painting in particular.

Whether directly quoted, or indirectly mediated via Symbolist descendants such as Khnopff, Rossetti's contemplative maidens are evocatively present in *Giulietta degli spiriti*. The frontal medium close-up of Laura bearing an absent gaze, for example, evokes characteristic representations of female insanity in late nineteenth-century painting, best exemplified in recurrent representations of Ophelia, the archetype of the deranged female who takes her own life. As widely demonstrated by Bram Dijkstra, late nineteenth-century painting manifested a predilection for images of mad (young) women, epitomized in the recurrence of hysterical postures and vacant gazes.[28] The Ophelia figure, Dijkstra shows, represented for the epoch what was then regarded as a specifically female inclination for insanity.[29] Ophelia was "the later nineteenth century all-time favorite example of the love-crazed self-sacrificial woman who most perfectly demonstrated her devotion to her man by descending into madness ... and who in the end committed herself to a watery grave, thereby fulfilling the nineteenth-century male's fondest fantasies of feminine dependency."[30]

In the Laura character, it now becomes clear, Fellini looks back to Shakespeare's tragic protagonist, and more particularly to representations of this figure in late nineteenth-century painting. Fellini introduces two significant shots where Laura is associated with late nineteenth-century representations of Ophelia. The shot of the absent-minded girl, gazing ahead with eyes that do not see, particularly brings to mind typical 1890s renderings of Ophelia, portrayed in half-length with unkempt hair and a vacant gaze. In fact, this shot quite strikingly recalls two of the paintings which Dijkstra elects as typical examples of this brand: *Ophelia* by Ernest Hébert (1890s), and Georg Falkenberg's painting of the same subject (ca. 1898). Both painters present Ophelia in a frontal half-length view, her flowing hair framing a contemplative gaze beneath raised eyebrows. Fellini positions Laura in a strikingly similar pose, her flowing hair, adorned with flowers, framing a vacant facial expression. This particular shot clearly reveals the late nineteenth-century "Ophelia" typology, woven into the cinematic text(ure).

But there is yet another shot in this film which invokes the Ophelia motif even more strongly, and that is the underwater shot briefly discussed earlier in this chapter (Figure 2.1). Laura, now dead, is seen floating in a stream, surrounded by waterweeds. She still wears her white dress and wreath of flowers. As shown earlier in this chapter, the shot manifests a distinctly painterly quality in its pronounced employment of *effetto pitturato* and its marked flattening of the human body. At this point I propose an intertextual reading of this shot, which seems to speak to a painting of the dead Ophelia by Pre-Raphaelite painter John Everett Millais (1829–96). At the same time, the shot evokes an 1865 painting by Federico Faruffini, the *Sacrifice of a Virgin to the Nile* (fig. 2.4). The latter painting, it is significant to note, is permanently exhibited at the GNAM in Rome, where Fellini could have seen it along with Previati's *Funeral of a Virgin*. It has, moreover, been the subject of a 1911 cinematic adaptation by Enrico Guazzoni, a major Italian film director of the silent era.

Fellini was undoubtedly familiar with Millais's *Ophelia* (Figure 2.3), if only through a reproduction printed in *Histoire de la Peinture Surréaliste* by Marcel Jean (1957), of which he owned a copy. Notably, Jean features Millais's *Ophelia* in the first section of his monograph, which bears the title "Surrealist Art before Surrealism." In this section of the book, which addresses proto-surrealist art, Marcel Jean refers to Millais's painting as representative of the Pre-Raphaelite interest in the dream state, a major concern of the surrealists and a highly significant concern of Fellini since his encounter with Jungian psychology. In the early 1960s, Fellini was immersed in Jungian thought. Furthermore, he was committed, by the advice of his Jungian mentor, Ernst Bernhard, to keeping detailed dream notebooks. Marcel Jean's text, in which psychoanalytic overtones are attributed to Millais's painting, would thus have doubled Fellini's interest in this painting.

Now, the reason that Millais's particular rendering of Ophelia had given rise to this psychoanalytical reading is that Millais was unique in representing Ophelia after the moment of death, with part of her body underwater. In the period under discussion, the majority of paintings of this theme tended to depict a living Ophelia, either seated on the river bank or having just fallen into the water. Millais's rendering of a dead Ophelia is therefore an exception in its suggestion of dream, so dear to Pre-Raphaelites, Symbolists, and surrealists alike. This would explain the appeal of this particular painting to Marcel Jean, and to Fellini in his turn.

As shown earlier, Laura and Giulietta are multilayered cinematic constructs, signifying receptiveness to otherworldly or unconscious materials. The emergence of Giulietta's demons from the depths of the sea must thus be strongly associated with Laura's death by drowning. Carolyn Geduld has rightly pointed out, in a Jungian reading of this

Figure 2.3 John Everett Millais, *Ophelia*, 1852. Oil on canvas, 76.2 × 111.8 cm, © Tate, London 2013.

film, the significance of Giulietta's clogged lily pond, indicating the protagonist's "troubled relationship with water – her unconscious."[31] What Geduld fails to note, however, is that the shot of Laura floating in an open-air stream connotes a way out, or rather in(to) the pregnant waters of the unconscious.[32] It is thus crucial to recognize Millais's *Ophelia* as a central constituent of the intertextual matrix undergirding this shot.

But the full gamut of the art-historical links embedded in this single shot has yet to be explored. If we unravel the intertextual tangle a bit further, another art-historical reference, briefly mentioned earlier, comes into sight. *La vergine al Nilo* (*Sacrifice of a Virgin to the Nile*, 1865; Figure 2.4), by the Italian Federico Faruffini (1833–69), belongs to the collection of the *Galleria d'Arte Moderna e Contemporanea* in Rome, and has been on permanent exhibit since its acquisition in 1886.[33] Faruffini's painting features a bare-breasted dead girl, bound to a cross-shaped wooden fixture floating in the Nile. A large audience on the riverbank appears to engage in a ritual of human sacrifice.[34] Although its theme and imagery draw on antiquity, the painting bears obvious Christian

Figure 2.4 Federico Faruffini, *Sacrifice of a Virgin to the Nile*, 1865. Oil on canvas, 123 x 243 cm, Rome, Galleria nazionale d'arte moderna e contemporanea. Su concessione del Ministero per i Beni e le Attività Culturali. Photo G. Schiavinotto.

connotations, indicated by the strange combination of virgin and cross. The connotation of human sacrifice becomes doubly significant in the present reading of *Giulietta degli spiriti*, if we recall the representation of innocent little girls playing willing martyrs, or "brides of God," for an audience of Catholic nuns, fascist functionaries, and coercive parents. "Putting a twelve-year-old on the flames ... Playing cannibals, you wretches! Go to Africa, if you have a flavor for roasted girls! Or go cook each other, you bitches," the rebellious grandfather bellows as he interrupts the ceremonious acting-out of Christian martyrdom, untying little Giulietta from the grill.[35] As the grandfather's text clearly implies, Giulietta and her schoolmates have fallen prey to just another version of human sacrifice.

The shot of Laura floating in the stream is, however, equivocal. It certainly draws on Faruffini's painting, notwithstanding obvious differences: the one bare-breasted, the other fully dressed, the one subject to the gaze of a crowd while the other drifts along in solitude. Its critical connotations notwithstanding, Fellini's very evocation of a pagan fertility rite – particularly one that involves immersion in water – again points to a deep-seated preoccupation with the unconscious and its accessibility, as crucial elements of the creative process. Moreover, Faruffini's portrayal of primitive ritual would particularly appeal to Fellini's Jungian awareness. The "Ophelia" shot clearly turns away from any note of irony. As distinct from the school-play scene, this particular shot seems to signal a deep concern on Fellini's part with the mystical, the irrational, and the unconscious.

And yet there is more to be unearthed in the intertextual layering of this art-historical *lexia*. Fellini's acquaintance with Faruffini's *Sacrifice of a Virgin to the Nile* may have been mediated by an early Italian film, *La Sposa del Nilo* (*The Spouse of the Nile*, 1911), made by Enrico Guazzoni, director of *Quo Vadis* (1912), *Messalina* (1910, 1923), and other well-known Italian films of the silent era. *La Sposa del Nilo* is a short film which takes Faruffini's painting as a point of departure for a story about two Egyptian lovers who are cruelly torn from each other's arms when the girl is randomly chosen as sacrifice to the gods of the Nile.[36] The climactic ending of the film features the sacrifice of the virgin, in a *tableau* which reconstructs Faruffini's *Sacrifice of a Virgin to the Nile*, complete with the cheering crowd on the quay, the priests in ritual garment, and the dead virgin floating in the stream.

Guazzoni's film, and this is most pertinent to the present discussion, does not end with a long shot of the *tableau*, as would be expected, but rather with the dead virgin alone in the frame, floating in the water. Guazzoni thus significantly deviates from the painting, creating a cinematic image which is distinctly different.[37] While, as mentioned earlier, Faruffini depicts a bare-breasted girl lying on a cross-shaped fixture, the virgin in Guazzoni's film is fully dressed, and lies covered with a gauzy bridal veil which allows but a blurred view of her face and body (Figure 2.5).

In fact, Fellini's "death of a virgin" appears closest to Guazzoni's final shot, albeit with distinct echoes of Millais and Faruffini. In Fellini, as in Guazzoni, the girl still wears the wreath and festive clothing that mark her as a "bride" in a rite of human sacrifice, whether symbolic or cruelly actual. In Fellini, as in Guazzoni and unlike Millais and Faruffini, the girl's body and face are blurred in a mystical haze. What is more, the scenes in *La Sposa del Nilo*, in which the young victims are adorned with veils and wreaths, resonate in the preparation of young Giulietta by the black nuns for the role of martyr.

Here, again, we become aware of Fellini's dialectical stance. His earnest engagement with mystical phenomena is always played against an ironical reflection on institutional power. While Guazzoni emphasizes the cruel abuse of the girl in the name of religious hegemony, Fellini's treatment of the subject – while critically representing

Giulietta degli spiriti 37

Figure 2.5 Enrico Guazzoni, *La Sposa del Nilo*, 1911. DVD frame capture. DVD courtesy of EYE Film Institute Netherlands, Amsterdam.

the faceless black nuns handling the tender girls – is more equivocal than Guazzoni. As I have shown earlier, Fellini is attentive to the frail young women of Pre-Raphaelite and Symbolist painting, whose introspective gazes signal heightened receptiveness to the unconscious. His Ophelia figure is conceived more in the spirit of Millais's Ophelia, sunk deep in the sleep of death, than in the spirit of a silent era costume film like Guazzoni's *Virgin in the Nile*.[38] It has been pointed out earlier that the drowning scene underwent extensive subtraction and elimination until it reached its final stage – a single shot of a floating body. In place of conventional cinematic narration, Fellini employs one enigmatic pictorial shot, evoking the "dead virgin" motif via image, colouring, and mise en scène. Privileging a single art-historical *lexia* over three fully developed scenes, Fellini gravitates toward pure pictorial suggestion. It is here that his new visual idiom emerges, revealing a nascent reliance on painting as potent catalyst of meaning, or rather of non-verbal experience. From this point on, for roughly twenty years, Fellini will distinctly privilege the visual suggestiveness of painting over text-based cinematic narration.

Suzy's Domain: Symbolist *Femmes Fatales* Roaming *Art Nouveau* Interiors

Three female characters, Suzy (Giulietta's promiscuous neighbour), Iris (the spirit of "free love" appearing in Giulietta's séances), and Fanny (a circus artist with whom Giulietta's grandfather elopes), make up the larger construct which, to facilitate the discussion, I will call "Suzy." Sandra Milo, Fellini's archetypal cast for the sensual lover, had been cast for all three parts. This triad embodies unrestrained sexual conduct and thus serves as a foil to the severe psychic inhibition epitomized in the characters of Laura and Giulietta.

Suzy is modelled as an overly sensual woman in extravagant attire. The appearance of this character communicates physical abundance, offering an alternative to the marked rejection of body in Laura and Giulietta. Conspicuous among the participants of Suzy's sexual revelry are dark men of Asian and African origin. Black performers, we may recall, are present also in the circus scene, where they feature a powerful contrast to the almost transparent silhouette of Giulietta. Suzy's world teems with dark, primitive figures, to whom the *soggetto* refers as "simultaneously divine and animal,"[39] and with whom she seems perfectly at ease. When Giulietta dares cross the boundary into her neighbour's world, a dark singer entices her to accept Suzy's (again dark-skinned) godson as a lover for the night.

Throughout his oeuvre, Fellini associates dark-skinned figures with primal sexuality. Whether he is merely exposing clichéd cultural coding, as Frank Burke maintains,[40] or rather expressing a deep concern with the workings of the primitive psyche, is a question worth considering. Burke believes that "far more than any of Fellini's preceding films, *Juliet of the Spirits* makes cultural representation its inescapable subject."[41] Any critical reading of this film, however, must take into account Fellini's deep engagement with Jungian concepts, one of which would be the Shadow archetype, incarnated in dark figures of a "hidden, repressed, for the most part inferior ... personality whose ultimate ramifications reach back into the realm of our animal ancestors."[42] Immersed as Fellini was at that point in Jungian literature, it is unlikely that he would have been ironical about the foregoing association of the dark figure with the primal depths of the unconscious. Rather, he would be disposed to conceive of dark oriental figures as embodiments of "the unconscious man, that is, his shadow."[43]

The dark-skinned Other thus assumes Jungian overtones, its manifest presence in Suzy's domain signalling access to primitive strata of the psyche. Notably, a direct passageway leads from Suzy's bedroom to an underground pool. The intimate proximity with the dark lover is thus explicitly associated with easy access to the subterranean waters of the unconscious. In fact, the script has a scene in which Suzy slides down to the underground pool in the company of her oriental lover, Momy.[44] In the final cut, a naked Suzy slides through the tubular passage in an unmistakable suggestion of reverse birth, regressing into the warm amniotic fluid of a maternal womb. Carrying obvious psychoanalytic overtones, this scene recalls a number of passages from Jungian literature which refer to regression into the maternal "fountainhead" as a necessary step toward psychic growth and revival of creative faculties.[45]

Water and dark men, so it seems, play a crucial role in this film. It is primarily on their rapport with these two elements that Fellini predicates the Suzy/Giulietta dichotomy. As mentioned earlier, Giulietta, unlike Suzy, struggles with a clogged lily pond. Again unlike Suzy, Giulietta's encounters with dark shadow figures are extremely problematic, and involve unnerving hallucinatory visions. A spirit named Olaf, which the script identifies as a Turk, brings Giulietta into a fainting fit. The *soggetto* associates this Turk, Olaf, with an Oedipal childhood fantasy in which Giulietta finds out that her much dreaded father is not her real father.[46] Although omitted from the film, the Oedipal suggestion further indicates Fellini's association of the oriental figure with repressed primal matter, which threatens Giulietta to the point of losing consciousness. In the beach scene, a gigantic man whom Geduld again identifies as a Turk[47] rises from the sea. Emerging from deep waters, the Turk is explicitly marked as an archetypal psychic element. Giulietta's horror at the sight signals suppressive forces powerfully at work. Giulietta, in sum, dreads the very Turks that Suzy easily communicates with.

Further underscoring the dichotomy, Fellini implants a neutralized, lifeless version of the Orient in Giulietta's bedroom. The room is hung with a wallpaper of orientalist landscapes. Fellini markedly distinguishes the flattened and domesticated image of the Orient in Giulietta's dwelling from Suzy's live "orientals." The wallpaper presents a muted version, a pale echo of the real thing, which at that point Giulietta dreads to explore.

Suzy's villa, in its turn, is alive with exuberant art nouveau interiors, which denote mental liberation in more than one way. In his construction of Suzy's domain, Fellini employs art nouveau, or *Stile Liberty*, as a central visual paradigm. I will be particularly concerned with the historical and cultural connotations of this style, and will offer a historically specific reading of *Stile Liberty* against the backdrop of Italy's fascist regime.

Suzy's villa is an endless maze of labyrinthine spaces, revealing yet unknown rooms and passages in each and every scene. In critical treatments of the film the villa is described as "lavishly extravagant,"[48] "eccentrically decorated,"[49] or "decorated like a brothel."[50] However, the precise art nouveau idiom that dominates the décor begs particular critical attention.

Although the *soggetto* is noncommittal in its description of Suzy's dwelling,[51] in discussion with his designers Fellini expressly specified the style as *Liberty*, one of the two terms denoting art nouveau in Italy.[52] The central decorative element in Suzy's hall is thus a colourful stained glass window featuring a peacock, a favourite art nouveau motif. The main hall of the villa, to name yet another example, boasts an elaborate spiralling staircase with a distinctly art nouveau curvilinear railing.

Stile Floreale, as art nouveau was alternatively tagged in Italy, was a style of voluptuous ornamentation. As in art nouveau, it epitomized the flow of vital energy. Fellini reverts to this style as yet another visual expression for the overflowing vitality of the Suzy character. A close look at the interior of the villa reveals Fellini's brilliant concretization of *Stile Floreale* in the live creeper which actually covers, as if with a live wallpaper, the staircase leading to Suzy's bedroom. Bringing to life the vegetal patterns of *Stile Floreale*, Fellini carries this ornamental style to its literal extreme. Significantly, the creeper spreads right up to Suzy's bedroom, from which one is able to slide into the subterranean pool of the "realm of the mothers," if we are to put it in Jungian terms. Whereas Giulietta's ambience has but a devitalized version of *Stile Floreale* in the vegetal pattern of her curtains and drapery, in Suzy's domain the graphic pattern of the creeper comes alive, thriving. In Giulietta's villetta, in turn, even the rose bushes in the garden are not allowed natural growth. Unnaturally trimmed, they suffocate under bizarre plastic hoods that cover them for the night.

But, Fellini's recourse to art nouveau, in its aspect of *Stile Liberty*,[53] has yet to be considered in its historical specificity. I therefore propose to look at what art nouveau might signal in the context of Fellini's childhood and early years of adulthood, under the fascist regime.

Even before the advent of fascism, the international aura of art nouveau gave rise to heated objection on the part of Italian nationalists.[54] In the late 1920s, the first years of the fascist takeover of Italy, the fascist establishment opted to encourage the emergence of an alternative style.

The idea of *Italianità* was conceived in terms of the classicist paradigm involving "symmetry and proportion such as Michelangelo asserted," to quote the Roman Quadrennial's secretary general. "In Italy," this fascist functionary asserted, "one is either a classicist or nothing."[55] The subsequent radicalization of the fascist dictatorship, and its growing affiliation with Nazi Germany, buttressed its antipluralist approach to culture, identifying modernism and internationalism as "the enemy." A demand arose for the forced formation of a "fascist art" purged of "impure" elements.[56] A typical example would be the pronounced classicism and rationality of the new façade of the Venice Biennial main pavilion, commissioned by the fascist government in 1932. The heavily ornamented, curved wall of the 1914 façade was replaced by a rectangular, functionalist façade in which smooth columns replaced the Corinthian pilasters, and the word ITALIA in sans serif letters took the place of the "pro arte" motto in the original façade.[57] A similar taste for classicist austerity can be detected in the plans for the *Palazzo della civiltà Italiana*, published in the official prospectus of the 1942 *Esposizione Universale* in Rome.[58] This building, as *comissario generale* Vittorio Cini wrote in the prospectus of the exhibition, was "the essence of Italian architecture." Its predominant architectural element, the arch, is regarded as the epitome of Roman architecture, one which "resisted outside influence" through the ages.[59]

At the specific historical moment in which Fellini's visual sensibility was being formed, the rich curvilinear forms of *Stile Liberty* were considered radically alien to the fascist formal dogma. The point I am making is that in *Giulietta degli spiriti*, *Stile Liberty* literally connotes liberty, or freedom from the coercion, enforced submissiveness, and inhibition of psychic growth, all of which Fellini associated with growing up in fascist Italy. I deem it highly probable that Fellini references art nouveau, or rather *Stile Liberty*, in its literal reading of "libertà," notwithstanding the historical reference of this term to the famous London store of art nouveau fabrics. The *Liberty* interiors are thus employed for their historically specific connotation of freedom of thought and, by extension, free access to the domain of primal instincts and insights.[60]

Further unravelling the intertextual tangle that constitutes "Suzy," more art-historical leads come to light. Again, they reference turn-of-the-century painting. I now wish to look at two female figures singled out from among the host of grotesque characters that orbit around Giulietta's lively neighbour, Suzy. These figures look back to the works of Italian Symbolist Giulio Aristide Sartorio, German Symbolist Franz

Von Stuck, and, first and foremost, to the graphic works of Aubrey Beardsley.

The first image to be considered appears in a brief sequence of love-making couples caught for a moment by Suzy's flashlight, as she escorts Giulietta to the bedroom connected to the subterranean pool. Significantly, the two women walk along the corridor grown over with the live creeper. Suzy's flashlight generates a series of brief tableaux, as she briefly sheds light on the couples hiding in the foliage. In the script, unlike the film, these tableaux were not conceived as live-action scenes but rather as paintings hanging on the corridor wall. Giulietta, the script notes, would gaze at the "little pictures of dubious taste," looking "a bit scandalized but interested." The paintings were to portray, "as if in a profane, blasphemous 'Via Crucis', the successive 'stages' of an amorous possession of a woman."[61] Notably, in the final cut Fellini elected to replace the paintings with a succession of live tableaux, each lit for a brief second as Suzy and Giulietta go by. One of these tableaux, at least, references a line of art-historical intertexts.

The tableau in question features an imposing red-haired woman, in a red shawl and gloves, kissing an apparently unconscious man about half her size (Figure 2.6). The same lady appears as well in an earlier shot of the party sequence. In this shot she is framed in

Figure 2.6 *Giulietta degli spiriti*. Red-haired *femme fatale*. DVD frame capture.

medium close-up which highlights her big breasts, wide shoulders, and enormous red hairpiece. The "lady in red" evokes characteristic late nineteenth-century portrayals of the evil woman. The shots under scrutiny are embedded with particular art-historical intertexts, the first of which is Aubrey Beardsley's figure of Salomé, extensively featured in his illustrations for Oscar Wilde's 1907 play of the same title.

The *tableau*, in which the "woman in red" administers what seems to be a vampire's kiss to the shrivelled little man, distinctly speaks to Beardsley's *Dancer's Reward* (Figure 2.7), in which Salomé bends in a similar posture over the severed head of Iokhanaan, bleeding on a platter. Another reference embedded in the same tableau would be the macabre kiss in *J'ai baisé ta bouche Iokanaan, J'ai baisé ta bouche*, from the same series. The other shot of the "lady in red," mentioned earlier, echoes the frontal position, stout build, huge curly hairpiece, and exposed breasts of Herodias in Beardsley's *Enter Herodias*. Beardsley's *femme fatale*, so it seems, is transposed onto film to add a shade of uncanny evil to the Suzy signifier.

However, where Beardsley's graphic figures are conceived in black and white, *Giulietta degli spiriti* employs colour as a major vehicle of signification. And thus the woman's red hair functions as yet another visual cue linking "Suzy" to the Symbolist *femme fatale*. Edvard Munch's *Vampire* (1893–4), to name but one typical example, depicts a woman with long red tresses, administering a lethal kiss to a young man whose head lies lifelessly in her lap. The woman's red hair falls over the man's head like a bloody snare. Italian Symbolist painting features this type extensively. One painting at least would have been known to Fellini from the permanent exhibit at Rome's GNAM, and that is *La Gorgone e gli eroi* (*The Gorgon and the Heroes*, 1897), by Giulio Aristide Sartorio. Sartorio's *Gorgon and the Heroes* portrays the mythological creature as a young and beautiful naked woman, at whose feet three men lie dead. Laying her winged feet upon the head of the right-hand figure, this victorious *femme fatale* towers over her male victims.[62] Fellini could also find the painting reproduced in *I grandi pittori dell'ottocento italiano* (1961), and in *Pittura italiana dell'ottocento* (1963), which lay on the shelves of his private library. A painting by Italian Symbolist Giovanni Segantini entitled *Vanità* (*Vanity*, 1897) demonstrates a similar conception of red hair as signifier of evil womanhood. In *Vanity*, Segantini depicts a naked woman displaying her ginger-coloured hair while examining her reflection in a pool, from which a snake-shaped monster emerges.

Figure 2.7 Aubrey Beardsley, *The Dancer's Reward*, illustration from *Salomé* by Oscar Wilde, pub. 1894 (line block print)/Private Collection/The Stapleton Collection/The Bridgeman Art Library.

The red-haired *femme fatale* is transposed and incorporated into Fellini's intertextual matrix. The serpent, an indispensable element of *femme fatale* iconography, is there too. In Suzy's party sequence, one shot frames a naked woman with a large black serpent coiled around her body. This image strikingly recalls two paintings: *Sensuality* (1891) and *Sin* (1893), by German Symbolist Franz Von Stuck.

The resemblance to Von Stuck's *Sensuality* is quite striking. The size and form of the snake, the way it emerges from between the woman's thighs to coil around her waist, reappearing from under her arm, and the woman's direct gaze at the spectator all suggest that this is a direct quotation, indicating (again) Fellini's reliance on master paintings as building blocks for his visual signifiers. Relying on Von Stuck's powerful evocation of Symbolist anxieties, Fellini embeds this visual cue as a means of augmenting the suggestive power of the cinematic image. Eliciting in this particular case a heightened sense of anxiety, painting functions as a conduit to concrete, almost embodied experience, signifying, or rather communicating, on the level of the *sémiotique*.

Needless to say, *fin-de-siècle* iconography of "evil womanhood" has much to do with the archetypes of the unconscious. To apply the Jungian terminology which Fellini was extensively studying at the time, one may construe the red-haired "Beardsley woman" in *Giulietta degli spiriti* as an anima figure of the hazardous brand. In Jungian thought and imagery, art, myth, dreams, and fantasy generally employ female figures as embodiment of "the feminine nature of a man's unconscious,"[63] that which ensures vitality and creativity.[64] Jungian literature puts a strong emphasis on the danger of becoming "devoured," or engulfed, by the unconscious to the point of pathological instability. For Jung, therefore, the recurrence of the evil woman type in dreams, myth, and art manifests the sense of danger that accompanies the subject's confrontation with "contents ... which till now were latent."[65] Erich Neumann, whose Jungian writings Fellini eagerly read and quoted,[66] dwells at length on the way in which this pending threat is personified in "terrible figures that manifest the black, abysmal side of life and the human psyche."[67]

Fellini's predatory woman in red resonates with the "terribleness" of the Jungian anima, the deadliness of Beardsley's Salomé, the red-haired menace of Sartorio's *Gorgon* and Segantini's *Vanity*, all woven into a concise visual unit effectively communicating the peril of Giulietta's condition.

A comprehensive outlook is now possible on the "Suzy" signifier, with particular emphasis on its participation in the production of meaning via art-historical reference. Suzy, it has been asserted earlier, is introduced as a foil to Giulietta, the inhibited, mentally blocked protagonist of this film. Both "Suzy" and "Giulietta" are complexly structured cinematic signifiers, meant to be sensed, or experienced, rather than read. Cinematic signifiers of this kind may be said to address Vivian Sobchack's "cinesthetic [sic] subject,"[68] one endowed with "an embodied intelligence that opens our eyes far beyond their discrete capacity for vision ... and opens language to a reflective knowledge of its carnal origins and limits."[69]

The Master's Bedroom and the Jungian *Shadow*

Giulietta degli spiriti reaches its climax in a scene that literally features a "return of the repressed." Throughout the film Giulietta is attacked by hosts of grotesque apparitions, whose aggressiveness increases as the film nears its conclusion. Only in the final sequence is she able to confront the demons that haunt her. As the spirits invade every corner of the house, Giulietta tries to find shelter in bed. Beside the bed she discovers a little door, hitherto unknown to her, behind which faint crying is heard. Giulietta defies the apparition of her domineering mother, and enters the room despite the mother's prohibiting command.

Bending to enter the undersized opening in the wall, much like Alice in the rabbit's hole, Giulietta finds herself in a claustrophobic room whose extreme perspectival recession is emphasized by sharply receding floorboards. The demons lurk in one corner, while in the centre her younger self, the little girl playing the martyr, lies fettered to the flaming grate of the school play scene (Figure 2.8). Giulietta bends lovingly

Figure 2.8 *Giulietta degli spiriti*. Giulietta in the claustrophobic room. DVD frame capture.

over the girl, unbinding and hugging her with affection and acceptance before she sets her free. The menacing spirits dissolve into thin air.

At least two visual intertexts are woven into Fellini's image of the sharply receding room inhabited by creatures of the unconscious.

I first wish to look at a drawing in Jung's own hand, portraying an embodiment of the Shadow archetype. The drawing derives from Jung's richly illustrated personal diary, the *Red Book*, which has not been published until recently, but is often referred to and quoted in the Jungian literature. The drawing under discussion is reproduced in *C.G. Jung, Word and Image*, edited by Aniela Jaffé (1979). To quote Jaffé's caption, the drawing presents a "meeting with the shadow."[70] A dark and grotesque embodiment of the Shadow archetype lurks in the farthest corner of a red-walled room, whose distorted perspective is indicated by a sharply receding checked floor and tiled walls that recede in a similar fashion.

The expressed eeriness of the room signals that it is a mental space that is represented. In Jungian theory, the Shadow represents "the inferior part of the personality; sum of all personal and collective psychic elements which, because of their incompatibility with the chosen conscious attitude, are denied expression in life and therefore coalesce into a relatively autonomous 'splinter personality' with contrary tendencies in the unconscious."[71] The red room in the drawing is inhabited by suppressed mental contents, the encounter with which, however unnerving, is a crucial stage of the individuation process.

As becomes clear, the confrontation with the spirits in *Giulietta* draws heavily on Jung. Moreover, Jungian imagery is extensively referenced. The claustrophobic room which Giulietta discovers concretizes the unconscious via a visual formula that strongly echoes Jung's image of the shadow. As in Jung's drawing, we enter a spatially distorted room, teeming with grotesque shadow figures. Only when she musters the courage to face her shadow does Giulietta gain final liberation.

But was Fellini acquainted with this particular drawing? As indicated earlier, the *Red Book* had certainly not been published before or during the conception of *Giulietta degli spiriti*. However, Fellini made personal contact with the Jung family subsequent to his introduction to Jung's writings. He may have been given access to this manuscript while negotiating with the family on a film project about Jung, which unfortunately was never brought to fruition.[72]

Critical treatments of *Giulietta degli spiriti*, particularly the reading offered by Carolyn Geduld, quoted earlier, have shown quite convincingly that Giulietta's journey of individuation is conceived in Jungian terms. The presence of Jungian imagery in the film's intertextual matrix highlights Fellini's growing reliance on direct visual suggestion as a signifying means.

Beyond its Jungian connotations, however, the mysterious room recalls the anxious spaces of Max Ernst's collages, particularly one gouache overpainting, *The Master's Bedroom* (1920; Figure 2.9). As in Fellini's "Ophelia shot," the anxious room forms a rich intertextual junction where Jung meets Max Ernst and Giorgio de Chirico.

Fellini could have had direct knowledge of Ernst and his work through a mutual acquaintance, the painter and film director Hans Richter, to whom he was introduced by Gideon Bachmann, a journalist and film critic close to Fellini in those years.[73] A copy of Jung's *Man and His Symbols* in Fellini's library bears a dedication from Richter, dated 1965. Written in Italian and in second person, this dedication indicates a close relationship between the two artists, who apparently shared a common interest in Jung.[74]

Considered in light of the foregoing, it seems that Richter's film *Dreams That Money Can Buy* (1944) could have constituted an important

Figure 2.9 Max Ernst, *The Master's Bedroom*, 1920, gouache, pencil, and ink, printed reproduction mounted on paperboard, 16.3 x 22 cm. © 2012 by ADAGP, Paris.

link between Fellini and Max Ernst, whose short film episode "Desire" forms part of Richter's film.[75] In "Desire," based on Ernst's collage novel, *Une Semaine de Bonté* (1934), a young woman, apparently in a state of dream or hallucination, lies on a bed lined with lace and crimson-coloured velvet. The woman mumbles unclearly about furry nightingales pursuing her, evoking Ernst's painting, *Two Children Are Menaced by a Nightingale* (1924). A man breaks into the room and carries the woman away unconscious, while Max Ernst himself is seen pulling mysterious male figures from beneath her bed, where they appear to be drowning. The man carries the unconscious woman through a claustrophobic underground passageway. However, as they emerge the lady seems to gain considerable strength, whereas the man becomes powerless and passive. This sequence of uncanny events reconstructs a series of collages from Ernst's *Une Semaine de Bonté*, compiled into a cinematic dream sequence by Ernst.

Certain similarities between the plot of Ernst's short film and *Giulietta degli spiriti* are notable. Both films feature the liberation of a woman from haunting apparitions that invade her bedroom. In "Desire" Ernst pulls mysterious drowning figures from the apparently flooded space beneath the bed. In Giulietta's dream, an old man draws a barge loaded with savage warriors out of the deep waters of the sea. Moreover, like Ernst's protagonist, who has to stoop while he carries the unconscious woman through low-ceilinged passageways, Giulietta has to bend low in order to pass through the miniature door of the claustrophobic room.

Given Fellini and Richter's personal acquaintance, it is plausible that Fellini had seen *Dreams That Money Can Buy*, with Ernst's highly suggestive episode. It is my assumption that the acquaintance with Ernst's work, whether mediated by Richter or via some other cultural route, would have aroused Fellini's interest in Ernst's paintings and collages. His personal friendship with Richter, and with the surrealist painter Léonor Fini, could have enabled first-hand acquaintance with works by Ernst that were not yet exhibited or published at the time, particularly the series of early gouache overpaintings to which *The Master's Bedroom* belongs. Thus, although *The Master's Bedroom* was not exhibited or published around 1965 or earlier, Fellini could have been acquainted with one or more of Ernst's overpaintings, or with this work in particular, in private collections.

Several of the works in this series feature sharply converging floorboards and distorted perspectives. The converging walls and floorboards of the anxious room in *Giulietta* seem to emulate those of *The Master's Bedroom*, as does, to a certain extent, the colour scheme predominated by greys, and the expressed painterly texture of the walls. In *The Master's Bedroom* Ernst eschews conventional arrangement of objects in deep space. Painting over a found catalogue page, on which various images are represented in arbitrary distribution, Ernst generates an uncanny interior where objects do not conform to the laws of perspective. The objects' "position in the different depths within the pictorial space," Haim Finkelstein notes, "remains somewhat indeterminate because of the ambiguities informing the various layers."[76] For Finkelstein, the "marked sense of spatial dissociation" manifested in this and other overpaintings by Ernst is generated by a layering of space into a succession of parallel surfaces. Ernst's conception of a layered mental space is informed by psychoanalytical theory and its spatial conception of the psychic apparatus, which he visually concretizes. Works like *The Master's Bedroom* forge "a pictorial space that analogizes a probing through the layered barriers deeper into the domain of the forbidden sight of some repressed infantile scene."[77]

The emphasis put on the floorboards is another conspicuous detail in Ernst's concretization of mental space. In the artist's early childhood, wooden floorboards triggered a hallucinatory re-emergence of primal fantasy, hence their crucial role in the evolution of his automatic technique of *frottage*.[78] The pronounced presence of wooden floorboards in *The Master's Bedroom* indicates a major concern of this particular work with primal psychic matter. The rapidly converging floorboards in Giulietta's claustrophobic room echo this central feature of Ernst's work, marking the anxious room as a space of the unconscious.

If we choose to follow this intertextual string just one link further, Ernst's indebtedness to de Chirico must be recognized. As Haim Finkelstein shows, the conception of space in de Chirico informs to a great extent the "spatial ambiguities and paradoxes" of Ernst's early works.[79] Fellini, in turn, seems to draw on both Ernst and de Chirico in his cinematic rendering of the anxious room. Taking perspectival distortion to its extreme, he forces the receding walls and floorboards into actual convergence. Inverting the scale of *The Master's Bedroom*, Fellini's room is so utterly compressed that it can barely contain even the *petite* Giulietta. With the low ceiling reaching just above her head, the room appears precisely fitted for Giulietta's miniature stature. The improbable size marks the room as an eerily unreal ambience. Fellini modifies Ernst's uncanny space according to his own cinematic requirements, preserving, however, Ernst's compelling evocation of the uncanny. A "'scenography' of the psyche," to quote Hal Foster on *The Master's Bedroom*,[80] Fellini's "anxious room" is precisely the right setting for a confrontation with the demons of primal trauma.

What Fellini seeks to appropriate from painting is thus the capacity for conveying the presymbolic stratum of experience, from which, Merleau-Ponty asserts in "Eye and Mind," Western critical thinking has long detached itself. Notwithstanding the cultural references embedded in the art-historical *lexiae* of *Giulietta*, their core function is that of powerful conduits to primal experience that precedes cultural coding. What is recuperated on screen, and in the spectator, is the director's "raw" experience of the paintings in question, rather than (or in addition to) recognition of their culturally dependent semiosis. While in *La dolce vita* the Morandi hangs on the wall, framed and demarcated as "a painting," or "museum piece," *Giulietta degli spiriti* initiates a phase in Fellini's oeuvre where painting bursts out of the frame, acquiring a pivotal role in the construction of film experience.

Chapter Three

Toby Dammit: Rembrandt Meets Velázquez on Screen

This chapter charts the network of art-historical hyperlinks which Fellini's *Toby Dammit* (1968) mobilizes for constructing the tormented mindscape of its protagonist. I wish to begin with a brief review of the circumstances of the film's production, and their close bearing upon Fellini's changing conception of the cinematic text.

Loosely based on a story by Edgar Allan Poe entitled *Never Bet the Devil Your Head*,[1] *Toby Dammit* is Fellini's first literary adaptation. The film was conceived in the wake of severe artistic and economic crises in the director's life, crises which entailed physical collapse and even life-threatening illness. During this critical period in his life and work, Fellini had to abandon a project entitled *The Voyage of G. Mastorna*. *Mastorna*, telling the story of a voyage into the domain of the afterlife, was induced by the sudden death of Fellini's Jungian mentor, Ernst Bernhard.[2] Fellini's expressed reason for giving up the much cherished project of *Mastorna* after two years' preparation and, naturally, vast expenses was a profound loss of confidence in his creative potency.[3] Experiencing ominous presentiments, Fellini decided to abandon the project, which was indeed never realized.[4]

The *Mastorna* crisis had severe economic consequences for Fellini. Legal threats on the part of his producer had a devastating effect on the director. In April 1967, while nervously waiting to resume work on *Mastorna* after having reached an agreement with the producer, Fellini fell seriously ill, believing, as did his friends and doctors, that his life was in immediate danger. In the summer of 1967 Alberto Grimaldi agreed to purchase the *Mastorna* project from Dino De Laurentiis, delivering the convalescing Fellini from economic pressure and eventually enabling him to give up the project altogether. It was at this point that an offer came from the French producer Raymond Eger, asking Fellini to contribute an episode to a film entitled *Histoires Extraordinaires*, in which four well-known film directors would adapt stories by Edgar Allen Poe. Fellini realized the project in close cooperation with his new scriptwriter, Bernardino Zapponi, with whom he would continue working closely until 1980.[5]

After much deliberation, Fellini decided to contribute a loosely adapted version of *Never Bet the Devil Your Head*, in which a boy named Toby Dammit actually loses his head in a bet with the devil, incarnated in a respectable elderly gentleman. In Fellini's version, the protagonist is a stage actor in acute mental and creative crisis, alcohol-ridden and probably also addicted to drugs. Fellini's substitute for Poe's gentlemanly devil is a satanic blond girl playing with an enigmatic white ball. This mysterious figure haunts the anxious actor when he arrives in Rome to participate in an absurd Catholic western. Simultaneously alarmed and attracted, Toby eventually surrenders to the diabolical summon to join the girl's mysterious ball game. In the ending sequence he attempts to jump an abyss with his new Ferrari, so as to reach the girl, who stands waiting on the other side. The leap – whether courageous or insane remains to be considered – costs Toby his head. The head, severed by a metal cord, is picked up by the blond devil, who lays the white ball on the ground in its place.

Both Peter Bondanella and Frank Burke regard Fellini's illness and creativity crisis as the primary motivating force behind his engagement in literary adaptation. Consenting to film *The Satyricon* by Petronius, eventually completed in 1969, and the Poe adaptation along with it, Fellini was acting in distinct contradiction to his expressed aversion toward literary adaptations, which in his view were no less than "monstrous and ridiculous."[6] It was Fellini's loss of confidence, Bondanella implies, that made him turn to literary works as creative triggers or stimulants. Thus, for Bondanella, it is "impossible to understand [Fellini's] decision to employ literary texts as the basis of his scripts without some consideration of his biography."[7] Frank Burke, in his turn, proposes to "link the personal to the cultural, particularly in relation to the death-of-the-subject and the death-of-the-artist."[8]

Burke consequently points out a profound conceptual change in Fellini's thought and practice in the aftermath of this "most severe creative block of his career: the inability to complete [...] *The Voyage of G. Mastorna.*" Fellini, Burke believes, came to question "the creative freedom of the ever-evolving individual," the death of the author/artist becoming increasingly manifest in his work. Bridging the gap between biographical fact and critical theory, Burke highlights a conceptual and structural shift in Fellini's work. From the high-modernism of *8½*, with Guido the cinematic artist as organizing centre, Fellini shifts to the much more loosely centred *Toby Dammit*, which pivots around the disjointed subjectivity of its mentally unstable, intertextually constructed protagonist. Toby Dammit, to quote Frank Burke, "can only resolve his crisis by [...] appropriating the figure of Christ [...] and [...] impersonating Macbeth (not only reciting Macbeth's lines but losing his head)."[9]

Intertextual construction is a major formal paradigm in Fellini's work of the late 1960s and onward. As shown in chapter 1, the script for *Toby Dammit* indicates Fellini's awareness of contemporary thinking on intertextuality, and the centrality of Joyce as the epitome of intertextual writing. Indeed, extant readings of *Toby Dammit* explain Fellini's increasing reliance on intertextuality as the reflection of an acute disillusionment with the agency of the author.[10] Such readings, however, often disregard the specificity of Fellini's intertextual choices, which, if closely considered, invite an altogether diverse reading of the film. Christopher Sharrett asserts that Fellini's particular cultural allusions "no longer have any autonomy, nor can they support authorial intentionality or broad notions of cultural tradition."[11] However, detailed analysis of the film's art-historical intertexts reveals a rich network of authorial experiments, designed to unleash the *sémiotique* in the filmic text. Fellini's intertexts have been carefully elected. They thus call for individual analyses. Each art-historical *lexia*, it will be shown, has a particular role in augmenting the film experience.

The Hanging Carcass: Rembrandt to Fellini via Soutine and Bacon

In the course of Toby Dammit's ominous car ride from the airport into Rome, the actor's (and with him the spectator's) eye glimpses a truck carrying butchered meat (Figure 3.1). The car ride sequence as a whole is a succession of disjointed scenes, not at all what Padre Spagna, the producer of the Catholic western, would define as *syntagmatic*, in the rigidly structuralist sense of the term.[12] The first scene in the script portrays a group of road workers moving half-naked in the midst of a "black cloud of tar," emanating from "monstrous iron mouths pouring the liquid asphalt."[13] Far from a banal "road crew paving the highway," as Sharrett insists on labelling them,[14] the script expressly describes these figures as a host of medieval devils. Admittedly, in the final cut

Figure 3.1 *Toby Dammit*. "Butchered meat" shot. DVD frame capture.

Fellini chooses to refrain from this explicit allusion to the otherworld, and portrays the workers fully dressed rather than half-naked. And still the uncanny atmosphere and sulphurous colour scheme of the entire scene communicate a sense of anxiety which permeates the sequence.

The script subsequently describes a group of fashion models, posing for photography in strange plastic garments fastened with gold chains. These puppet-like models are positioned next to a dried-up baroque fountain, and appear to be manipulated by a blond photographer to whom the script refers as "a pederast." A butcher shop window was to appear next, followed by a display of garden decorations. According to the script again, a lean, yellow-faced man was to eat spaghetti in a miserable *trattoria*, seated at a table placed on a narrow sidewalk. This image was to be succeeded by another group of models seated at a bar, wearing jeans, boots, or tennis shoes in "almost a parody of the beatniks."[15]

The reading I am proposing bears on the final cut, however, rather than the script. The final cut presents a significantly modified version of the car ride sequence, with some scenes added and others extremely changed, their uncanniness enhanced. My discussion will hinge on the shot of the truck carrying butchered meat. This enigmatic image, which the script does not mention at all, was elected to open the sequence.

It probably replaces the shot of the butcher shop window, planned for a later segment of the same sequence.

Framing the rear of the truck for but a brief instance, the camera tracks right, gliding over a display of chandeliers in a large store, which probably substitutes for the garden decorations mentioned in the script. The fashion models appear next, posing motionless upon a mobile platform which slides along an incongruous background of construction works. The road works scene, which in the final cut includes a motorcycle accident, ends the anxious journey into the city of Rome.[16]

Each and every scene in this sequence pronounces its contrived nature, primarily via *effetto pitturato*, or the "painted effect." In the opening shots, a flat orange surface blocks the view from the car window, totally obstructing the presentation of deep space. The sequence is thus immediately invested with a sense of irreality, aroused by its treatment of colouring and space, both of which evoke the distorting effect of hallucinatory drugs. Piero Tosi, the film's set designer, remembers that he was asked by Fellini to actually take hashish as a preparatory step for designing this sequence.[17] According to Tosi, Fellini provided him with a portion of hashish before sending him out on a drive along the road from the airport into Rome, in which he was to take random photographs of whatever he saw on the way. Given that Fellini himself had experimented with LSD at that period, as part of his deep engagement with the mysteries of the psyche,[18] it becomes evident that he conceived the car ride sequence as a voyage through a distraught, drug-affected consciousness.

There is more, however, to Fellini's employment of *effetto pitturato* in this sequence. The sequence simultaneously offers a romantic exploration of the artist's consciousness and a self-referential exploration of a quasi-filmic succession of "pictures," framed by the car window. Whether this marked self-referentiality arises from an essentially modernist project, or rather exposes the "tired cliché" of self-reflexivity, calls for consideration. This will be possible at a later stage and on the basis of further data. At this point I propose to have a particular look at the "meat shot" and its employment of *effetto quadro* in a chain of art-historical evocations.

Notably, the "meat" image under scrutiny has been subject to extreme change on its passage from script to final cut. These changes are highly revealing. The script, as mentioned earlier, features a butcher shop window displaying a gigantic ox-head in bronze, beside "whole dismembered and bloody oxen hung on hooks" and "detached calf-heads [that] seem to be sleeping in the shop-window, with their closed eyes shedding tears."[19]

As Figure 3.1 clearly shows, the final image radically departs from the script version. The shop window does not exist anymore, nor do the bronze head and the weeping calves. Instead, a rear shot of a truck produces a flattened image in which the beef carcasses are pushed to the forefront, framed by the rectangular outline of the vehicle. Two metal bars and an obscure black background obstruct depth altogether, intensifying the sense of painterliness that prevails in the shot. Framing the image, the truck's flapping wrap evokes a spread-armed torso.

Although the shot includes within its frame a road on the left of the truck and a blurred cityscape on the right, differences in colour saturation distinguish the central image, in intense ochre and red, from the dull, monochrome images on its sides, which seem to merge into the flat, yellowish background. To augment the emphasis on surface, rather than depth, the camera faces the rear part of the truck frontally, and then abruptly abandons the vehicle, tracking right to scan the display of chandeliers. A side view of the truck would have afforded perspectival depth, which Fellini markedly avoids, forcing the image to retain its pronounced depthlessness.

A fundamental change is thus clearly discernible in the scene's passage from textual to cinematic rendering. The apparently realistic depiction of a butcher shop in the script is eliminated, giving place to an expressly painting-like composition: framed, unrealistically coloured, emphasizing surface while obstructing depth.

But there is more. Not only is this shot pronouncedly "painted" on film, but also it explodes with intertextual hyperlinks that participate in signification via cultural reference, even as they enable instinctual recognition of what Merleau-Ponty has called "the fabric of brute meaning."[20]

First and foremost, this shot harks back to Rembrandt's *Slaughtered Ox* of 1655 (Figure 3.2). Rembrandt's painting portrays a dark and empty slaughterhouse interior, with a flayed ox hanging spread-eagle on a rectangular wooden fixture. On its right a barely discernible female figure peeps from behind a semiclosed door. This canvas is the first "hyperlink" in a succession that continues in Chaim Soutine's bloody "beef paintings" of the 1920s and 1930s, and Francis Bacon's paintings in which the bloody sides of beef often serve as background for tortured human figures. Evolving from sixteenth- and seventeenth-century allegories, the images of bloody, anguished beef carcasses have come to denote human suffering and martyrdom.

In his comprehensive review of this motif in art history, Avigdor Poséq maintains that "in modern art the butchered animal has been given two kinds of meaning: it is used as an autobiographical allegory of the creative individual's ordeal and as an emblem of inhumanity."[21] As Poséq points out, the employment of this motif relies on "iconographical precedents where the slain beast is a metaphor of cruciation evoking ancient sacrifices."[22]

Figure 3.2 Rembrandt van Rijn, *Slaughtered Ox*, 1655. Oil on panel, 94 × 67 cm, Louvre Museum, Paris © RMN-Grand Palais (Musée du Louvre)/Gérard Iot.

As early as 1965, scriptwriter Brunello Rondi remarked on Fellini's profound interest in Rembrandt and his "favolosa tragicità" (fabulous tragicity).[23] Moreover, two monographs on Rembrandt in Fellini's private library bear direct evidence of his interest and acquaintance with the master's work.[24] Fellini's "butchered meat" shot closely echoes Rembrandt's masterpiece, although it certainly eschews meticulous reconstruction of the painting in tableau vivant. To begin with, the shot features three carcasses instead of one, only the left one hanging from its legs as in the painting. As in the Rembrandt, however, a dark background highlights the carcasses while obscuring the person standing next to them. Recalling Rembrandt's peeping maid, the male figure in Fellini's shot is hardly discernible on first sight. As for the imposing monumentality of Rembrandt's "crucified" carcass, this is evoked in Fellini by means of the flapping wrap, whose spread wings strongly suggest a spread-armed torso. The Fellinian image thus evokes a crucifixion, albeit implicitly, recalling the iconographic tradition that links the slaughtered ox to Christ's universal sacrifice.

Yet another shot included in the car ride sequence seems to reference the Passion of Christ in direct association with Toby's psychic torment. Non-existent in the script, like the butchered meat shot, it appears to be a last-minute addition. An ecclesiastical procession passes beside the car stuck in the heavy traffic. Fellini does not provide the conventional long shot that would introduce the procession. Rather, he elects to begin with a medium close-up of Toby's anguished visage, visible through the car window, with a halo superimposed on it. The halo, constituted by the reflection of a sacred icon carried in the procession, invests the film's protagonist with an aura of martyrdom, connoting, like the butchered carcass, what Poséq calls "the creative individual's ordeal." As mentioned earlier, the procession scene, the reflected halo, and the changes made in the butchered meat scene are not mentioned in the script. It thus appears that these significant modifications were conceived during the actual shooting, with the probable intention of enhancing the visual suggestiveness of the scene, giving rise to an intense experience of anxiety and mental torment.

Returning to the art-historical matrix undergirding the "meat shot," reference to Soutine's imagery of flayed beef must be noted, adding a second layer to the suggestion of pain and mental torment.

Chaim Soutine, a Russian Jewish painter who immigrated to Paris, the seat of the *avant-garde* in the first decades of the twentieth century, had a particular attraction to Rembrandt's works, which he encountered in the Louvre. Under the strong impression of Rembrandt's *Slaughtered Ox*, Soutine purchased a beef carcass in the neighbourhood abattoir and placed it in his studio, creating a series of variations on Rembrandt's subject. Rembrandt's *Slaughtered Ox* provided Soutine, as per Poséq, with "a kind of aesthetic validation for his own neurotic attraction to morbid subjects."[25]

The "beef" paintings are widely associated with Soutine's social and mental tribulations. Soutine himself had remarked that he wished to "show Paris in the carcass of an ox," in light of which the series of carcasses has come to be associated with "the brutality of the metropolis,"[26] aside from the loneliness and misery of the artist.

Soutine's macabre imagery did not escape Fellini's attention, so it seems. In fact, Rinaldo Geleng, a painter and Fellini's lifelong friend and collaborator, has mentioned Soutine to me as one of the painters in whom Fellini took interest.[27] Geleng, an intimate friend of Fellini since 1939, and sharing his profound love of painting, was probably the most suitable companion with whom such interest could be shared. I also risk an assumption that Fellini's interest in Soutine may have been aroused by Ernst Bernhard, the Jewish psychotherapist (a refugee from Nazi Austria) who introduced Fellini to Jungian psychology, and with whom Fellini maintained a close relationship for about five years, until Bernhard's sudden death in 1965.[28]

Significantly, Fellini introduces the motif of the butchered carcass into the sequence of the nervous entry into metropolitan Rome. Constructing this sequence as a highly troubling projection of an anxious mindscape, Fellini appears to rely on Soutine's compelling rendering of the painter's loneliness, guilt, and creative anxiety. This visual hyperlink (as I have proposed to define Fellini's signifying units) invokes the "raw," physically felt sensation of angst emitted by the Soutine and the Rembrandt alike. The "meat shot" thus calls for reflection on the mechanism of its embodied effect and its indebtedness to painting, and to the particular paintings that it addresses and evokes.

In her suggestively titled essay, "Dead Flesh, or the Smell of Painting," Mieke Bal highlights the "daring roughness of the handling of the paint" in Rembrandt's *Slaughtered Ox* in the Louvre.[29] The crux of Bal's argument is what she sees as the work's strongly felt association of paint with flesh, putrefying flesh. But the paint, Bal emphasizes, does not function primarily on the level of representation – that is, as "expressing *something else*"[30] – but rather as a medium for making present the experience of death via powerful suggestion of the rotting flesh.

Painting, Bal writes, "becomes here the medium for overcoming the nonrepresentability of death."[31] Fellini, I am arguing, mobilizes precisely this capability of painting to reach beyond representation, toward Merleau-Ponty's "imaginary texture of the real."[32]

Probing further and deeper into the intertextual layering of Fellini's "meat shot," I presently wish to draw attention to the reverberation of Francis Bacon's hanging cadavers in this multilayered signifying unit. The oeuvre of the Irish-born British painter (1909–1992) is situated in a historical period in which the iconography of animal slaughter takes on an even more macabre tone.

From an early stage of his career, Bacon collected photographs of abattoirs, complete with their gruesome contents. Some of these items have been published in the Vienna Kunsthistorisches Museum catalogue, *Francis Bacon and the Tradition of Art* (2004). Among the colour-stained scraps of paper torn out of magazines and catalogues, one finds Rembrandt's and Soutine's "beef" paintings, beside photographs of butcher shop windows and even a carcass hanging in a car trailer, curiously recalling Fellini's "meat shot."[33]

Bacon incorporated images of slaughtered beef into his work as early as *Painting 1946*, which features an open-mouthed figure seated under a black umbrella against a split beef carcass. The human figure, a male, is flanked by dismembered meat parts, in a setting that has the appearance of a butcher shop. Ziva Amishai-Maisels regards the split cadaver as a "sliced open and crucified human carcass," and proposes to read *Painting 1946* as "a juxtaposition of torturer and tortured," and the grinning (or yelling) man as a specific reference to Mussolini.[34]

In 1952 Bacon had himself photographed by John Deakin, holding two sides of a split carcass. His 1954 *Figure with Meat* features a screaming Pope Innocent X with two parts of a carcass, suggestive of a crucifixion, and in the right-hand panel of Bacon's 1962 triptych, *Three Studies for a Crucifixion* (Figure 3.3), the crucified creature clearly derives from Soutine and Rembrandt. In Bacon, however, it is an expressly human creature that hangs upside down with its mouth open in a horrible scream.

In a 1962 conversation with David Sylvester, Bacon explicitly associated the motifs of slaughterhouse and raw meat with the Crucifixion and its connotation of pain, cruel mutilation of the human body, and atrocious death.[35] Unlike Rembrandt, who places the hanging cadaver in the concrete context of a slaughterhouse, or Soutine, who isolates it against an expressionistic background, Bacon couples his animal

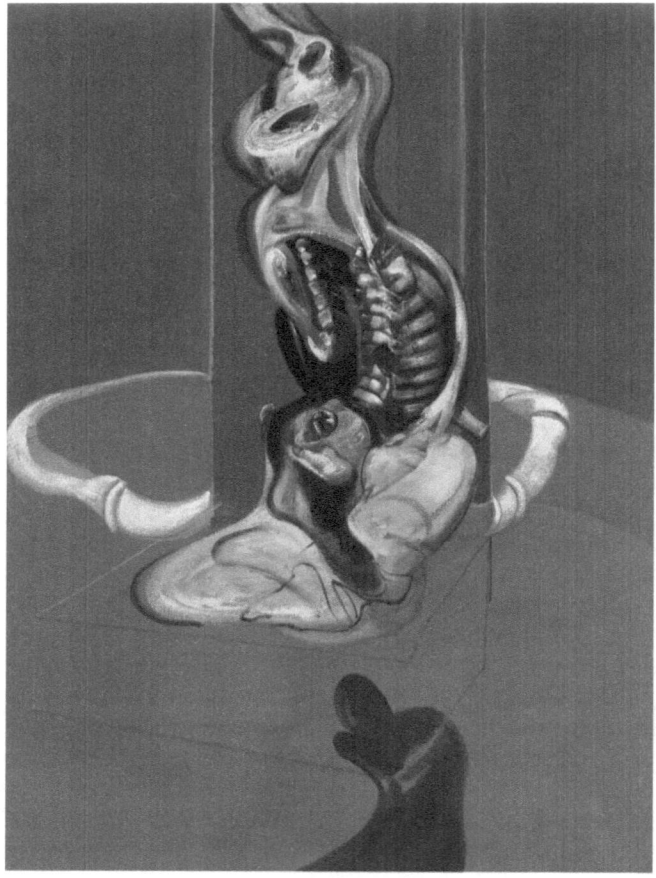

Figure 3.3 Francis Bacon, *Three Studies for a Crucifixion*, March 1962 (detail). Oil with sand on canvas, three panels, 78 × 57 inches (198.1 × 144.8 cm) each. Solomon R. Guggenheim Museum, New York, 64.1700 © 2012 by The Estate of Francis Bacon. All rights reserved. ARS, New York/DACS, London.

carcasses with living humans in alarming circumstances. As Norman Bryson has pointed out, "with Bacon, the death-drive is not deflected or warded off into a safely separated zone, it inhabits life from the inside, at the deepest level of the body's tissue and bone."[36]

Fellini, who was in the habit of frequenting art exhibitions both in Italy and abroad, often upon the invitation of friends,[37] could have had an opportunity to see Bacon's *Three Studies for a Crucifixion* in the retrospective exhibition launched in May 1962 at the Tate Gallery, or as it travelled with sensational success to other European cities, including Turin, Italy.[38] Alternatively, he could have become acquainted with this and other of Bacon's paintings at the exhibit of the painter's new works held in Rome in January 1967,[39] very close to the conception of *Toby Dammit*. In the latter exhibit Fellini could most probably have seen Bacon's 1965 *Crucifixion*, in which the central figure echoes Soutine's writhing carcasses. In this painting, again, the crucified cadaver has a suggestively human spine, with bandaged limbs prostrate on a red surface, and a foetal skull hinted at just above them.

The acute anxiety and profound involvement with death in Bacon's meat paintings would have hit a responsive chord in Fellini, deeply affected as he was at the time by the unexpected death of his Jungian mentor, Bernhard, and profoundly disturbed by the consequences of his own illness and failure to complete *Mastorna*. The "meat shot" seems to evoke paintings of the hanging carcass, relying on the embodied effect made possible via their non-verbal communication of anxiety, mental torment, and death.

In his monograph *Francis Bacon: The Logic of Sensation* (1981), Gilles Deleuze has addressed Bacon's treatment of the body as raw flesh, materialized in paint. "The painter," Deleuze writes, "is certainly a butcher."[40]

What this suggestive formulation implies is a certain capacity of painting – particularly via the material sensation aroused by paint – to "[come] across directly onto the nervous system."[41] Like Merleau-Ponty, Deleuze conceives of painting, particularly Bacon which for him is apparently the epitome of painting, as having to do primarily with embodied experience. "There are no feelings in Bacon," Deleuze writes. "There are nothing but affects: that is, 'sensations' and 'instincts.'"[42] And thus, Deleuze seems to posit, the flesh, that unstructured, primal "zone of indiscernibility,"[43] materializes on Bacon's canvas in a distinctly nonsymbolic, preverbal mode. Sensed as a presence, rather than re-presentation, "[w]hat is painted on the canvas is the body, not insofar as it is represented as an object, but insofar as it is experienced as sustaining *this* sensation."[44]

In his quest for the *sémiotique* within cinematic language, Fellini seems to recognize the strong sense of presence elicited by Bacon's "meat" paintings, which he successfully reevokes in Toby's fleeting view of the truck. Vivian Sobchack, in her phenomenological study of film, elaborates at length on the embodied nature of the film experience. Sobchack posits, "[w]e cannot meaningfully abstract vision from the spectator's lived body."[45] It is an embodied spectator, a "lived-body" or "body subject," to say it with Sobchack, that shares the filmmaker's experience "through the respective mediation of camera and projector."[46] The film is the site where "filmmaker and spectator are brought into indirect perceptual engagement with each other ... They are brought also into perceptual engagement with each other's perceptive and expressive acts."[47] Film is thus not a neutral object for vision, but rather a site of exchange and engagement, where the spectator is able to recapture, or reexperience, the author's original experience of the profilmic material. It is thus that Fellini's spectator is enabled to experience the intensity which particular paintings, in this case the sequence of butchered carcasses, from Rembrandt to Bacon via Soutine, bear for Fellini. The "meat shot," and this is crucial to my argument, does not function primarily, or exclusively, as a cultural signifier. True, the motif of the slaughtered ox carries widely recognized cultural connotations, best realized via erudite recognition of its art-historical references. Nonetheless, it is capable of arousing an unnameable, embodied sensation of *angst*, irrespective of its cultural coding.

What Fellini seeks to appropriate from painting, then, is not so much its cultural codedness as its compelling capacity to convey that "brute" or primal meaning so central for Merleau-Ponty in his elaboration on the ontology of painting in "Eye and Mind," discussed at some length in chapter 1.

Notably, Fellini's idiom does not conform in the least to the tradition of the tableau vivant, which in the 1960s had already become paradigmatic for any cinematic endeavour of referencing painting. Fellini's meat shot by no means constitutes, or seeks to constitute, a tableau vivant in the same way that this formal trope is employed in Pasolini, or Godard, to name but two major examples from the same period. The "meat shot" does not bear the conventional markers of tableau vivant, such as halted or suspended motion, nor does it display the shifts in colour scheme or soundtrack which conventionally mark the passage from cinematic narration to the tableau form.

Rather, Fellini's smooth and seamless weaving of the shot into the fabric of the sequence is dialogic in the Bakhtinian sense, in that it eschews the modality of tableau vivant altogether, declining to formally mark painting as cinema's Other. As shown in chapter 1, Bakhtin's conception of dialogism and *heteroglossia* hinges on the idea that the heteroglot utterance incorporates diverse languages in "*concealed form ... without any of the formal markers usually accompanying such form.*"[48]

Luckily enough, film history has provided probably the best foil against which to consider Fellini's incorporation of painting(s) in *Toby Dammit*. Only three months after Fellini finished shooting *Toby Dammit*, Pier Paolo Pasolini began his work on *Teorema*, with Terence Stamp, Fellini's cast for Toby Dammit, playing the lead role of a mysterious visitor upsetting the life of a bourgeois household. *Teorema* was filmed in Rome between March and May 1968, when *Toby Dammit*, begun in October 1967, was already projected in Cannes. This close circumstantial proximity calls for a comparative look at Pasolini's treatment of some paintings by Francis Bacon, in light of the foregoing discussion.

The sequence of shots I wish to reference features Terence Stamp as the enigmatic visitor seated on a bed beside the son of the host family. As the film insinuates, the two are involved in a homosexual relationship. In the scene under scrutiny the two are seen leafing through an illustrated monograph on Francis Bacon. Shots in which the paintings fill the frame are intercut with reaction shots of the boy's anxious face as he gazes at these paintings.

Pasolini employs Bacon's paintings as a concrete visualization of the character's anxiety, pivoting on the homosexual liaison. Lingering for several minutes over Bacon's *Two Figures in the Grass* (1954), and then on *Two Figures* (1953), the camera reflects the expressed concerns of the scene. Special weight is given to reaction shots of the boy's anxious expression, as he examines the screaming creatures in *Three Studies for Figures at the Base of a Crucifixion*, or the bloody meat parts in *Painting 1946*. The paintings are thus embedded in the cinematic text(ure) as explicitly coded for homosexuality and anxiety.

While *Teorema* and *Toby Dammit* seem to engage in a similar endeavour of incorporating painting into a cinematic text, they diverge extremely in their formal devices. Unlike Fellini, Pasolini places actual paintings (or, to be more accurate, printed reproductions of the paintings) in front of the camera. The images are immediately recognizable both as "paintings" and as "Bacons" – that is, culturally sanctioned "museum pieces." In *Teorema*, the incorporated paintings are expressly marked as foreign to the cinematic flow. Framed by a camera that rests longer than usual on each single painting, they are further alienated by recurrent moments of arrested motion. Pasolini not only underscores the foreignness of these embedded paintings but also makes sure to foreground the process of cinematic mediation through which they are presented to the spectator. Sabotaging the auratic integrity of the museum masterpiece, he employs oblique camera angles that distort the paintings, cropping and skewing the original "Bacons." Foregrounding elements of the cinematic apparatus such as camera angle and framing, Pasolini engages the cinematic mediation of painting in a self-referential stand. As the man and the boy leaf through the pages, the resultant succession of paintings comes to suggest a "flipbook," or archaic prototype of film. Pasolini's astute juggling of still painting and filmic flow undermines the sacred stillness of the painting. More particularly, it highlights the serial – or should we say cinematic – quality of Bacon's triptychs.

The director of *Teorema* seems intent on marking painting as an alien element within film, asserting, in the process, the supremacy of the cinematic medium. Fellini's *Toby Dammit*, in turn, does not support such clear demarcation of painting within the filmic text. The shallow space and painterly, monochrome colour scheme pervade the car ride sequence in its entirety, rather than the meat shot alone. Painting in *Toby Dammit* is seamlessly woven into the fabric of the film, giving rise to a Bakhtinian "hybrid construction." In fact, the manifest *heteroglossia* of Fellini's filmic text constitutes a primary parameter by which his idiom may be distinguished from that of Pasolini, both in *Teorema* and in earlier films like *La Ricotta* (1963), where tableau vivant plays a major role.

A brief look at *La Ricotta* may clarify this point. In *La Ricotta* Pasolini makes a clear formal distinction between two diegetic planes that simultaneously overlap and clash, the one associated with painting, the other with "real life" or rather social reality. The film thus follows two diverse narrative lines that converge in the film's tragic conclusion. In the first storyline Orson Welles is cast as a tyrannical film director who unsuccessfully attempts to reconstruct the Passion of Christ in tableaux based on two Mannerist paintings of the Deposition, dating from the 1520s. The film's parallel narrative line follows the story of Stracci, a lower-class worker hired as an extra to play one of the thieves crucified alongside Christ. Stracci feeds his hungry family with the lunchbox he receives on the set, and suffers humiliation from extras and professional actors alike. He ends up dying on the cross in the process of shooting a crucifixion scene. Stracci dies of a mixture of starvation and overeating, having gorged on the remainders of the "last supper" chucked at him by the abusing actors.

The *mise-en-abŷme* of "outer" and "inner" film is elaborated in an expressed clash between the reality of Stracci's story, filmed in black and white, and the expressed artificiality of the tableaux, presented in colour and expressly marked as unfilmic. The marking is achieved first and foremost by abrupt alternations between colour and black and white. The colour shots employ a palette of primary colours: blues, reds, yellows, and white, as well as orange, green, and brown. This unnatural, or "painterly" palette, and the formal arrangement of local colour, expressly deviate from the cinematic aesthetic. Furthermore, the shifts from black and white to colour are not explainable within the diegetic logic. What is more, the tableaux vivants appear to be located in a studio, against an artificial flat background, whereas the Orson Welles character is clearly seated in an outdoor location while directing these scenes. Unexpected, brief cuts from colour tableau to the black-and-white outside world and back enhance the incongruence of this peculiar cinematic construct.

Another formal marker of painting in film is naturally the suspension of movement. Pasolini introduces stillness only to sabotage it. The figures in *La Ricotta*'s living pictures never manage to stay still. They move their eyelids, pick their noses, fall unexpectedly, and altogether subvert the aura of noble mourning that pervades the paintings.

Distinction on the level of sound is the last framing device employed by Pasolini. The tableaux are accompanied by classical music, while the domain of "real life" is marked by the Twist, to which the actors dance in carnivalesque disrespect for the sacred scene featured in the tableau. When the set assistants mistakenly play the Twist in the background of the Rosso tableau, the director responds with furious exclamations about sacrilege and blasphemy.

In *La Ricotta*, therefore, Pasolini markedly delineates the boundaries of the painterly within the filmic, "stag[ing] a conflict between two semiotic models: the painterly and the cinematic," as per Rumble.[49] The frustration expressed by Orson Welles's character stems from the impossibility of achieving the full stillness and auratic atmosphere required for a successful imitation of painting. His attempts to reconstruct the tone of sacred reverence are repeatedly aborted by the actors' irreverent conduct and poor acting skills. In a cinematic tour de force, Pasolini aggressively appropriates the paintings, dissecting and exploring them by bits and fragments, zooming in on individual characters, changing viewpoints, gaze directions, and colour, and even tampering with format and *mise en scène*, adding figures and other elements to the composition. The paintings are cinematically modified in various ways, their unity and authorial authenticity sabotaged. Pasolini's cinematization of painting thus conforms to François Jost's "*picto-film* type II," where trans-semiotization of painting is effected via the cinematic device and its essential tools.[50]

Notably, Pasolini undermines the canonical masterpieces in ways that exceed formal manipulation. The Passion of Stracci, who actually expires on the cross, is Pasolini's competing version for the canonical representation of the Passion. A politically engaged cinematic version is thus juxtaposed with the canonical imagery of art history.

Fellini's concerns, however, lie far from the film/painting dialectic which Pasolini openly engages via quotation and appropriation. The three art-historical intertexts – Rembrandt, Soutine, and Bacon – embedded in Fellini's "meat shot" are not encountered as "museum pieces," that is distinctly marked units of painting. The actual paintings are never shown on screen, as in Pasolini's *Teorema*. Neither are they brought to the viewer's attention via an easily recognizable tableau, as in *La Ricotta* or *Il Decameron* (1971). Fellini is obviously not concerned with enabling facile recognition of cultural clichés. Neither is he concerned to elicit that "awareness of the power of the code itself" which Patrick Rumble finds in Pasolini.[51] At the heart of the matter lies Fellini's trust in painting as a conduit to a stratum of "raw", or pre-symbolic experience. His transposition of painting into the "moving pictures" breeds a unique hybrid, neither purely painting nor entirely film.

And thus, while *Toby Dammit* and *Teorema*, respectively, strive to signify anxiety via painting(s), they diverge extremely in terms of formal idiom, in a way that recalls the distinction made by Julia Kristeva between the *sémiotique* and the *symbolique*. In Pasolini we are presented with a systematically constructed cinematic "sentence," where Bacon's paintings constitute discrete, recognizable units conveying a definitive meaning. The undifferentiated form and augmented visual suggestiveness of the Fellinian text, in turn, strongly gravitate toward the *sémiotique*, or toward Deleuze's "zone of undecidability."[52]

The motif of butchered meat resurfaces in *Fellini's Roma* (1972), where three brief shots of hanging beef carcasses appear in a context quite similar to that of *Toby Dammit*. Again it is a young man's entry into metropolitan Rome. This time it is a young boy (widely recognized as an alter ego of the young Fellini) who arrives in Rome for the first time in his life. A streetcar ride from the Stazione Termini into town initiates the provincial youngster into the unsettling chaos of 1940s Rome. The first "meat shot" in *Fellini's Roma* closely recalls the shot of the meat truck in *Toby Dammit*, only to undermine the similarity by eliminating from the *Roma* version the pronounced painterliness so crucial to *Toby Dammit*. Unlike the flat, hazy, and monochromatic shot in *Toby Dammit*, in *Fellini's Roma* the "meat shot" retains a realistic sense of depth and colour.

Effetto dipinto, both in the capacity of *effetto pitturato* and *effetto quadro*, reappears at a later stage in the film, where Fellini resorts to an image of a butcher-shop window, recuperating the scene originally suggested in the script for *Toby Dammit*. The monochromatic colour scheme of this shot, the pronouncedly painted background behind the hanging cadavers, and the lighting that renders them starkly artificial all create a distinct sense of *effetto pitturato* (Figure 3.4). The hanging carcasses are bathed in an eerie blue light emanating from the electric cables of the streetcar. The glass doors of the butcher shop suggest a diptych-like partition. Together with the shop window on the left a triptych emerges, evoking Bacon's characteristic triptych form.[53] In fact, the large carcass in the middle "panel" of Fellini's triptych closely recalls Bacon's rendering of the meat motif, particularly his emphasis on the ribcage and contorted spine, as in the right panel of *Three Studies for a Crucifixion*, and the middle panel of the 1965 *Crucifixion*. Fellini eliminates Bacon's strong suggestion of blood, substituting the cold blue flashes of the electrical short circuit for Bacon's reds and oranges. Nonetheless, the alarming noises of explosion on the soundtrack augment the connotation of wartime disquiet.

Figure 3.4 *Fellini's Roma*. A butcher shop window. DVD frame capture.

Two portraits of Mussolini, posted on the wall to the left of the butcher shop, mark the historical specificity of the scene. And then, as the camera tracks right and passes the display of hanging carcasses, it reveals a poster depicting a truncated visage of a girl, where only the point of a nose and a wide open mouth are visible. Posted on the lower part of the placard is a banner calling the public to enlist. Interestingly enough, this image seems to reference another recurrent motif in Francis Bacon, the motif of the screaming, bare-teeth human mouth, as in *Three Studies for Figures at the Base of a Crucifixion* of 1944. With Fellini's joining of the wide open mouth, the hanging carcass, and the tripartite triptych-like framing, recognition of Bacon's imagery as an embedded intertextual reference is practically inevitable.

Fellini's Roma introduces this art-historical *lexia* in a context of life in Rome during and after World War II. Cultural and social concerns outreach the suffering of the individual, whereas in *Toby Dammit* it is the inner voyage of the creative artist that is evoked via the *angst* of a Rembrandt, a Soutine, a Bacon. Fellini thus employs the butchered meat motif in diverse modes, according to the particular concerns of the film text in which it is embedded. Nonetheless, in both films Fellini's "meat" *lexiae* are predicated upon painting, of which the director apparently conceives as the most effective catalyst, or conduit of the *sémiotique*.

The *Bambina Diavolo*, or "Velázquez on Film"

The figure of the devil-girl, or *bambina diavolo*, requires unravelling as yet another multilayered intertextual construct. As mentioned earlier, Fellini substituted Poe's male devil, a respectable elderly gentleman, with a blond girl holding a white ball. Peter Bondanella, tracing the gradual change in the figure of the devil from script to film, asserts that Fellini had left no trace of Poe's male devil in the final cut. Nonetheless, it is possible to recognize a hint of the male devil in the old man grinning menacingly at Toby, just prior to his fatal leap over the bridge. Employing no other means but backlighting, Fellini astutely suggests a couple of devil's horns on the two sides of the man's dark beret. Subtly hinting at the literary origin of the film, Fellini foregrounds its intertextuality.

In the present discussion I wish to engage a number of shots portraying the *bambina diavolo*, mostly in oblique view and dramatic backlighting (Figure 3.5). Figured this way, I will argue, the image of the girl constitutes a pregnant art-historical *lexia*. This assertion is based first and foremost on archival findings from Fellini's private library, indicating

Figure 3.5 *Toby Dammit. Bambina diavolo.* DVD frame capture.

his interest in Velázquez's masterpiece, *Las Meninas* (1565; Figure 3.6), with particular focus on in the figure of the Infanta Margarita.

The most significant piece of evidence is a line in Fellini's handwriting on the inside cover of a 1952 monograph by Francisco Javier Sánchez Cantón, *Las Meninas y sus personajes*. The note makes reference to page 23 in the book. Page 24 in turn has a paragraph describing the royal child, marked on the side by Fellini, who even took the trouble of translating it into Italian on a scrap of paper inserted into the book. As it appears, Fellini also collected reproductions of other portraits of the royal *infanta* by Velázquez. These he also kept inserted between the pages of the *Las Meninas* monograph. A typical example of these inserts is a detail of *Las Meninas*, with the girl in its centre, bearing a handwritten note that specifies the whereabouts of the painting ("Madrid – Prado"), beside the name of the figure ("Infanta Margarita Teresia"), and the fact that it is a detail of *Las Meninas*. While these scraps of paper clearly indicate that Fellini took active interest in Velázquez's royal Infanta, there is no mention of *Toby Dammit*, or any other film for that matter, in these intriguing notes. Whether the figure of the Infanta Margarita is indeed incorporated into Fellini's imagery, and precisely how and where, whether a scene or a single shot, is left open to speculation.

Figure 3.6 Diego Velázquez, *Las Meninas*, 1656 (detail). Oil on canvas, 26.7 × 23.1 cm, Museo del Prado, Madrid, Spain/Giraudon/The Bridgeman Art Library.

Fortunately, historical circumstances support the association of Fellini's devil girl with the blond empress of *Las Meninas*, as proposed in the following pages. In 1966 Michel Foucault addressed *Las Meninas* in an article by that name, which aroused a heated debate that lasted well into the 1980s. Two years after the publication of Foucault's essay, Pier Paolo Pasolini introduced *Las Meninas* into the opening scene of his short film *Che Cosa sono le nuvole?*, featuring a marionette theatre production of Othello.[54] As in *Teorema*, Pasolini incorporates the paintings in discrete units of filmed tableaux embedded in the cinematic text. In the scene opening the film Pasolini lets his camera travel over publicity posters reproducing four Velázquez masterpieces, which in turn constitute backgrounds for advertisement of what seems like a traveling theatre company.[55] In the shot that concludes this scene, the camera rests for an unusually long moment on the *Las Meninas* poster, made to serve as background for the credit titles of the film we are about to watch, *Che cosa sono le nuvole?* (Figure 3.7). The film's self-reflexive engagement with cinematic representation is thus denoted via overt recourse to *Las Meninas*. The static shot of *Las Meninas*, and the preceding shot

Figure 3.7 Pier Paolo Pasolini, *Che cosa sono le nuvole*. DVD frame capture.

traveling over the other Velázquezes, constitute a "bracketed phrase" within the cinematic flow. In superimposing his name, professional title, and the title of his work, *Che cosa sono le nuvole*, upon the violently cropped Velázquez masterpiece, Pasolini blatantly posits painting as film's contested Other, appropriated by the cinematic medium of which he is the master.

Fellini was bound to be aware of the intellectual stir and rekindled critical interest in *Las Meninas* in Italy's intellectual and artistic circles. Most probably, he was also aware of Pasolini's cinematic endeavour and his overt presentation of *Las Meninas* on screen. *Le nuvole* was filmed in Cinecittà between March and April 1967,[56] about five months before the onset of studio work on Fellini's film. It was released in April 1968, a month before the debut of *Toby Dammit*. In those years, Pasolini and Fellini were working in close proximity, employing in some cases the same actors, set designers, and cameramen. The two directors were thus bound to follow each other's work with attention. Given that *Le nuvole* was shot in Fellini's home base, Cinecittà, it is practically beyond doubt that he had at least some knowledge of what was going on on Pasolini's set.

Foucault's seminal essay of 1966 is concerned with systems of representation and signification. The essay ascribes a focal role to the interchange of gazes between figures within and outside of the picture space, the gaze of the former group implying the presence of the latter.

Las Meninas thus constructs "three 'observing' functions" that "come together in a point exterior to the picture."[57] These are (1) the actual, historical figure of the painter in contemplation of his painting, (2) the king and queen, who are his assumed models and are not seen in the painting, and (3) the spectator. All three are connoted by the gazes directed outward from the painting. Foucault emphasizes the fact that the Infanta's gaze, which should interest us most in the present discussion, constitutes the centre of the composition. "A vertical line dividing the canvas into two equal halves would pass between the child's eyes," where "beyond all question, resides the principal theme of the composition ... the very object of this painting."[58] The enigma that is constituted by the implied gazes, inverted canvas, and fuzzy mirror reflection lies at the core of Foucault's conception of *Las Meninas* as "representation in its pure form."[59]

In the critical debate over Foucault's essay, probably the most interesting note was contributed by Joel Snyder and Ted Cohen, who argued, in an essay of 1980, that in this "painting about painting" the mirror reflects not the actual king and queen but rather their painted portrait on the inverted canvas. "Velázquez wants, and he wants the viewer to understand that he wants, the mirror to depend upon the unseeable painted canvas for its image.... The mirror image is only a reflection. A reflection of what? Of the real thing – of the art of Velázquez .... In the presence of Velázquez, a mirror image is a poor imitation of the real."[60] In the cultural discourse of the late 1960s–1980s, *Las Meninas* was featured as a visual riddle on the problematics of visual representation as seen from postmodernity.

Returning to Fellini, although his interest in *Las Meninas* may have been triggered by Foucault, perhaps through the mediation of Pasolini, it is not primarily the self-referentiality of *Las Meninas* and its metadiscursive overtones that he seeks to evoke in *Toby Dammit*. Rather, Fellini invokes Velázquez's blond empress-to-be in the figure of the *bambina diavolo*, engaging her in a fatal exchange of gazes with Toby Dammit, an artist in crisis. The spectator, implicated in the exchange as addressee of the gaze, is made strongly aware of the disturbing sensations it arouses.

Fellini's recourse to the evocative power of painting is again made evident. Reliance on painting enables him to forge an intense cinematic experience on the level of the *sémiotique*, one in which the spectator acquires the quality of a "body subject," to adopt Vivian Sobchack's phenomenological term, rather than remaining a disembodied, deciphering mind.[61] Unlike Pasolini's *Le nuvole*, which leaves the painting in its original and recognizable state – albeit visibly cropped and blatantly appropriated – Fellini does not make any effort to reproduce *Las Meninas*, nor does he make overt reference to this painting, neither as "a painting" nor as the culturally sanctioned entity that is "*Las Meninas* by Velázquez." Rather, he extracts a suggestive detail, the penetrating gaze of the blond empress, appropriating its heightened capacity for visual communication.

Although, as in *Le nuvole*, we are dealing with a stage actor as the focal figure of the film, what is at stake is not a self-reflexive examination of the creative apparatus. Rather, Fellini's film engages the intense experience of the creative process, speaking through Velázquez's painting to evoke anxiety and distress. In this sense Fellini is far from the notion of subject-less cultural construction as the paradigm for all artistic endeavour. For Fellini, despite premature announcements of its death, the (creative) subject is alive in postmodernity as it was for romantics and modernists alike.

Fellini, Picasso, and *Las Meninas, after Velázquez*

But the intertextual fabric of Fellini's film has yet to reveal more of its art-historical fibres. In a brief but significant shot from the car ride into Rome, Fellini effects a dislocation of Toby's facial features in the manner of Picasso, by means of a reflection cast on the car window, through which the actor is partly visible. A schematic, elongated face, considerably larger in proportion to Toby, is superimposed on the actor's face, resulting in a strange fragmentation and distortion of the protagonist's features.

Fellini's art-historical *lexiae* do not stop at invoking painting in the general sense of *effetto pitturato*. The present shot speaks again to *Las Meninas*, this time via Picasso's series *Las Meninas, after Velázquez*.

In this 1957 series of forty-five canvases, Picasso grapples with the revered Spanish masterpiece. In the first canvas of the series, the painter's visage is split into opposing profiles, one eye positioned lower than the other, one nose penetrating the opposite profile. As Susan Galassi has observed, in Picasso's version of *Las Meninas* the painter is "in the process of dissolution."[62] For Galassi, Picasso's modification of Velázquez connotes an "absence of certainties."[63] Fellini appears to turn to Velázquez's Infanta as a paradigm for self-assured sovereignty, at the same time resorting to Picasso's twist on Velázquez when he needs to render the creative subject as crumbling apart.

Fellini had an expressed and pronounced interest in Picasso. He even made the master's acquaintance at the Cannes film festival of 1957.[64] This would have been about three months before Picasso began work on the *Las Meninas* series. Did the two artists discuss Velázquez, or *Las Meninas* in particular, on that occasion?

Laying aside this wild suggestion, which lamentably cannot be verified, it must still be noted that Fellini, quoted in Bondanella, regarded Picasso as "the eternal embodiment of the archetype of creativity."[65] "Last night I dreamt of Picasso," he writes in *Fare un film*. The two "Picasso dreams" recounted in *Fare un film* occur at times of "confusion and loss of confidence."[66] One dream encounter takes place among the waves of a stormy sea, with Picasso confidently leading the way toward "the best fishing."[67] Navigating the deep, turbulent waters of the unconscious, Picasso is able to bring the creative process to a promising conclusion. Whether authentic or contrived, the dream posits Picasso as a major Fellinian signifier for creative potency.[68]

Fellini could have had a few opportunities of seeing the *Las Meninas* series on exhibit. The series was first shown at the Galerie Louise Leiris in Paris in 1959, and, closer to the conception of *Toby Dammit*, in a 1966 Picasso retrospective in Paris.[69] Moreover, in February 1968 Picasso donated the entire series to the Picasso Museum in Barcelona. This must have received wide publicity, which in turn would have drawn Fellini's attention to the *Las Meninas* series precisely when post-production work on *Toby Dammit* was initiated.[70] That Picasso had chosen to tamper with Velázquez may have doubled the appeal of his series for Fellini, given his own involvement with *Las Meninas* at that period.

Las Meninas after Velázquez may thus be recognized as yet another visual intertext woven into the rich fabric of Fellini's *Toby Dammit*. Moreover, and now I am returning to the mesmerizing one-eyed gaze of the *bambina-diavolo*, it seems that Fellini predicated it on Picasso's depiction of the girl no less than on the Infanta in Velázquez.

In *Las Meninas, after Velázquez* Picasso depicts the royal Infanta more often than any other detail of Velázquez's painting. Realizing the focal role of the girl's penetrating gaze, Picasso detaches this figure from Velázquez's compositional framework, dedicating several of the canvases exclusively to her. In these works, extra visual emphasis is put upon a single eye, in expressed elaboration on the gaze that is only hinted at in Velázquez. Picasso's pronounced emphasis on the single eye as the epitome of the gaze seems to resonate in Fellini's *bambina diavolo*, whose one-eyed stare drives Toby to his death.

It should be noted, however, that Fellini transposes this highly charged exchange of gazes from the painter's studio, as in Velázquez and Picasso, to the artist's mindscape. The entire occurrence unfolds in a Rome that is hallucinatory and uncannily labyrinthine, far from a realistic urban setting. Transplanting the artist and the blond empress into a mind-scenery, Fellini involves them in a series of ghastly gaze exchanges. In the power struggle that ensues, the girl is clearly the stronger party.

But who is this girl? To attempt an answer to this question, some further unravelling is required. It is at this point that I propose to turn to Jung, and more particularly the Jungian literature on Fellini's shelves.

Severed Head and White Ball: Fellini's Jungian Universe

Characterized as a sovereign of the artist's psyche, the *bambina diavolo* represents an archetypal psychic force. As such, this figure is predicated to a great extent on the Jungian anima archetype. Given Fellini's extensive reading and exploration of Jung, one may expect to find Jungian imagery incorporated into the visual and conceptual matrix of this film, particularly in the figure of the *bambina diavolo*.[71]

The film brings Toby's anxious journey to its end in a gory decapitation. Fellini's final shots portray the severed head as it lies on the ground, the girl's white ball bouncing in its direction until it comes to rest next to Toby's head. The head is picked up by the diabolical girl, while the white ball remains on the ground where it had come to rest, substituting for the head.

While the theme of decapitation derives directly from Poe's story, the white ball is an addition, attributed by Fellini to the devil figure.[72] The conjunction between white ball, blond girl, and severed head calls for attention, particularly in light of its possible association with a couple of dream illustrations in C.G. Jung's edited volume, *Man and His Symbols*.

The white ball has been widely overlooked in critical treatments of *Toby Dammit*. It is, however, a key image in this film. Fellini's doomed protagonist, irresistibly drawn to the girl's enigmatic ball game, is ready to disregard her blood-chilling stare and take a fatal leap over the abyss, only to reach the white ball held up in her hands as a promised trophy. In light of Fellini's deep involvement with Jungian thought, at that period in particular, Toby's seemingly suicidal act may turn out to constitute a "creative leap," to adopt a term denoting extremely risky acts taken as a way out of crisis situations.[73]

As mentioned earlier, Fellini's collection of Jungian literature included a copy of the richly illustrated *Man and His Symbols*. Intriguingly, this book reproduces a still from Fellini's own film, *La Dolce Vita* (1959). Even more significantly, the *Dolce Vita* still is assigned to illustrate a chapter on depressive crisis. To quote Marie Louise Von Franz, Jung's disciple and the author of this chapter, depressive crisis must be regarded as the "initial stage of the individuation process."[74] One cannot underrate the importance of this Jungian text for Fellini, experiencing physical and mental crises during these very same years.

A couple of dream illustrations in *Man and His Symbols* particularly stand out in relation to the girl-and-ball signifier. The first of these photographic illustrations portrays a blond girl staring obliquely at the camera. The particular posture, angle of the gaze, and of course the physical characterization of this figure strongly resonate in Fellini's *bambina diavolo*. Besides the powerfully penetrating stare and sharp tilt of the head, Fellini's shots of the *bambina diavolo* recall the dramatic backlighting and ominous atmosphere of the Jungian illustration.

The photograph of the staring girl in *Man and His Symbols* is captioned thus: "the anima accuses the dreamer of being inattentive to her." The adjacent image, which portrays a skull and a detached head that gradually dissolve into a red ball, is captioned as follows: "here the man may try to reject the unconscious (kicking the skull) but it asserts itself by means of the ball ... and the anima figure [i.e., the female head]."[75]

A personification of the anima archetype, the blond, staring figure amalgamates a promise for vitality and creativity[76] with a sense of imminent danger.[77] According to the dream interpretation proposed by Von Franz, a struggle takes place between the dreamer and his anima, the latter asserting her power via round objects like the clock and the red ball. The required plunge into the unconscious, the dream seems to say, is dangerous and potentially destructive.

A couple of other images from *Man and His Symbols* substantiate the proposed Jungian reading of Fellini's *bambina diavolo*. I am referring to a drawing and a film still, both accompanied by explanatory captions that present them as anima personifications. In the first image, a drawing by William Blake, Dante's Beatrice is presented as a "guide, or mediator, to the world within and to the Self."[78] Adjacent to Blake's drawing, on the same page, we find a still photograph from a film, in which a woman in white beckons a man to cross an abyss, for which he must step over a dubious-looking wooden beam. The female figure, the caption explains, embodies the anima as a "death demon," one which arouses suicidal drives.[79] The striking similarity between this image and the final state of affairs in *Toby Dammit* is hard to miss. The camera first frames the *bambina diavolo* in extreme long shot as she beckons to Toby across the collapsed bridge, displaying the white ball as an award. In response, the delirious artist drives forward in full speed, attempting to leap the abyss.

But there is more. As the captions in *Man and His Symbols* make clear, the photo-illustrations we have been discussing "present a few examples of mandala imagery ... to indicate the vastly different form in which this archetype can manifest itself, even in one individual's unconscious."[80]

The Jungian *mandala*, from the Hindu *magic circle*,[81] embodies an idea of integrity and wholeness via round or oval objects such as an eye, a fish, and other spherical bodies. Presented in Jungian thought as "a symbol of human wholeness or as the self-representation of a psychic centripetal process," the *mandala* is conceptualized in terms of "a system of order which superimposes itself, so to speak, on the psychic chaos."[82] Jungian texts, moreover, explain spontaneous irruptions of *mandala* imagery (as in dreams, fantasies, or automatic drawing) as "an unconscious attempt at self cure in states of psychic disorientation."[83] The *mandala* symbol is closely associated with the creative process, as Von Franz asserts in the following paragraph of *Man and His Symbols*, which I deem highly pertinent to the present discussion:

> [The mandala] also serves the creative purpose of giving expression and form to something that does not yet exist, something new and unique ... What restores the old order simultaneously involves some element of new creation.[84]

Fellini's indubitable acquaintance with these texts must inform any reading of his ending of *Toby Dammit*. The white ball in the hands of the satanic girl is a Jungian *mandala*. For the artist in creative crisis it bears a promise of revival. Bondanella tells us that Fellini cherished the apparition of bright, floating spheres in his childhood fantasies. He often lamented the loss of his visionary faculty in adulthood, and the consequent disappearance of these glowing globes.[85] But, looking closely, one realizes that glowing spheres hover above Toby's head all along the anxious drive through the labyrinthine Rome of his mindscape. Tauntingly close yet unachievable, these spheres of light resonate with the white ball in the hands of the *bambina diavolo*.

Fellini's intense involvement with Jung implies an attempt to counter postmodern anxieties about art's capacity to touch on, and convey, an experience of the real. Here I am in complete disagreement with the vein of reading represented by William Van Watson's assertion, that the only way left for Toby is substituting wholeness with "holeness," turning to "death rather than transcendence."[86] True, heavy doubt has been cast in postmodernity on the capability of art to recapture or regenerate primal sensation, if such exists at all in an age of hollow simulation. Fellini, however, stubbornly holds on to the option of wholeness, which for him is still an open possibility for the (cinematic) artist. The piercing gaze of the diabolical girl is a case in point. By means of its strong corporeal appeal, this visual moment elicits a highly embodied response. Fellini appropriates from Velázquez, Picasso, and Jung the sensually flowing hair and penetrating gaze of the blond figure, leaving aside such informative details as dress, entourage, and physical surroundings. With the gaze extracted from its narrative context, the stage is clear for the archetypal intensity of the anima, bringing the film image close to "real" experience, as close as art can get.[87]

The Severed Head: Symbolist Intertexts

But aren't we overlooking yet another powerful image that participates in the ending shots of this film? In fact, the film's concluding shots are not exclusively about the devil-girl. Rather, the spectator is presented with Toby's severed head lying on the ground, as the white ball quietly bounces toward it. This image appears to speak to a Symbolist theme, the decapitation of Orpheus.

In the Symbolist discourse, Orpheus was the archetypal artist, at once a "poet, martyr, priest, and magician."[88] An occultist belief in the transcendence of art, and in the artist as priest and initiate, pervades the Symbolist set of ideas on art as a vehicle of mystical revelation and spiritual transcendence. A key figure in this frame of thought, Orpheus is featured time and again in Symbolist painting. In various versions of the myth, Orpheus is torn to pieces by the Thracian Maenads. His severed head, floating down the river Hebrus, acquires oracular powers. In other sources, the head emits divine music, "by which his art transcends his brutal death."[89]

Toby Dammit, an artist in crisis, meets a similar fate. Like Orpheus, he is beheaded. The resonance of the Orpheus myth in the film's concluding shots, it will be shown, relies particularly on the representation of the myth in Symbolist painting. Recognition of a couple of relevant art-historical evocations may enable a more complex reading of *Toby Dammit*, that veers away from the notions of "holeness," to quote Van Watson, that pervade practically all critical readings of this film.

I shall return to the Symbolist Orpheus shortly, but first I propose a brief detour that will further highlight the art-historical undergirding of Fellini's character. The film expressly marks Toby as a martyr, particularly in the many shots that frame his anguished expression. In one such shot, mentioned earlier, the corona of a sacred icon in a religious procession is reflected in the window of Toby's car, crowning his forehead in perfect superimposition. A similar instance of visual marking occurs in another shot featuring Toby inside the car. In this low-angle shot, the figure's intense anguish is indicated by the sharp backward thrust of the head. Dramatic contrast lighting hints at the protagonist's fate, virtually "severing" the head from the neck, which is hidden in deep shadow.

Intriguingly enough, the physical traits, facial expression, and particularly the position of the head in this shot recall a drawing by Odilon Redon, entitled *Christ* (1887). This drawing appears in André Mellerio's monograph on Redon, which Fellini had in his library. The book was published in 1968, the very same year when *Toby Dammit* was completed.

The dispirited, absent gaze on Toby's face, the backward thrust of the head, and the dramatic highlighting of the forehead and one half of the face closely recall those of Redon's *Christ*. The one distinction between the two portraits lies in the direction of the gaze, which in Redon is turned upward right, and in Fellini downward left.[90]

Relying on Redon's *Christ* as a visual paradigm for martyrdom, the shot under discussion marks the artist as martyr. Or is it, as Burke might have it, only the cliché of the martyred artist being exposed? Further exploration of embedded intertexts is required before an attempt is made to resolve this question, although it must be stressed that ambiguity is the hallmark of Fellini's idiom, making closure and conclusion practically impossible.

In Mellerio's monograph, Fellini could have found a collection of severed heads, as for example in the lithograph *The Eye, Like a Strange Balloon, Mounts towards Infinity* (1882), in which a head lies upon a platter attached to an eye-shaped balloon. This work derives from Redon's lithographic album *To Edgar Poe*, as is clearly indicated in Mellerio's caption. Bearing in mind that *Toby Dammit* is a Poe adaptation, the lithograph becomes doubly salient. *The Eye, Like a Strange Balloon* appears, as well, in *Il Simbolismo* by Renato Barilli, part of the series *L'Arte Moderna* (1967), which Fellini owned.[91] Fellini was undoubtedly familiar with Redon's homage to Poe.

The Eye, Like a Strange Balloon thus bears significant relevance to the present reading. Redon's lithograph implies a cycle of crisis and transcendence, countering the downward inclination of death by the lightness of the ascending balloon. As Barbara Larson has pointed out, Redon's interest in the balloon as image of transcendence was aroused by his observation of a tethered hot-air balloon presented for public view in a Paris fair. The balloon's struggle to overcome the binding cords embodied for Redon "[m]an's struggle to free himself from gravity and the material realm," and "the attempt at ascent toward spiritual realms," shadowed by the inevitable failure of this struggle.[92]

The reverberation of Redon, and Jung, in the ending shots of *Toby Dammit* carries an implicit suggestion of transcendence through art. A kinship is thereby forged between Fellini's beheaded protagonist and Orpheus, the archetypal, beheaded artist. It is not surprising to find, therefore, that the film's ending shots evoke Symbolist renderings of the Orpheus myth. Jean Delville's *Orpheus* (1893) particularly comes to mind, bearing a similarity of composition and colour scheme. In Delville, the head lies on an elaborately decorated lyre, and the scene is bathed in a greyish-blue haze, with the ripple of water filling the background. As in Fellini's ending shots, Delville isolates the severed head, leaving only the lyre on which the head lies, and with which it practically merges.

Evoking Delville's painting, *Toby Dammit* features an isolated head lying on a bluish grey surface. The colour scheme of the shot closely recalls that of the watery background in Delville's *Orpheus*. As in Delville, the head is positioned along a diagonal axis that stretches from lower left to upper right. The position of the head is inverted, however, rendering the face almost invisible. As in the painting, the source of light in this shot is invisible and hard to locate. The overall atmosphere is likewise hazy. As the shot proceeds, the white ball bounces into the frame, coming to lie beside the severed head. It is in this state that the composition most resembles Delville's *Orpheus*. The white ball provides a focal spot of light that either reflects an outside source or, in the Symbolist spirit, connotes an otherworldly light.

The concluding shots of *Toby Dammit* thus resonate with echoes of the Symbolist Orpheus, connoting transformation and transcendence rather than "holeness" and death. Coupled with the Jungian references pointed out earlier, the present intertextual reading makes it possible to think about Toby's leap and beheading as a magical resolution of the artist's crisis. Courageously leaping the abyss, the artist is not annihilated, but rather undergoes radical transformation. In fact, he acquires the magical mandala-ball in exchange for his (rational, logocentric, symbolic?) head.

What emerges in this reading is what Roland Barthes has called the "third meaning," or "other text." Once recognized, this "other text" powerfully counters the sense of annihilation so strongly implied by the gory imagery of the film's ending shots. The focal argument made in the present study is that Fellini's reliance on embedded art-historical hyperlinks makes possible the emergence of a "third meaning." A Bakhtinian "double-voiced discourse" is thereby forged, weaving painting seamlessly into the cinematic text.

Toby Dammit: The Creative Artist as Mystical Initiate

Symbolist painting emerges as the major visual and conceptual matrix of Fellini's cinematic fabric. Fellini's ventures into the world of the occult during this very same period, the late 1960s, may be regarded as another manifestation of the same project, in that they express a deep-seated belief in the possibility of transcendence and mystical initiation.

At the same time, Fellini was well aware of the intellectual currents of thought of his time. As shown in chapter 1, he was acquainted with post-structuralist thinking and concepts to a larger extent than has formerly been acknowledged. The manifest artificiality and pronounced intertextuality of *Toby Dammit*, particularly in the first car ride sequence discussed in detail in this chapter, reflect Fellini's awareness of notions of the death-of-the-subject, and author, in postmodernity. This said, I wish to insist that the film's expressed intertextuality does not necessarily imply the ultimate end, or loss, of authorial agency. In this chapter, and the ones to follow, I propose to pay closer attention to Fellini's particular choice of visual intertexts, and how they function, "site-specifically," in each signifying unit, or *lexia*. It has been shown earlier that the motif of butchered meat, appropriated from painting, has a crucial role in generating an immediate, almost physical experience of torment and anxiety in Toby's car ride into Rome.

What Fellini's mode implies is a desire to reach through to the *sémiotique* via visual suggestion, largely dispensing with narrative means.

Christopher Sharrett, ignoring what the film potently communicates via the *sémiotique*, concludes that Fellini had reached a point of "distrust of representation itself," expressing a "nihilistic sense that artistic poetics has been exhausted."[93] However, when we read the film via its visual hyperlinks, it becomes evident that Fellini's cinematic signs preserve a power of suggestion able to counter the alienation of the "hollow signifier." William Van Watson rightly concludes in his thought-provoking essay that, even though "like a postmodernist [Fellini] concedes and revels in the artifice of the signifier [...] for Fellini this does not mean that the signifier's relationship to the signified is completely arbitrary [...] the Fellinian umbilical reties them as sign."[94]

Fellini's project, which is re-establishing the sign as a conduit to the real, relies primarily on painting. In constructing an intertextual network of art-historical references he consciously treads a liminal path, between postmodernist and romantic, or modernist conceptions of art and the artist. In his overt intertextuality and structural fragmentation, Fellini seems to call on the formal tropes of postmodernism only to subvert them by reasserting the agency of the artist and the potency of art for conveying real human experience.

Chapter Four

Fellini Satyricon: Bruegel Meets Klimt in the Sewers of Imperial Rome

Fellini Satyricon is doubtless the most painterly of Fellini's films.[1] Several frames *en-abyme* juxtapose live and painted figures, and the film seems quite explicit about its art-historical sources. *Fellini Satyricon* is less a psychoanalytically conceived private dream than a culturally conscious one. As indicated in the preface to this book, the preparatory notes for *Fellini Satyricon* present an eclectic list of visual sources, featuring an improbable conjunction of Byzantine and pop art, the psychedelic and the Pompeian, beside modernists such as Mondrian and Klee. Although the preparatory note quoted here should be approached with due reservation, as but a very partial clue to the film's intertextual network, it is highly revealing as to the crucial role of painting in Fellini's late 1960s idiom.

As pointed out by Frank Burke, *Fellini Satyricon* lacks the organizing centre of a stable, individuated protagonist. Rather, Burke notes, Fellini turns to art as "a kind of last-ditch opportunity to maintain the kind of affirmative vision that characterizes ... *The Nights of Cabiria, 8½, Juliet of the Spirits, Toby Dammit*, and perhaps even *Fellini Satyricon*."[2]

While the extent of art-historical intertextuality in *Fellini Satyricon* has been strongly intuited by critics and scholars,[3] a systematic analysis of specific images in light of their various intertexts has yet to be proposed. This chapter sets out to trace, if not the whole intertextual network which informs this film, at least some of the major art-historical *lexiae*.

Fellini's (re)Presentation of *Romanità*

Fellini's representation of imperial Rome in *Satyricon* is rooted in the historical specificity of his own biography to a greater extent than might be expected, or has been acknowledged. Analyses of *Fellini Satyricon* have tended to read its representation of antiquity as a reflection of the late 1960s social and cultural upheaval.[4] Gianfranco Angelucci alone has acknowledged a possible hint in *Fellini Satyricon* to fascist representations of imperial Rome. For Angelucci, Fellini's film offers a reconsideration of the myth of Rome, obscured over the past twenty centuries, above all by the rhetoric of fascism and Hollywood cinema.[5] I will expand on this point, and argue that the rhetoric of fascism, and the idea of *Romanità* in particular, is a central concern of Fellini in this film, as becomes manifest via an art-historically informed reading.

My discussion of *Giulietta degli spiriti* has touched on its implicit reference to fascism, via the "barba-rossa" headmaster and the figure of the fascist father appearing in the *soggetto* and the script. The exuberant *Liberty* style of Suzy's villa has been shown to flout the severe classicism of the fascist, *Romanità*-oriented style. While *Amarcord*, *Roma*, and *I Clowns* engage fascism in an overt manner, many of Fellini's other films employ subtle visual hints that implicitly evoke this dark period of Italian history, which coincided with and significantly affected Fellini's childhood and adolescence.[6]

In an interview given to Valerio Riva and titled "*Amarcord*: The Fascism within Us," Fellini expressed his view that fascism persisted in a certain state of mind still pervasive in contemporary Italian society, and thus formed an ever looming potential threat. Traveling second-class in Italian trains, Fellini remarked, one feels that things had not changed since the fascist era. "Italy, mentally, is still much the same [and] fascism and adolescence continue to be, in a certain measure, permanent historical seasons of our lives: adolescence of our individual lives, fascism of our national life."[7]

Fellini's view of Italian fascism as "a past which is nearby and still very much present"[8] offers a new perspective on his pronounced alienation from the figures of *Fellini Satyricon*, to whom he referred as "these human beings who lived two thousand years ago and don't mean a damned thing to us."[9] Alienating himself from the fascist rhetoric of *Romanità*, Fellini's intense resentment is turned not so much toward his historical Roman ancestors as toward the mates of his teens and early twenties. It is notable that in the preparatory notes for *Satyricon*, published in *Fare un film*, Fellini openly refers to the figures of his film as "Nazzisti" and "razzisti [racists]."[10] The *Satyricon*, then, seems to reference the 1920s and 1930s more than it does the 1960s.

One of the central ideological premises of Italian fascism was the concept of imperial mission, a myth of Roman glory which the regime constructed and disseminated.[11] In *Fare un film*, Fellini condemns this sort of exploitation of antiquity as an "abject, [...] a bit racist curiosity."[12] Albeit not specific as to the precise object of this critical comment, Fellini is evidently referencing fascist propaganda. In *Fellini Satyricon* he thus posits a de-idealized image of antiquity, one in which brutal power reigns over a depraved host of grotesque subjects. It is worth noting that the *trattamento* (or primary story version) of *Fellini Satyricon* begins with a scene of brutal gladiator fights at the *Circo Massimo*. Roman citizens of both sexes and all ages, headed by the empress, watch the atrocious spectacle with indifference, laughing, eating, and making bets while humans and animals die a bloody death in the arena.[13] Notably, this scene does not exist in Petronius, and is an addition made by Fellini or his scriptwriters. Notwithstanding the omission of this scene from the script version and the final cut, the fact that it opens the *trattamento* highlights Fellini's attribution of idiocy and cruelty to the very same Romans whom fascism went so far to idealize.

I commence with a look at Fellini's treatment of imperial portraiture in *Satyricon* and *Block-notes di un regista* (*Fellini: A Director's Notebooks*). *Block-notes*, made for NBC contemporarily with the production of *Satyricon*, features a sequence of shots in black and white in which famous Roman bust portraits emerge gradually from a dark background, only to be swallowed anew by the darkness that surrounds them. These shots are intercut into a sequence in full colour, taking place in a slaughterhouse in contemporary Rome, where Fellini and his crew arrive in order to search for and audition "authentic" Roman butchers for the film *Fellini Satyricon* (Figure 4.1).

Taken at face value, Fellini's introduction of Roman portraits into this sequence may be read as a reassertion of an ancestral link between antiquity and contemporary Rome. However, this scene is set in a slaughterhouse, where, by implication, the descendants of the glorious Roman emperors are to be found. The film thus disturbs the fascist myth by positing an analogy between the glorious Roman warriors and modern Roman butchers.[14] The slaughterhouse sequence could in fact be read in conjunction with the *Circo Massimo* butchery scene, presented in the *trattamento* of *Fellini Satyricon*. What we are offered is rather sarcastic commentary on the valorization of the Roman warrior during the fascist era.

Fellini Satyricon surpasses even *Block-notes* in its grotesque twist on the Roman bust. A case in point is the improbably grotesque amputee appearing in the temple of the Hermaphrodite. Loudly hailed as "the

Figure 4.1 *Block-notes di un regista*. Contemporary Roman butchers and imperial Roman busts. DVD frame capture.

unfortunate hero of the battle at Quadragesimo," the monstrous figure is carried around on a stretcher, receiving the veneration of the surrounding crowd (Figure 4.2). This grotesque personage, who is nowhere to be found in the script, constitutes a veritable "living bust." Notably, it recalls the well-known bearded imperial portraits. Manifesting the self-assurance that befits a Roman general, this "living bust," amputated up to the chest and shoulders, receives the onlookers' adoration with calm dignity. As in the slaughterhouse sequence in *Block-notes di un regista*, the ridiculous hybrid creature presents an ironic twist on the militaristic ideal of the "citizen-soldier," which, Emilio Gentile points out, was central to the fascist discourse of *Romanità*.[15] Fellini's pun on the glorious Roman bust debunks both the notion of the Roman hero and the art-historical aura of imperial portraiture.

Military heroism is deflated in *Fellini Satyricon* in more than one way. The parade of the usurping Caesar toward the capital merits a look. In what seems to be a direct reference to Mussolini's "March on Rome," the script features a host of grotesque warriors parading onto the capital, led by a general who has brutally seized political power.[16] As this

Figure 4.2 *Fellini Satyricon*. "The unfortunate hero of the battle at Quadragesimo." DVD frame capture.

scene is envisioned in the script, all of the "vecchi combattenti" (war veterans) participating in the parade are physically crippled. Some are blind, and others are lame or maimed in different ways.[17] The shot that follows, in the script version, presents a view of cadavers of Roman generals, rotting inside their armature.[18] The heroic armour, readily recognizable from Roman portraiture, is juxtaposed with the decaying flesh in an uncanny hybridization of the glorious and the grotesque, as in the amputated "hero of the battle at Quadragesimo." The crippled *combattenti* and the generals rotting inside their armour offer an ironic statement on this major trope of fascist propaganda – namely, the myth of Roman military glory.

But Fellini does not settle solely for ironic treatment of Roman portraiture. Turning to the painting of Pieter Bruegel the Elder as a reservoir of ready-made signifiers of grotesqueness and idiocy, Fellini is able to construct the Romans, and by implication Italian fascists, as a host of passive, lazy, stupid, and immature sexual exhibitionists.[19]

Fellini's interest in Bruegel is well documented. Gianfranco Angelucci lists a few that most attracted Fellini's attention in the Flemish master's oeuvre. He mentions *Lust*, from Bruegel's series of the *Seven Deadly Sins*, the *Tower of Babel*, and the *Land of Cockaigne*.[20] In addition, Fellini's private library has a copy of *Das Bruegel Buch*, a small volume bearing a dedication from Ennio Flaiano, a close collaborator, dated January 1954, beside another monograph on Bruegel published in 1955.

Fellini's merciless image of *Romanità* appears to be informed to a great extent by Bruegel's idiom. The temple of the Hermaphrodite, where the "Quadragesimo hero" is encountered, swarms with deformed humans (Figure 4.3), one of which particularly recalls Bruegel's *Beggars* of 1568, while another echoes the contorted postures of the figures in Bruegel's *Parable of the Blind* of the same year.

The "Bruegel itinerary" embedded in *Fellini Satyricon* takes the viewer further, to Trimalchio's dinner party, where an entire scene is devoted to the gutting of a roasted pig from whose slit belly an enormous amount of meats and sausages pours out. This scene immediately brings to mind Bruegel's slit-bellied creatures. Best known among these is probably *Big Fish Eat Little Fish*, of 1556, portraying a giant fish from whose mouth and dissected belly a host of smaller fish pours out, some holding smaller fish in their mouths. A man with his face completely covered by a helmet is cutting at the belly of the fish with a disproportionately big knife, while another man, his face similarly unseen, uses a ladder to climb atop the giant fish. A fish with two human legs is seen in the background holding yet another fish in its mouth, presenting an inhuman and merciless system of power relations.

But Bruegel's oeuvre teems with creatures whose slit bellies expose visceral contents. In *Gluttony* an unidentifiable object protrudes from a creature's stitched belly, and in the *Fall of the Rebel Angels* a creature in the lower right-hand corner holds open the slash in its belly to expose its viscera. While in *Gluttony* the slit-bellied creature obviously

Figure 4.3 *Fellini Satyricon*. A Bruegelian cripple featured in the Hermaphrodite scene. DVD frame capture (frame detail).

refers to concrete issues of the stomach, in the *Fall of the Rebel Angels* the bladder-like creature is an angel transformed into a monster, suggesting the sin of lust through its obvious sexual connotations. Bruegel's creatures with exposed viscera address themes of gluttony, lust, and human alienation. All of these powerfully resonate in *Fellini Satyricon*, particularly via the figure of Trimalchio and its monstrous gluttony, lust, and cruelty. A slave become *nouveau riche*, Trimalchio embodies the entire gamut of vices evoked in Bruegel's painting, gluttonously feasting on absurd amounts of food, lusting for his young male lover, abusing his slaves, and insulting his guests.

Notably, the script references Bruegel directly in conjunction with Trimalchio's dinner party. Subsequent to the scene with the gutted pig, the script features a shot of a barrel wheel on which hang "as on the tree of Cockagine, ham, birds, decanters of wine and bunches of grapes."[21] *The Land of Cockaigne* (1567), counted by Angelucci as one of Fellini's favourite paintings by Bruegel, depicts a legendary glutton's paradise, where "pigs and geese run about already roasted, and pancakes and tarts grow on the rooftops, and fences consist of fat sausages."[22] The focal point – and central axis – of Bruegel's composition is a tree from which hangs a circular wooden tray, set with various foods. Under the "tree of Cockaigne," three unconscious men are sprawled, obviously fallen victim to their own gluttony.

Unlike Pasolini, who only two years later re-created Bruegel's *Land of Cockaigne* in a tableau featured in *Il Decameron* (1971), Fellini apparently discarded the idea of explicit reproduction. True to his commitment to open form and *heteroglossia*, he chose to eschew tableau vivant. Rather, he privileged a seamless incorporation of painting into the fabric of the film. And still the script's explicit mention of the tree of Cockaigne sheds light on the thought processes and working methods underlying this film. The script discloses the considerable art-historical awareness involved in Fellini's working process, and the particular relevance of Bruegel's idiom to the representation of imperial (or is it fascist?) Rome.

But the "Bruegel itinerary" has not been exhausted as yet. Fellini refers to the tenement named *insula felicles*, where the two protagonists, Encolpio and Ascilto, live, as a "terrifying skyscraper-palace, immense, dark, swarming like Bruegel's *Tower of Babel*,"[23] and, in another place, as "that monstrous Tower of Babel."[24] Quite surprisingly, therefore, we find that the visual rendering of that structure diverges significantly from Bruegel's *Tower of Babel* (1563). In the two versions of this subject

Figure 4.4 *Fellini Satyricon, insula felicles*. DVD frame capture.

painted by Bruegel, both in 1563, the tower evokes classical Roman architecture, with which Bruegel became acquainted on his visit to Rome. Bruegel's tower particularly references the arched openings of the Colosseum, and its separation of outer shell and inner structure.[25] In Fellini's *insula felicles*, however, the arches are replaced by irregularly dispersed rectangular openings (Figure 4.4).

Why is it, then, that, after having made the explicit textual association with Bruegel, Fellini elects to make this significant modification, practically annulling the analogy between the film image and Bruegel's painting?

The answer to this question may again be found in the film's pervasive sarcasm vis-à-vis the concept of *Romanità*, or the idealized image of imperial Rome in the fascist rhetoric. While Bruegel celebrates the Colosseum as the epitome of architectural achievement, Fellini often referred to this Roman monument with overt hatred, as "that horrendous catastrophe in stone, that immense skull consumed by time, stuck in the middle of the city."[26] Fellini was undoubtedly ambivalent about this emblem of *Romanità*, whose arches resonate in fascist architecture, as for example in the *Palazzo della civiltà Italiana* mentioned in chapter 1, a strictly Roman-style edifice designed for the 1942 *Esposizione Universale* in Rome. In fact, the *insula felicles* evokes the austereness of this brand of fascist architecture, much more than it does Bruegel's *Tower of Babel*. However, the austere regularity of the fascist style is disrupted by the varying sizes and irregular distribution of the apertures.

The public edifice of the fascist era is thus evoked in *Fellini Satyricon* only to be ironically debunked, as with the Roman bust transformed into a living amputee, or the honourable Roman landlord transformed into the gross landowner, Trimalchio. The Roman (or fascist) edifice of the *insula felicles*, swarming with grotesque humans who indulge in the seven deadly sins, is modelled upon the template of Bruegel's *Tower of Babel*, the ultimate signifier of human depravity and corruption, with a subtle nod at fascist architecture.

Fellini's "Byzantium"

Fellini's image of the declining Roman Empire is not informed, however, exclusively by Bruegel. It also draws on late nineteenth-century or *fin-de-siècle* painting, predominantly on the Decadents. In his overview of the Decadent aesthetic, Mario Praz has named two characteristic features, the "beauty of inertia" and the "necessity of richness."[27] Both of these central aesthetic qualities resonate in *Fellini Satyricon*.

Inertia, a key feature of this film, is manifested first and foremost in its privileging of the static camera and expressed rejection of dollies and other means of motion. From the script one learns that Fellini meant Trimalchio's guests to freeze suddenly when coming into frame, as if they had just finished speaking or still had their lips twisted in a laugh.[28] Fellini's decision to shoot *Satyricon* with minimal camera movement strongly indicates that he was opting for a strong sense of detachment and alienation.

In its project of alienation, the film obstructs spectatorial identification. Bondanella, quoting Stuart Rosenthal, asserts that *Fellini Satyricon* prevents identification by avoiding the POV pans that conventionally simulate the protagonists' subjective gaze.[29] Intentionally faulty and unsynchronized dubbing is another technical means for subverting illusion, and with it identification.[30] The lethargic alienation, or *inertia*, which permeates *Fellini Satyricon* strongly evokes the atmosphere that suffuses Decadent painting.

Praz's second characteristic, the "necessity of richness,"[31] is highly pertinent to Fellini's "baroque" style, as it has widely been described. Visually overdetermined, *Fellini Satyricon* manifests a large number of characters and extras, fantastic sets, elaborate costumes and jewellery, and pronouncedly artificial makeup and hairdo abounding with golden ornament. All of these closely evoke what Praz refers to as "voluptuous, gory exoticism."[32] Shortly after the release of *Satyricon*, Alberto Moravia wrote that Fellini was "a decadent who is magnetized by the most celebrated and most historic of all decadences." Fellini,

Moravia wrote, was "attracted by Antiquity precisely because he sees it as corrupt and moribund."[33] However, while Moravia was referring to Roman decadence, I propose to look to late nineteenth-century Decadence as a major constituent of the art-historical matrix which undergirds *Fellini Satyricon*.

Beyond formal aspects of style, Fellini's very choice of imperial Rome as subject matter repeats the *fin-de-siécle* "turn to the decaying Rome and Byzantium as historical metaphors for their own age."[34] Fellini seems to draw on Byzantium as a Decadent concept, a ready-made signifier of historical and cultural degeneration.

Notably, the Decadent conception of Byzantium involved elements of occultism, black magic, and satanism, reflecting the period's renunciation of rationalism.[35] Judging by the number of books on magic and the occult in Fellini's private library, it appears that Moravia's definition of Fellini as a decadent was not far from the truth. *Il Demoniaco nell'arte* (1952), *Histoire en 1000 images de la magie* (1961), *Incontri con Satana* (1961), *Leggende del Diavolo* (1957), and a *Dizionario di scienze occulte* (1910), all preserved in Fellini's library in its current state, indicate beyond doubt his avid reading of and fascination with the subject of the occult. A preparatory drawing for *Satyricon* confirms Fellini's immersion in this brand of literature. The drawing depicts a goat-headed figure with a lit candle on its head, closely recalling a photograph appearing in Fellini's copy of *A Pictorial History of Magic and the Supernatural* by Maurice Bessy (1964). The figure in the photograph, described as a "contemporary European sorcerer," engages in some ritual of black magic, connoted particularly by the goat costume.[36] The drawing, which Fellini entitled "Satyricon," actually copies the image from Bessy's book, associating it with his film. Fellini's image of Roman antiquity and its representation in *Satyricon* thus appear to be mediated to a great extent by the concerns and imagery of *fin-de-siécle* Decadent art.

As mentioned earlier, commentators on *Fellini Satyricon* have pointed out at random some of its art-historical references. In what follows I reject some of these proposals, while enforcing others by additional research. I will thus begin with Philippe Jullian's brief mention of Beardsley, Klimt, and Böcklin, to which list he adds Rochegrosse and Alma-Tadema, as possible sources for the imagery of *Fellini Satyricon*.[37] Jullian, a scholar of late nineteenth-century painting, may have been more disposed than other critics of *Satyricon* to discern the reverberation of Decadent painting in this film. However, like other generalizing attempts that associate *Fellini Satyricon* with Cubism, surrealism, or abstract expressionism, Jullian does not offer any particular analysis of individual images so as to substantiate his claim. Moreover, he binds together the Decadents and Alma-Tadema, who cannot be counted as one by any means. Since Jullian does not point out individual shots or scenes that in his opinion derive from Rochegrosse, Alma-Tadema, or Klimt, his assertions remain regrettably vague.[38]

The association of Alma-Tadema with the imagery of *Fellini Satyricon* is particularly debatable, given marked differences in style and atmosphere between the idealized genre scenes of Roman life presented by Alma-Tadema and Fellini's unsettling tableaux of corruption and disintegration. One may consider, for example, the visible disparity between Alma-Tadema's representation of the Roman baths, as in the brightly illuminated and idealized imagery of the *Apodyterium* of 1886, and the dark, uncanny environment of the baths in *Fellini Satyricon*. Fellini expressly resented the brand of exotic genre or costume scenes epitomized in Alma-Tadema's painting. As his set designer Danilo Donati told Eileen Hughes on the set of *Satyricon*, Fellini was opting for décors and costumes that would be evocative without indicating specific period imagery.[39]

Not only the sets and general atmosphere of *Fellini Satyricon* but also its representation of Woman departs significantly from Alma-Tadema's typical costume scenes. The reclining prostitutes in the "lupanari," for instance, are a far cry from the idealized, unselfconscious, unthreatening objects of desire which Alma-Tadema sets against brightly illuminated backgrounds in *The Tepidarium* (1881). Fellini's women are posed in cavernous dark cells, gazing directly at the spectator with the assured self-consciousness of a *femme fatale*. The "lupanari" prostitutes may rather be associated with an 1885 painting by Belgian Symbolist Fernand Khnopff, *Of Animality*, in which a woman is presented in a context of primitive ritual, her naked body flanked by two multibreasted pagan idols.

Trifena, the character played by the French actress Capucine, is a fully elaborated Decadent type. Trifena is the female partner of Lica in his predatory mission, collecting "human curiosities" for Caesar's diversion. In her physical attributes, dress, and gestures, this figure particularly evokes Gustave Moreau's rendering of Salomé, and even more so Gustav Klimt's portrait of yet another beheader of men, *Judith I* (1901).

Klimt was undoubtedly an object of interest for Fellini. Notably, Fellini owned the comprehensive 1967 catalogue of the painter's works by Novotny and Dobai. As Rossana Bossaglia notes, the late 1960s had seen a revived interest in Liberty style, of which Klimt was considered a central representative.[40] This revival of interest in Klimt, just about the time when Fellini was conceiving *Satyricon*, is significant in this respect. *Fellini Satyricon* evokes Klimt in more than one way, beginning with its pronounced decorative excess, particularly manifest in the elaborate golden jewellery of the women.

Trifena, probably the major female protagonist of this film, first appears in Trimalchio's dinner party. Gazing fixedly at Encolpio, she causes him to freeze "as if subjugated," to use the words of the script.[41] As she slowly leans to touch a table with her lips, in an explicit summons, Trifena is immediately identified as a sexual predator (Figure 4.5).[42] A few episodes that appear solely in the script involve Trifena in ritual scenes of sex and bloodshed. All of these scenes take place on board Lica's ship, which the script describes as a microcosm of monstrosities.

In fact, the sequence of scenes on board the ship has two versions in the script, none of which is fully realized in the film. The first scene in version 1 features Trifena and Encolpio in a boat, sailing toward the ship. Trifena watches the pale and depressed Encolpio as though she were "a huntress who had captured a precious animal."[43] In shots 513–14 Trifena acts as a judge between Encolpio and Ascilto, distributing orders and penalties, and in shots 535–6 she sinks her teeth into an enormous live crab, proceeding to kiss Ascilto while holding him "in a possessive gesture."[44]

Figure 4.5 *Fellini Satyricon*. Trifena. DVD frame capture.

The second version of this sequence features Trifena in the nude, in an obscure sexual liaison with a giant. Two shots later she cuts off the head of a chicken, letting its blood drip upon the naked buttocks of a young girl. Then, skipping two shots, Trifena is seen mounting a wooden idol with an erect phallus. The scene is watched by an audience chanting and clapping rhythmically.[45] This image, which like the earlier scenes is absent from the final cut, curiously recalls a watercolour by Félicien Rops, *The Idol*, from the 1883 series *Sataniques*. This fleeting nod in the direction of Rops, a Belgian Decadent, indicates the unmistakable Decadent matrix of *Fellini Satyricon*.

Trifena is a fully elaborated fatal woman, a sexually assertive sovereign, judge, huntress, and predator, a woman who "unmans man," to quote Charles Bernheimer on the Decadent *femme fatale*.[46] In shot 631 we find Trifena ritually transforming Lica into a bride, applying makeup to his face, rouge to his lips, and a blond wig to complete the transformation.[47]

Very few of these scenes made it to the final cut. Trifena's most significant appearance in the film occurs in two scenes in which she acts as a pagan priestess. The first of these is the wedding of Lica and Encolpio, which derives from the second version of the script, and the second is Lica's decapitation by the usurper's soldiers. A significant change occurs between the script's first and second versions of the wedding. While in the first version it is an old man, and not Trifena, that is cast as the priest examining the sacrifice and declaring the good omens, in the second version, and in the final cut, it is Trifena who performs the ritual. A few scenes ahead, still dressed as a priestess, Trifena reacts with undisguised pleasure to the gory sight of Lica's headless body lying at her feet.[48] Notably, the theme of decapitation does not derive from Petronius, where the character named Lichas drowns in a shipwreck. The distinct evocation of Salomé owes purely to Fellini's conception of Trifena as a *femme fatale*, Decadent style.

Trifena and her peers are represented with pronounced artifice. They seem more painted than alive. In one significant shot, for example, a woman's face and body are painted white, her strange rectangular headdress accentuating the unnaturalness of this human figure. The women in *Fellini Satyricon* are invested with a distinctly inorganic quality. According to Eileen Hughes, Fellini had a few of the actresses shave off their eyebrows,[49] dehumanizing them to an even greater extent by transforming them into decorative objects, then filming them against flat colour backgrounds. In the Trifena character in particular, the

98 Federico Fellini

shaved eyebrows render the heavily made-up face more of a painted visage than a living human. The elaborate headdresses, richly ornamented with gold, enhance and underscore this impression. In fact they recall Klimt's play of flat ornamental surface against fully voluminous living bodies. In *Judith I* (1901; Figure 4.6), Klimt's representation

Figure 4.6 Gustav Klimt, *Judith*, 1901. Oil on canvas, 84 × 42 cm, Belvedere, Vienna.

of Judith/Salomé oscillates between the organic and the inorganic, her live, naked body stifling under the pressure of the gold leaf decoration.

As noted earlier, Fellini would have had quite thorough knowledge of Klimt's oeuvre, if not through direct acquaintance with the canvases, which is itself highly possible, then at least through his copy of the 1967 comprehensive catalogue. I therefore propose to take a closer look at Klimt's works and their resonance in *Fellini Satyricon*.

Judith I, Klimt's 1901 version of the story of Judith and Holofernes, was exhibited under the title *Salomé* both during the artist's lifetime and in later periods. This mistake owed to the association of this story with the favourite *fin-de-siècle* theme of Salomé, as it was rendered by Moreau, Beardsley, and Max Klinger. During the second half of the nineteenth century, the figure of Judith, originally conceived as a pious and heroic woman, came to be portrayed as a sexually frustrated widow who fancies the enemy general and eventually kills him for her own satisfaction.[50] The association of decapitation with castration in late nineteenth-century thought probably contributed to the analogy between Judith and Salomé.

Clutching the severed male head with a spasm of her long fingers, Klimt's Judith/Salomé expresses ecstatic pleasure in this gruesome situation. In fact, her half-closed eyes and parted lips have been considered to connote orgasmic excitement.[51] The ecstatic backward thrust of the head, accentuated by the low-angle viewpoint, renders the spectator inferior, as if subjugated to this mighty female. In Klimt's *Medicine*, a panel of the university murals in Vienna, the goddess Hygieia was rendered in a similarly hieratic and commanding stance.

Klimt's close association of decapitation with sexual gratification seems to resonate in *Fellini Satyricon*. A case in point is the overt smile of pleasure on Trifena's face as she witnesses Lica's brutal beheading, thrusting her head backward and partly closing her eyes. This is not the only shot in which Trifena bears a facial expression that closely recalls Klimt's *Judith I*. Figure 4.6 features a low-angle shot in which she is set against a flat red background, her head slightly thrust backward, eyes closed and lips extended forward in desire. Rendered in low angle and in a frontal pose of sovereignty, Fellini's Trifena speaks to Klimt's Hygieia, Judith/Salomé, and Pallas Athene.

Klimt's idiom resonates in more than one way in *Fellini Satyricon*. Klimt's extensive use of stylized ornamentation is echoed in the hairpieces, clothing, and backgrounds of *Fellini Satyricon*. In one sequence in particular Fellini's elaborate use of stylized body-decoration brings together Klimt and Moreau on the film screen. In the sequence suggestively dubbed the "Garden of Delights," the poet Eumolpo takes the sexually incapable Encolpio on a visit to an oriental brothel, situated in an unrecognizable desert ambience. A host of young prostitutes, played by gypsy girls hired for the scene,[52] treat Encolpio to a lashing ritual, while others ride a large swing together with Ascilto, mocking Encolpio from above.[53]

The scene under discussion features a belly dancer whose face we don't see. The camera frames exclusively her naked abdomen, which bears a pattern of dotted lines, produced on the set by means of little beads that were glued onto the girl's bare skin.[54] This contrivance works to enhance the sense of artifice in this image, hybridizing living body and decorative plane. The dancer's face is never shown. Her breasts and abdomen fill the screen in medium and close-up view, endowing the ornamented surface (which is the dancer's belly) with an autonomous signifying capacity.

Fellini's superimposition of an inorganic pattern over living flesh distinctly recalls Moreau's application of elaborate ornamental patterns to the naked skin of *Salomé Dancing before Herod*, also known as the "Tattooed Salomé" (1876). The dotted patterns on the naked bodies of Klimt's *Water Serpents I* (1904–7) also come to mind. In Moreau, the living flesh is overburdened with inorganic ornament. In *Salomé Dancing before Herod* (1874–6) the seductress wears an elaborately ornate garment and heavy jewellery. Moreau himself tellingly defined her stiff garment as a reliquary.[55] In *The Apparition* of 1874–6, Salomé's naked body is partly covered with stylized jewellery, repeating the "tattooed" effect of the 1874 oil painting.

As in Moreau's "Tattooed Salomé," the body of Fellini's dancer is converted into a ground for abstract ornament. Furthermore, this figure is denied the sacred integrity of the human body. Truncated by the cinematic frame, it is objectified into an ornamental piece.

In playing living flesh against artificial overlay, late nineteenth-century painting foregrounded its concern with the dialectic of life and death, authenticity and artifice, or "art" and "life." In Huysmans's *A Rebours* (*Against the Grain*), which comes to mind as an appropriate example, the Decadent protagonist Des Esseintes has a live tortoise encrusted with gold and inlaid precious gems. As expected, the creature eventually dies, unable to bear the burden of the artificial shell.[56] Huysmans engages at the same time the dialectic of life and death and of art and life. In the Decadent vein of thought, the death of the turtle is a desired transformation, sacrificing coarse, natural existence for a superior and more refined form. Artifice and death have the upper hand. A similar dialectic, again epitomized in an excess of ornament and jewellery, underlies Klimt's excessive use of gold. The oscillation between representation in depth and abstract pattern in Klimt's "golden" works addresses the same dialectic of life and death, or rather life and art.

The female figures of *Fellini Satyricon* manifest an analogous combination of sensuality and detachment, organic and inorganic matter, life and art, life and death. According to Fellini's makeup consultant Piero Tosi, the figures of the film were envisioned as veritable "walking mummies."[57] The imperial Rome of *Fellini Satyricon* is inhabited by "dead men walking," so to speak, living figures turned into stiffly stylized structures. Like the turtle in Huysmans's *A Rebours*, the human figures of *Fellini Satyricon* are dead beneath their armour of jewellery and makeup. Fellini draws on the excessive artifice of Decadent painting in order to mask and neutralize human expression, thwarting identification and promoting alienation.

Picasso's Minotaur Meets Encolpio in Fabrizio Clerici's Labyrinths

Between the opening scene in the baths and the ending of the film, Encolpio evolves from a mere shadow on a graffiti-covered wall into a fully elaborated wall painting.[58] That Encolpio undergoes moral evolution is indicated by his growing sympathy toward fellow humans and, finally, his transformation at the house of Oenotea.[59]

The Labyrinth sequence, which will constitute the focus of the present discussion, is a turning point in Encolpio's story. The sequence opens with a sudden cut to Encolpio, brutally hurled by a group of armed people down a barren slope of earth.. He finds himself in a vast open-air arena, around which an excited audience is rhythmically clapping and cheering. Handed a burning torch and a huge boxing glove, Encolpio is urged into a labyrinth in the centre of the arena. Inside the labyrinth lurks a tall figure wearing a Minotaur mask. Encolpio is to fight him.

The apparent seriousness of the situation is mitigated by the presence of a cheering audience, investing the whole affair with the theatricality of a dramatic performance or a sports contest. And yet the pronounced unreality of the event is undercut by Encolpio's genuine anxiety. It is obvious that for him the Minotaur presents mortal danger.

The scene intercuts extreme long shots of the cheering audience with medium and long shots of the labyrinth interior, and close-ups of Encolpio's sweating, anxious countenance, shifting continuously between "show" and genuine terror. Only in the end is narrative justification provided for this ambiguity, when the whole event is explained as a ritual of Risus, the god of laughter, whose annual festival must begin with a joke played at the expense of an unaware stranger.[60]

Bearing in mind that Fellini conceived the creative process as a voyage through a labyrinth, his drawings and "doodles" playing the role of Ariadne's thread, it seems that this sequence tells a psychoanalytical tale of regression into the unconscious. What is most pertinent to the present discussion is Fellini's recourse to painting in the construction of Encolpio's mindscape.

It should be noted at the outset that the story of the labyrinth is in no way rooted in Petronius, in whose text such scene does not exist. Rather, the primary intertextual premise of this sequence is an episode in *The Golden Ass* by Apuleius.[61] However, Fellini's version has very little in common with the story as it is told in *The Golden Ass*, except for the general reference to the festival of Risus, celebrated by playing a joke on a stranger who is genuinely scared to death.[62] This is why Bondanella asserts quite convincingly that Fellini "had more in mind than a mere classical footnote." The passage through a labyrinth, Bondanella points out, is widely acknowledged as a metaphor for an inner journey.[63] Bondanella, and later Burke, regard the labyrinth scene as a key to the psychic evolution of Fellini's protagonist.[64]

Fellini's version of the "voyage in" was bound to be informed by Jungian theory and imagery. A look into the place of the labyrinth in Jungian thought is thus required. A chapter in *Man and His Symbols*, written by Joseph L. Henderson, will serve as a useful reference, particularly given its immediate availability for Fellini, in his private library.[65] The chapter, "Ancient Myths and Modern Man," directly addresses the myth of the Minotaur and its struggle with Theseus, which for Henderson is an archetypal "hero myth" representing the liberation of the ego from "unconscious demonic maternal powers."[66] Henderson relates to the Minotaur as "the devouring aspect of the mother image," and to the labyrinth as "an entangling and confusing world [...] of matriarchal consciousness [that] can be traversed only by those who are ready for a special initiation into the mysterious world of the collective unconscious."[67] Encolpio traverses a labyrinth that is a Jungian site of archetypal struggle, leading to full individuation.

It is thus doubly notable that the first shot of the labyrinth in *Fellini Satyricon* literally quotes a Jungian illustration from the first chapter of *Man and His Symbols*. The chapter, "Approaching the Unconscious," was written by Jung himself. Fellini's shot offers a view of a rectangular stone-lined passage, which strikingly resembles the dark, rectangular entrance to an Egyptian tomb featured as an illustration to the Jungian text. In fact, the photograph occupies an entire page in *Man and His Symbols*, and apparently represents a portal to the unconscious, which is exactly the role assigned to the entrance of the labyrinth in *Fellini Satyricon*.[68]

Not even the newly acquired friendship with the Minotaur, however, can save Encolpio from the sudden loss of sexual potency brought about by his abortive encounter with Arianna (or Ariadne), the archetypal female awaiting him on the exit side of the labyrinth.[69] In the Jungian version of the myth, which Fellini would have read in *Man and His Symbols*, Ariadne represents "the anima as an inner component of the psyche that is necessary for any true creative achievement."[70] That Fellini conceives of Arianna in Jungian terms is strongly hinted by the image of archetypal fertility goddess visible in the background.[71] The fact that Encolpio fails to achieve physical union with this figure connotes a disturbance in the process of individuation. This disturbance, which further complicates events, will be resolved only through liaison with another archetypal female, Oenotea the sorceress, who preserves the primal fire in her womb.

Several intertexts converge in the figure of Arianna. Attention must be drawn to the posture in which this figure reclines on a pedestal, which distinctly speaks to the reclining Ariadne in the works of Giorgio de Chirico. In de Chirico, Ariadne is a classical marble sculpture placed in deserted Italian piazzas.[72] Fellini's Arianna is as cold and unresponsive as de Chirico's "petrified mothers," thwarting the prospect of return to primal unity. *Man and His Symbols* actually reproduces de Chirico's *Anxious Journey* (1913), to illustrate a text by Marie Louise Von Franz. De Chirico's "gloomy passages," the caption says, represent "the first contact with the unconscious when the individuation process begins."[73] The Jungian text could thus have played a mediating role in the formation of Arianna in *Fellini Satyricon*, suggesting to Fellini the association between de Chirico's labyrinthine passages and psychoanalytical theory. In the figure of Arianna, Fellini brings together classical mythology, Roman sculpture, de Chirico's painting, into the psychoanalytical discourse which informs *Fellini Satyricon* in its entirety.[74]

The Minotaur constitutes yet another multilayered art-historical *lexia*. I turn to Jung's *Man and His Symbols* again as a rich visual source at Fellini's immediate disposal. Practically loaded with art-historical references, this book reproduces Picasso's 1935 *Minotauromachy*. No less important is the Jungian caption for this painting: "a symbol of man's uncontrollable instinctive forces."[75]

While it may have been the reproduction in *Man and His Symbols* that drew Fellini's attention to Picasso's engraving, it is highly probable that he had sufficient acquaintance with Picasso's oeuvre to be aware of it independently. It is noteworthy that when Eileen Hughes interviewed Danilo Donati, set and costume designer for *Fellini Satyricon*, he made several references to Picasso.[76] This interview, made on the set during the actual shooting of the film, is a reliable indication of the concerns at stake between Fellini and his designer, and of an overall engagement with Picasso on the set of *Fellini Satyricon*.

Picasso's interest in the myth of the Minotaur owed to his collaboration on the surrealist magazine *Minotaure*. Although he was never a formal member of the movement, Picasso was certainly part of the surrealist scene in Paris, and was invited to produce the cover for the first issue of *Minotaure*, whose title reflected the growing interest among French intellectuals in the psychoanalytical aspects of the myth. For the surrealists, Theseus came to represent a conscious agent successfully crossing unknown regions of the human mind, where the minotaur is to be confronted.[77]

In Picasso's work, the Minotaur is conceived as an "indirect self portrait,"[78] a tragic figure.[79] In a 1933 dry point, a melancholy Minotaur crouches over the sleeping Marie-Thérèse, while in 1934–5 a blind Minotaur, its head tilted back in torment, is led by a young girl resembling Marie-Thérèse. An "element of self-pity" is pointed out by Kirk Varnedoe in this "self-aggrandizing myth," in which Picasso adopts the identity of a wounded Minotaur.[80] Mary Mathews Gedo, in her turn, suggests a strictly psychoanalytical reading of Picasso's Minotaur scenes, in terms of sexually related guilt. For the first time in his life, Gedo asserts, Picasso realized that there was a destructive aspect to his sexual voracity, embodied in the figure of the Minotaur who "invades the sculptor's studio."[81] According to Varnedoe, Picasso tended to see himself at that period as a "freak of nature," controlled by his creative powers rather than having them at his disposal. Thus, for Varnedoe, in Picasso's oeuvre the Minotaur reflects a conception of the artist as "part-man, part-animal who is both blessed and cursed by his transcendence of the conventions of human society."[82]

Picasso's representation of the artist as Minotaur was bound to appeal to Fellini, who conceived of the creative process in similar terms.[83] One may recall his remark about drawing and "doodling" as a creative way out of the labyrinth. It is thus interesting to note the significant resemblance between Fellini's Minotaur (Figure 4.7) and a 1933 charcoal drawing by Picasso portraying a Minotaur's head (Figure 4.8). Both seem pronouncedly humanlike, with human nose and mouth counterbalanced by a pair of bovine ears and curved horns. A 1936 gouache by Picasso entitled *Minotaur and Dead Mare before a Grotto* makes a clear distinction between the Minotaur's mask-like head and its smooth, human body. *Fellini Satyricon* manifests a similar hybridization of beast and human.

In Picasso's gouache, the Minotaur shows compassion toward the dead mare carried out of the dark labyrinth. Similarly, in *Fellini Satyricon* the terrified Encolpio receives deep sympathy from the "Minotaur." In Fellini, as in Picasso, the Minotaur evokes the *shadow*, which in Jungian thought is the primal, instinctual, and creative element in man. Encolpio and the Minotaur meet in the labyrinthine recesses of the unconscious, destined to engage in the archetypal struggle between "hero" and "dragon," to evoke the Jungian imagery of *Man and His Symbols*.

Figure 4.7 *Fellini Satyricon*. Minotaur, DVD frame capture.

Figure 4.8 Pablo Picasso, *Minotaur*, 1933. Charcoal, 51 × 34 cm, Musée Picasso, Paris. © Succession Picasso – Gestion droits d'auteur, Paris, musée Picasso, © RMN-Grand Palais/Michèle Bellot.

Beyond the Minotaur, and Arianna, there is the labyrinth, presented in a variety of shots that alternate between high-angle views of the overall structure and eye-level shots of inside passages through Encolpio's subjective point of view. The exceptional high-angle shots of the labyrinth require particular attention (Figure 4.9).

The overall theatricality of the labyrinth scene, the large audience viewed from afar as a host of minuscule figures, and primarily the high-angle view of the labyrinth itself point to Fabrizio Clerici's *Minotaur*

Figure 4.9 *Fellini Satyricon*. High-angle shot of the labyrinth. DVD frame capture.

series as a possible visual reference. Created between 1948 and 1969, Clerici's series of pen drawings, temperas, and one oil painting feature a Minotaur performing onstage. The audience is perched on raised galleries supported by wooden scaffoldings, suggesting theatrical sets. In Clerici's series, the labyrinth constitutes an extension of the proscenium, viewed from above in a pronounced high-angle view, as in *The Labyrinth* of 1966, the 1967 *Afternoon in Knossos* (Figure 4.10), or the earlier *The Minotaur Publicly Accuses His Mother* (1952). Clerici's pseudo-architectural structures have been associated by Maurizio Fagiolo with Bruegel's *Tower of Babel*.[84] Given the reverberation of the *Tower of Babel* in *Fellini Satyricon*, Clerici's labyrinth-theatres emerge as a significant cross reference in the intertextual network charted in these pages.

Clerici, who was an intimate friend of Alberto Savinio, Giorgio de Chirico, and Léonor Fini,[85] had a close acquaintance with Fellini.[86] In 1968 Fellini invited Clerici to design the sets for *Toby Dammit*, along with Renzo Vespignani. Fellini particularly needed the two painters' help in conceiving and designing the collapsed bridge featured at the ending scene of the film. While the proposed collaboration between Clerici and Vespignani eventually failed,[87] it appears that only one year later Clerici's *Minotaur* series came to resonate in Fellini's conception of the labyrinth.

A preparatory drawing made by Fellini strikingly recalls Clerici's unique combination of labyrinth, theatrical stage, and audience. As in Clerici, Fellini's drawing provides a high-angle view of a labyrinth

Figure 4.10 Fabrizio Clerici, *Pomeriggio à Cnosso (Afternoon in Knossos)*, 1967. Tempera on panel, 75 × 105 cm, courtesy of Archivio Fabrizio Clerici, Rome.

which is an extension of the stage area, the audience flanking it on two sides.[88] If this was indeed Fellini's initial conception of the scene, then it appears even closer to Clerici's imagery than the final cut reveals. In a few similar cases discussed in former chapters, an art-historically informed scene evolved through a process of elimination. This pattern emerges as central to Fellini's working process. Suffice it to recall the gradual elimination of detail in Giulietta's encounter with the dead Laura, or the evolution of the "meat-shot" in *Toby Dammit*, from a butcher shop window to a brief view of a hanging carcass carried on a truck.

Clerici's labyrinth series touches on two central concerns of *Fellini Satyricon*, the history and myths of ancient Rome and the psychoanalytic connotations of the labyrinth. Exhibited alongside Dalí, Duchamp, Ernst, and Léonor Fini, Clerici was obviously well acquainted with the surrealist concept of the Minotaur. For Patrick Waldberg, the labyrinth series pivots on the primal mélange of desire and aggression toward the mother.[89] In *The Minotaur Publicly Accuses His Mother*, the Oedipal theme is clearly suggested. The judicial connotation is further enhanced in a 1966 pen and watercolour drawing entitled *The Minotaur Accuses His Old Mother*, where the stage and labyrinth are eliminated to enable a closer view of the ghostly audience watching the Minotaur face a majestic old lady. The Minotaur in this drawing appears more vulnerable and less theatrical than in the 1952 painting. Stripped of the shredded cloak he wears on stage, his gesture appears more natural and human. The creature's hairy back, bent in pain, conveys a sense of dolefulness akin to Picasso's *Minotauromachy*. The creature's mother does not seem to heed his complaint. Avoiding his gaze, she stares indifferently ahead.

The Minotaur is featured as a tragic figure, struggling under the double burden of ancient myth and tribulations of the unconscious. Waldberg regards it as a self-portrait,[90] and indeed the trial scenes recall a miserable period in the painter's life, when his family went bankrupt and subsequently separated and dispersed.[91] Clerici's father was subjected to a series of trials that lasted several years,[92] a biographical fact that resonates in the recurrence of judicial situations in the labyrinth series.[93] The audiences in the Minotaur paintings may thus be identified as a mass of merciless judges.

Returning to *Fellini Satyricon*, it may be suggested that the labyrinth sequence echoes Clerici's strange combination of law court, stage performance, and labyrinthine mindscape. Fellini's labyrinth is at once a theatrical set and a locus of mystery and pervasive anxiety. Like the artist, Encolpio faces a merciless audience witnessing his abortive encounters with the Minotaur and the woman. As in Clerici's labyrinth series, suffering and anxiety translate into art.

To conclude the discussion I propose to look closer at Clerici's labyrinths as archaeological sites and how their proximity of archaeology and unconscious reverberates in *Fellini Satyricon*. A close examination of *The Minotaur Publicly Accuses His Mother* reveals a dark hollow underneath the stage boards, hinting that the labyrinth extends beneath the proscenium. Although the Minotaur does not dwell inside the labyrinth, as in *Fellini Satyricon*, it apparently treads a very thin and fragile surface just above it. The broken floorboards of *The Minotaur Publicly Accuses His Mother* reveal an even deeper stratum of underground space, a sort of archaeological unconscious. Two other works by Clerici come to mind as a further illustration for his engagement with the mindscape as an archaeological site. *La Stanza* (*The Room*) of 1954 and

Il Sonno Romano (*Roman Slumber*) of 1955 afford a closer look into the underground recesses which are only suggested in the labyrinth series.

La Stanza portrays findings from the 1950s excavations of the Roman colony of *Leptis Magna* in Africa, which Clerici visited in 1953. Fascinated by the ancient sculptures unearthed in these excavations, Clerici incorporated one of the sculptures into this painting.[94] *Il Sonno Romano*, in turn, is populated by a larger number of classical and baroque sculptures from the churches and museums of Rome, including the *Dormant Ariadne* from the Vatican Museums,[95] recurrently featured in the paintings of de Chirico, and discussed earlier as a visual intertext embedded in the Arianna figure.

At this point the intertextual network which undergirds *Fellini Satyricon* seems to fold upon itself, as double and triple intertextual knots agglomerate into a tightly knit tangle. Clerici's work, it may be noted, manifests a sort of Decadent inertia in its privileging of art and artifice over life and nature. In its own peculiar way, Clerici's imagery of antiquity recalls the Decadent theme of Byzantium, discussed earlier. Waldberg, in fact, regards Clerici as a twentieth-century Symbolist, and associates him with such Symbolists as Khnopff, Moreau, and Redon,[96] all of whom have come up as constituents of Fellini's intertextual matrix. Clerici and the Decadents, Picasso and de Chirico, and Bruegel and Jung cross resonate in Fellini's filmic text.

Fellini Satyricon exhibits an intertextual intricacy and complexity that render it distinctly postmodern, but only apparently postmodernist. As shown with regard to *Toby Dammit*, one realizes that while *Fellini Satyricon* indeed exploits the devices of postmodernist form, particularly intertextual construction and pronounced contrivedness, what is at stake is rather a (romantic) project, committed to forging a bridge to Merleau-Ponty's "brute meaning." As suggested in previous chapters, Fellini reasserts the potency of art as conduit to the real, the real conceived in terms of primary psychic matter. Fellini's project, it now becomes clear, involves intertextual construction, while at the same time it completely disregards the meaning of this formal device in the postmodern aesthetic. Rather, Fellini weaves a cinematic utterance that relies on the power of the *sémiotique* to convey primal anxiety and desire, operating simultaneously on the symbolic and presymbolic levels of the film experience. Embedded evocations of painting serve as his primary tools.

Chapter Five

Fellini's Casanova: Casanova Meets de Chirico on Böcklin's *Isle of the Dead*

Fellini's Casanova (1976) is loosely based on the memoirs of Giacomo Casanova, composed around 1785. The *Memoirs*, published in full edition only in 1960, make up six volumes and over two thousand pages in the German edition. Although it was he who suggested the idea of filming Casanova's memoirs to producer Dino De Laurentiis, Fellini was reluctant to read this mass of printed material, which, he said, he had never really tackled before.[1] After reading the *Memoirs*, Fellini remarked that they recalled a "telephone book of artistically non-existent and sometimes most boring occurrences."[2]

The film was released in December 1976. Production lasted about three years, due to several setbacks, which included a disagreement on casting. The American producers demanded that a *divo* like Marlon Brando, Al Pacino, or Robert Redford play the part of Casanova. Fellini's objections could only be expected. One producer after another withdrew from the project, until Alberto Grimaldi finally agreed to take it up on condition that the film be shot in English. In return, Fellini obtained the producer's consent to film the entire movie in Cinecittà, complete with costly sets of the Venetian lagoon and the Rialto Bridge.

This was certainly not the first time that Fellini privileged artificial sets over location shooting, but *Casanova*, Fellini's most expressly artificial film, manifests an expressed concern with copies, replicas, and simulations. The film addresses the problematic of subjectivity in postmodern thinking. In Dale Bradley's phrasing, Fellini's Casanova is a hollow figure existing only as sign or simulacrum.[3]

The pervasive preoccupation of this film with the collapse of the real is manifest in many of its scenes. The carnival scene which opens the film is a case in point. Flat masks posted on poles gaze directly at the camera, presenting human subjectivity as a hollow masquerade. In fact, these masks are the first protagonists the viewer encounters on screen. What is more, the real humans that appear later in this scene are unrecognizably masked. The film thus states its interests from the very first moment.

In the following sequence, Casanova is invited to the villa of French ambassador De Bernis, where he is to make love to the ambassador's mistress, dressed as a nun. Catering to the nobleman's taste for voyeurism, a peeping hole enables a view on the amorous affair. Significantly, the scene is set in a hall of mirrors, where hundreds of tiny mirrors fragment the figures of Casanova and his lover to a point where all that remains of Casanova is a splintered reflection. The character's material existence in the real is denied altogether. Featuring Casanova as a compilation of disjointed mirror images, the film evinces a deep concern with the hazardous condition not only of the human subject but also of the cinematic sign.

In yet another shot, Casanova is flanked by mannequins, with an Arcimboldesque painting hanging in the background. Placing Casanova in line with the mannequins and a pastiched Arcimboldo, Fellini highlights the borderline situation of his protagonist, between human subject and contrived simulacrum.[4] Casanova thus degenerates from masked figure to splintered mirror reflection to mannequin, only to be reduced in the film's ending to a shadow falling upon a drawing of himself as a young man. An immaterial shadow, superimposed upon a drawing, Casanova is categorically denied existence in the real.[5] The very existence, or presence, of a fully formed subject, let alone its representation in art, is thus problematized by means of visual configuration. A look at the intertextual underpinnings of Casanova may begin with the intriguing involvement of a *Golem* figure, complicating Fellini's polyvalent cinematic signifier.

Casanova as *Golem*

It is a widely known fact that Fellini purported to actually change the facial features of actor Donald Sutherland, creating the expressly unnatural appearance of Casanova. Fellini modified Sutherland's chin and nose with the aid of rubber appendages. In addition, he heightened his brow by seven centimetres, again with the aid of a rubber mask, then shaved and repainted his eyebrows. A working sketch demonstrates the liberty with which Fellini approached the actor's natural features, which he intended to mould into a visual construct that was wholly contrived. The miserable Sutherland had to arrive on the set three hours before everybody else and endure veritable torment, in order to be transformed into the Casanova that Fellini had in mind.[6]

Of all the facial distortions I have mentioned, the fake chin turns out to be more significant than appears on first sight. It certainly does not derive from Casanova's memoirs, or from any other historical source. Archival evidence found in Fellini's private library indicates that this facial trait could be said to draw on a 1966 image of the Golem (or "artificial man"), as it was featured in a 1966 film by Jean Kerchbron, *Le Golem*. This film would have been brought to Fellini's attention through reportage published in the French film magazine *midi/minuit Fantastique*, in the issue dated December 1966/January 1967. A copy of this magazine issue is preserved to this day in Fellini's private library.[7] The first item in this particular issue of *midi/minuit Fantastique* reviews in detail the film *Le Golem* (1966), which is based on a novel of the same title by Gustave Meyrinck. Part of chapter 5 of Meyrinck's novel is reprinted in the magazine. It is illustrated with behind-the-scenes photographs portraying the application of an artificial chin to actor André Reybaz, transforming him into a Golem with the further aid of a rubber mask.[8] The resemblance between Fellini's drawing and the photograph in *midi/minuit Fantastique* is remarkable, particularly in light of the close association one may draw between the Golem, which the magazine dubs "un homme artificiel,"[9] and Casanova as a "mechanical man," to use the words of Joseph Markulin.[10] I attribute major significance to the preservation of this single issue, no. 15/16 of *midi/minuit Fantastique* in Fellini's library. The feature article on *Le Golem* in this issue, particularly its photographs, very probably had a role in the formation of Fellini's Casanova.

The foregoing calls for a closer look at the story of the Golem in Meyrinck's novel. Fellini, it seems, must have at least leafed through the fifth chapter, reproduced in the magazine. This chapter follows a legend recounted by Zwakh, an old marionette artist who admits to having seen the Golem twice in his life thanks to his artist's receptiveness to unnatural apparitions. The Golem, which Meyrinck describes as an "homme artificiel," or alternatively "l'inconnu" (the unknown), is conceived in the novel as the archetypal work of art, "une oeuvre d'art sans connaissance."[11] Regrettably, it is impossible to ascertain whether Fellini had read the entire novel, or seen Kerchbron's film. If indeed he had read the book or seen the movie, Fellini could have learned more about Meyrinck's conception of the Golem as the bearer of a life force, capable of augmenting creative powers in any person receptive enough to recognize it. It suffices to mention but one scene in the novel, where the Golem presents a character called Pernath, an artist and the narrator of the story, with a magical book imprinted with the Hebrew title *Ibbur* (Conception).[12] Regardless of whether he read the novel, Fellini could have gleaned the general idea from the excerpt published in the magazine.

Meyrinck's notion of the Golem as epitome of creation accords with the Jewish mystic tradition. The Golem and its symbolic rituals embody "a mysterious knowledge of the inwardness of creation."[13] In a comprehensive study of the motif of the Golem in Jewish thought, Moshe Idel points out that "by creating an anthropoid the Jewish master is not only able to display his creative forces, but may attain the experience of the creative moment of God, who also has created man in a similar way to that found in the recipes used by the mystics and magicians."[14] A "creative contact with the divine" is thus inherent in all legends of the Golem.[15]

Fellini had most probably seen in *midi/minuit Fantastique* the photos of André Reybaz transforming into a Golem,[16] and probably also read chapter 5, if not the entire novel by Meyrinck. He would thus have become acquainted with the association of the Golem with mystical knowledge and creative powers. The Golem would have constituted the perfect conceptual template for the "artificial man" paradoxically conceived as creative artist, in an inherent dialectic that pervades Fellini's film from beginning to end.

Casanova is a dialectical Golem. The one aspect most commented upon is the expressed connotation of inhumanity, with Casanova featured as a soulless robot engaging in mechanical sexual performance. As he dances with the mechanical doll in the film's concluding scene, the non-human quality of this character is underscored. And indeed Fellini's interviews about *Casanova* have greatly encouraged critics to read into the film an "absence of the real, the death of the subject and author," as Frank Burke characteristically concludes.[17]

However, such readings neglect to recognize the inherent dialectic of *Fellini's Casanova*. Admittedly, the film strongly implies the death of the subject, or author-artist. At the same time, conceived as a Golem, Casanova acquires an aura of magic and the occult, evoking mystical rituals of creation. Fellini's expressed interest in the occult, which coincided with his intense study of Jung in the first half of the 1960s, is significant in this regard. The myth of the Golem as the archetype of magical creation charges *Casanova* with a romantic note, one of mystification vis-à-vis the creative process. The film thus gives powerful expression to Fellini's deep-seated creative anxiety.

Fellini's Casanova embraces a double-edged project, romantic in its re-establishment of the creative subject, and at the same time postmodern in its splintering of the very same subject into a multitude of simulacra sans origin. This dialectic underlies the film's art-historical references, which acquire a crucial role in the construction of Casanova as an equivocal "portrait of the artist."

As the previous chapters have shown, the presence of art-historical allusion becomes more pronounced in Fellini's films toward the late 1970s. Consequently, critics and scholars have set out to name and identify the more explicit art-historical references which *Fellini's Casanova* offers its spectator. These critical attempts, however, rely chiefly on Fellini's overt remarks, which conceal more than they pretend to reveal.

Antonio Costa, for example, grounds *Fellini's Casanova* in eighteenth-century Venetian painting, exclusively.[18] Roberto Campari, as well, looks to Venetian painters of this period, particularly Pietro Longhi and Giacomo Ceruti, as the sole visual sources for the film's genre scenes.[19] John Stubbs, in his turn, regards the London of *Fellini's Casanova* as a direct reflection of the representation of this city in the works of Hogarth.[20] My discussion of *Casanova* and its embedded art-historical *lexiae* will thus commence with a critical examination of the foregoing readings, only to suggest that the film's most intriguing and significant art-historical evocations are to be looked for elsewhere.

Pietro Longhi's genre scenes from the life of Venetian nobility indeed provided Fellini and Zapponi with historical data. Longhi's *Ridotto* paintings with their masked figures come to mind as possible points of departure for the carnival scenes in the opening of the film.

Similarly feasible is Pier Marco De Santi's reference to Giacomo Ceruti as the painter who might have provided the template for the costume of the nun in the De Bernis scene.[21] Although De Santi does not name a specific work, he probably had in mind Ceruti's *Portrait of a Young Nun* (early 1730s), in which the white headdress closely resembles the one worn by the French ambassador's lover.

Other associations suggested by critics are less convincing. A case in point is Roberto Campari's recourse to Ceruti as the source for Fellini's circle of seamstresses in the Annamaria sequence.[22] Campari must have been thinking of *Women at Work* (ca. 1720–5), although, like De Santi, he does not specify this or any other painting as reference. However, the foregoing seems like a slightly forced and unnecessary attempt to identify for each and every scene in *Casanova* an eighteenth-century source. The association of Ceruti's painting with Fellini's portrayal of seamstresses seated in a circle is grounded exclusively in the similarity of the situation, and completely overlooks Fellini's strong emphasis on the perfectly circular embroidered garment, a formal feature which is clearly absent from Ceruti's plain genre scene.

John Stubbs, as well, is only partly convincing in his association of Fellini's London Fair with William Hogarth's scenes of grotesque debauchery.[23] Indeed, Stubbs predicates his assertion on remarks made by Fellini and Zapponi, in which they indicate overt reliance on Hogarth as an aid for reconstructing the general atmosphere of eighteenth-century London. In Zapponi's literary version of *Casanova*, the London of Casanova's times is described as "twisted, deformed, as in the caricatures of Hogarth and Rowlandson," and Fellini, in his turn, remarked that the London scenes were conceived "in the milieu of Hogarth, according to the taste of Gustave Doré."[24]

Fellini, however, was inclined to divert attention from his deeper strata of art-historical evocation, astutely leading critics to the more obvious "costume" sources. Stubbs, like Campari, does not escape this trap.[25] Basically, Stubbs's assertion that Fellini, in his representation of the fair, shares with Hogarth a sense of grotesque riotousness is highly debatable. The atmosphere in the Fellinian fair is one of enigma, rather than "hurly burly." Unlike Hogarth's crowded and chaotic compositions, most of the shots of the fair in *Fellini's Casanova* feature a small number of figures in very concise *mise en scénes*, with enough vacant, hazy space among them to convey a sense of mystery. The feeling of enigma is greatly enhanced by the image of the embalmed whale and the monstrous slide show of *vagina dentata* imagery which takes place inside.[26]

And thus, while the remarks made by Fellini and Zapponi may indeed indicate their utilization of Hogarth for period reconstruction, they are far from providing a clue to the film's rich and complex reliance on painting. Upon close analysis, Fellini's London Fair is a far cry from Hogarth's scenes of bawdy revelry. Imbued with a sense of the bizarre, the mystic, and the metaphysical, the fair in *Fellini's Casanova*, seen as if through a misty screen or gauze, evokes Romantic or Symbolist painting rather than Hogarth and his grotesque sarcasm.

This is also the case when it comes to Fellini and Zapponi's explicit mention of Tiepolo in the script of *Casanova*, in association with the hunchback Du Bois. In the scene of Du Bois's party at his country residence, the script describes a black servant standing "motionless as in a painting by Tiepolo."[27] What Fellini, or Zapponi, probably had in mind were the numerous black servants that populate Tiepolo's scenes of aristocratic entertainment in eighteenth-century Venice. However, not much can be gleaned from this remark beyond a reaffirmation of the basic notion that Fellini's working process involved art-historical associations.

The instances where Fellini reveals his art-historical sources, albeit seemingly telling, actually obscure the most intriguing and deeper embedded hyperlinks, which Fellini was not inclined to expose or lend to facile interpretation. I propose a look at three unrecognized intertextual links that do not serve as mere points of departure for costume or period reconstruction. Rather, the art-historical *lexiae* to be discussed function as catalysts for the emergence of the *sémiotique*, introducing what could be conceived in the phenomenological terms of Merleau-Ponty as an experience of "brute meaning." In what follows I shall highlight the film's expressed bent toward de Chirico and Metaphysical painting, on the one hand, and nineteenth-century Symbolism, on the other. In this choice of intertexts Fellini reaches far beyond the banal use of eighteenth-century genre painting, which he regarded as intolerably exploited. In his interview with Aldo Tassone, Fellini explicitly expressed his opinion that "from the figurative point of view, the eighteenth century is the most worn-out century, exhausted and impoverished in every respect."[28] Rather than eighteenth-century painting, then, the imagery of *Casanova* speaks to de Chirico and Savinio, Böcklin and Whistler. Fellini's intertextual preferences, it turns out, orbit around fantastic and spiritual currents of painting.

Through the Half-drawn Curtain: Casanova, de Chirico, and *The Enigma of the Oracle*

The story of Casanova's amorous liaison with the anaemic seamstress, Annamaria, spans seven scenes in the published script, which the final cut condenses into a single nocturnal encounter between the two. In the course of a late-night stroll in the garden, the feeble creature suddenly faints. Casanova carries Annamaria to his bed and possesses her while she is still unconscious.[29] I wish to focus on a brief shot of Casanova's empty canopy bed, just before the girl abruptly appears on screen as she is thrown onto the bed by her excited lover (Figure 5.1). As the

Figure 5.1 *Fellini's Casanova*. Shot of Casanova's bedpost. DVD frame capture.

camera gradually zooms in upon a single bedpost, visible through the drawn curtain, the bedpost comes to suggest a mysterious human silhouette. The shot unmistakably evokes *The Enigma of the Oracle* by Giorgio de Chirico (1909–10; Figure 5.2), or its sequel, *The Oracle*, a drawing by Alberto Savinio (1909–10).[30]

De Chirico's painting, it should be noted, harks back to Arnold Böcklin in *Odysseus and Calypso* (1883), where the figure of Odysseus (or Ulysses) is conceived as a lonely silhouette gazing into the far distance. In de Chirico, the contemplative silhouette is situated within an architectonic structure, which de Chirico identified as a ruined temple, where "the broken statue of a god spoke in a mysterious language."[31]

De Chirico's romantic philosopher-hero first appears in *The Enigma of the Oracle* and is then recast as a statue in *The Enigma of an Autumn Afternoon*. Various critical readings have addressed this enigmatic figure. The readings span Willard Bohn's detailed iconographical analysis and Hal Foster's psychoanalytical reading. For Foster, de Chirico's concept of "enigma," "surprise," and "revelation" – forged around the time when Freud was postulating the uncanny – epitomizes "the estrangement that comes of repression and returns as enigma."[32]

The emphasis put by Paolo Baldacci and Willard Bohn on the overt metaphysical concerns apparent in de Chirico is more pertinent to

Figure 5.2 Giorgio de Chirico, *The Enigma of the Oracle*, 1909–10. Oil on canvas, 42 × 61 cm, private collection. © Estate of Giorgio de Chirico/SODRAC (2012)

Fellini's romantic engagement with the enigma of creation. Bohn has shown that the contemplative figure, which derives primarily from Böcklin, connotes philosophical meditation and metaphysical revelation. Identifying the architectonic structure in the painting as a temple of Apollo, Bohn elucidates the hooded figure as a priest of Apollo engaged in the ancient oracular ritual. The priest is thus seen waiting in contemplation, expecting the divine inspiration to be transmitted through a female agent, the Pythia.

Most pertinent to the present discussion of *Casanova* is Bohn's and Baldacci's identification of the contemplative figure as what could be called a "portrait of the artist as seer." Baldacci highlights the "correlation between the author and the pensive figure to the left,"[33] while Bohn agrees that "[a]s a priest of Apollo, god of the plastic arts, the soothsayer must necessarily be an artist."[34] Returning to the enigmatic shot of the curtained alcove in *Fellini's Casanova*, with the bedpost suggestive of a mysterious silhouette, we find that the evocation of *The*

Enigma of the Oracle charges Casanova with connotations of mystical "seeing" and archetypal creativity.

The half-drawn curtain, yet another compositional element which *Fellini's Casanova* appropriates from *The Enigma of the Oracle*, augments the suggestion of mystical epiphany. The half-drawn curtain, hanging on rings, makes its first appearance in de Chirico's oeuvre in this painting, subsequently becoming a signature of Metaphysical painting.[35] It is thus significant to note that in Fellini's film, the scenes which feature Casanova's liaison with Annamaria include not one but two major shots that present a similar "curtain of enigma." The first shot was discussed earlier. The second is the immediate reverse shot, where the two wings of the curtain frame a nervous and sweating Casanova that apparently speaks to a 1925 self-portrait by de Chirico, where the melancholy painter is framed by the wings of a half-drawn curtain. Notably, the painting has belonged to the permanent collection of the *Galleria nazionale d'arte moderna e contemporanea* in Rome since its acquisition in 1925, and has been almost constantly on display.[36] Fellini's acquaintance with this particular painting is thus practically certain. The reverse shot of Casanova through the curtain weaves the self-portrait of de Chirico as artist-seer into the fabric of the film, further enhancing its romantic undertones. Notably, the alcove scene does not provide two-shots of Casanova and Annamaria. Nor does Fellini offer any long shot by which to establish an overall view of the scene. The setting thus remains disorientingly enigmatic, and the reality of the scene ambiguous.

Carrying this reading a step further, an analogy may be suggested between the curtained alcove and the curtained temple of Apollo in de Chirico's *Enigma of the Oracle*, with Annamaria cast as a Pythia, the female agent of divine revelation, and Casanova as priest or seer, about to get a glimpse of the mystery behind the curtain. In *La mia Rimini* (*My Rimini*), an autobiographical text written in 1967 in the wake of severe illness, Fellini reveals that as a high school student he identified with the figure of Ulysses in the *Iliad*. "We read it and learned it by heart," he writes. "Each one of us identified himself with one of Homer's characters. I was Ulysses, keeping himself a little apart and looking on from a distance."[37] Quite strikingly, Fellini's description of Ulysses, written only a few years before the conception of *Casanova*, evokes the solitary, meditative figure in the paintings of Böcklin and de Chirico. Fellini's early identification with this Homerian figure may have heightened his interest in the two paintings, which strongly reverberate in *Casanova*.

In his first encounter with Annamaria, Casanova declares that the girl awakens the artist in him: "I shall be your Pygmalion," he announces, "and like Pygmalion I shall give life to my creation."[38] As this desire to give life evolves into a sexual act – performed, we note, in a setting suggestive of the temple of Apollo – it becomes clear that this film weaves artistic creativity and sexual potency into an inextricable complex.

The alcove scene, then, features a sexual act between the artist and his artwork, or model, which immediately brings to mind Picasso's series *Raphael and La Fornarina*, a series of boldly erotic etchings making up a segment of the *Suite 347* (1968).[39] In an explicit association of phallus and paintbrush, Picasso depicts a young painter simultaneously painting and having sexual intercourse with his model, a phallic finger protruding from his palette. In most of the engravings in this series one notices an aged voyeur looking on from underneath the bed or another hidden corner. David Sylvester has read this figure as suggestive of the aging painter's fear of (creative) impotence.[40]

Picasso appropriated the theme of La Fornarina and the painter from a painting by Ingres bearing the same title (1813–40). As Dominique Dupuis-Labbé suggests, Picasso's etchings engage "mystery of creation," the nude model representing "Painting in person." The painter's gesture, Dupuis-Labbé further asserts, is "not only love play or erotic metaphor, but an illustration of the act of painting itself, the painter 'attacking the virgin canvas.'"[41] Unlike Sylvester, Dupuis-Labbé believes that it is the young and exuberant painter who is to be identified with Picasso, rather than the older voyeur. In this reading, the voyeur does not begrudge the younger artist his superior capabilities but rather bestows paternal benediction upon him.[42] It may safely be asserted that both the old voyeur and the young painter embody aspects of the anxious artist. What is most pertinent to the present discussion is that Sylvester and Dupuis-Labbé agree upon the association of sexual potency and artistic creation in Picasso's etchings.

A similar association of phallus and paintbrush is found in Fellini's drawings, particularly in an unpublished drawing portraying his long-time friend and set-painter, Rinaldo Geleng, using his penis as a paintbrush.[43] Geleng is applauded by a young girl, who makes the following suggestive remarks: "What colours! What a paintbrush!!! Once more!!!!" The humorous aspect of the drawing should not obscure the significance of the red paint dripping from the artist's phallic paintbrush. One must also note the effort exacted from the painter in order to hold his paintbrush erect while performing the act of creation.

This drawing is obviously laden with creative anxiety. Indeed, Millicent Marcus has pointed out the reverberation of performance anxiety in *Casanova*, contending that Casanova constitutes "the perfect vehicle for the artist's anxieties about the loss of his own creative powers ... a power whose evanescence is analogous to the sexual potency of even the liveliest of men."[44]

What Marcus is implying is that the director's obsessive concern with the instability of the creative process is mirrored in his protagonist's need to reaffirm time and again his sexual potency. However, it appears to me that *Fellini's Casanova* engages the creative and the sexual act in more than a metonymical relation, the one simply substituting for the other in the passage from life to film. Rather, the possession of Woman in *Fellini's Casanova* is conflated with the creative process. In *Casanova*, particularly if elucidated in a Jungian key, woman is the ultimate conduit to creativity.

In Jungian thinking, which greatly informs Fellini's concept of Woman, the Great Mother and the anima archetype are closely associated with creativity. Since this issue has been discussed by Bondanella[45] and Stubbs,[46] a brief review will suffice to highlight the resonance of Jungian concepts and imagery in the Annamaria scene.

Jungian texts associate the anima, or female aspect of the male psyche, with a primal and irrational stratum of the psyche.[47] Human fantasy and dream embody the anima in various female forms, which stand for "the living thing in man, that which causes life."[48] The female factor is conceived as an irrational or prerational life force. In Jung, the Mother "constitutes the first incarnation of the anima archetype, personif[ying] in fact the whole unconscious."[49] Thus, as Erich Neumann has put it, the desire to merge with the archetypal feminine indicates a quest for an "unreachable treasure" hidden in the dark abysses of the unconscious.[50]

The anima archetype is explicitly associated with artistic creation, as is made clear in volume 5 of Jung's *Collected Works*, which Fellini owned in Italian translation.[51] In this volume, Jung asserts that creativity crises are solved solely by regression into the archetypal womb: "Whenever some great work is to be accomplished, before which man recoils, doubtful of his strength, his libido streams back into the fountainhead," inducing the "birth of creative thought from introversion."[52] Articulated in a slightly different way, this idea is found in *The Great Mother* by Erich Neumann, of which Fellini's library holds a 1955 edition. For Neumann, "[t]he Great Goddess as a whole is a symbol of creative life and the parts of her body are not physical organs but numinous symbolic centres of whole spheres of life. For this reason [...] her display of her breasts, belly, or entire naked body, is a form of divine epiphany."[53] Neumann grounds his conception of woman in what he calls the three "blood-transformation mysteries," menstruation, pregnancy, and childbirth (or "the transformation of blood into milk").[54] In Neumann's formulation, these three phenomena constitute "blood-transformation mysteries that lead [woman] to the experience of her own creativity and produce a numinous impression on the man."[55]

Fellini predicates the enigma of Annamaria on one such "blood transformation mystery". "She does not have her periods, you understand? It's a sort of internal haemorrhage. Poor thing, they bleed her daily," goes the dialogue.[56] What is more, Casanova (as Pygmalion) performs a "life-giving" act that miraculously sets right the girl's periodic bleeding. "Annamaria had regained her strength: I nourished her daily with my passion and my blood [...]. She even got her periods. She was transformed into a beautiful, flourishing young girl, full of the joy of life. Where there was death, I have brought life."[57]

Casanova's conquest of Annamaria addresses the mystery of creation. The Jungian anima, to quote Neumann again, is conceptualized in precisely these terms. It is "the vehicle par excellence of the transformative character. It is the mover, the instigator of change, whose fascination drives, lures, and encourages the male to all the adventures of the soul and spirit, of action and creation in the inner and the outward world."[58] *Fellini's Casanova* weaves together the Jungian anima archetype with the mystical Golem, further layering it with de Chirico's contemplative "seer" and the half-drawn curtain of enigma. The portrait of the artist thus constructed is invested with romantic mystification vis-à-vis the creative process.

To further unravel this pregnant intertextual network, I wish to draw attention to the recurring appearance of mannequins in the film (Figure 5.3). The presence of faceless tailors' mannequins is most expressed in the first scene of the Annamaria sequence, where an explicit analogy is suggested between Casanova and those wooden androids. However, Fellini's association of Casanova with the mannequin, as with the Golem, is multivalent, particularly in light of the usage of the same motif in the painting of de Chirico.

The theme of the mannequin made its appearance in de Chirico's painting in 1914, and was to dominate his oeuvre for the coming fifteen years. In *The Seer* (1915), the featureless head is endowed with one

Figure 5.3 *Fellini's Casanova*. Casanova in the company of mannequins. DVD frame capture.

staring eye, significantly placed in the centre of the forehead. For Willard Bohn, the eye, or "mask-scar," connotes transcendence of physical limitations. The mannequin-poet, much like the veiled philosopher (or priest) in *The Enigma of the Oracle*, is endowed with the gift of vision, which compensates for physical paralysis.[59] In Bohn's reading, de Chirico conceives of the mannequin as "a symbol of the Poet, and of the creative artist in general."[60]

In *Fellini's Casanova*, the mannequin assumes a dialectical quality. The "mannequinization" of Casanova is undoubtedly informed by postmodern patterns of thought. Casanova, as has been widely agreed in critical treatments of this film, is a fragmented, decentred, dead subject. At the same time, recognition of the embedded art-historical hyperlinks, which speak to de Chirico and Jung and strongly connote transcendence in the spirit of Metaphysical painting, immediately counters the Baudrillardian note which has quite rightly been discerned by the critics. The proximity of Casanova and the mannequins is essentially dialectical, playing the industrial inhumanity of the mannequin against the metaphysical overtones it is charged with in the oeuvre of de Chirico. A possibility of transcendence is thus connoted via the very image widely read as the epitome of the hollow signifier.

Fellini's Isoletta di San Bartolo, Böcklin's *Isle of the Dead*

At this point, the intertextual itinerary takes the reader back to Arnold Böcklin, one of de Chirico's major influences, whose painting (or rather series of paintings) *The Isle of the Dead* (1880) seems to resonate in the film's portrayal of Casanova ashore the Isoletta di San Bartolo. Alone on the dark island Casanova awaits a mysterious emissary approaching in a boat (Figure 5.4).[61]

Fellini seems to have transposed Böcklin's upright figure from the boat onto the island, leaving the rowing woman as sole person on board the boat. However, a look at the script indicates that Fellini envisioned a male figure in this scene. The man, as the script version goes, would stand motionless on board the boat as in Böcklin's painting: "Casanova looks about anxiously. Suddenly he sees ... a gondola approaching. Inside there is a human figure standing up, motionless, almost a phantasm."[62] But with Fellini equivocality is always the rule. As the script subsequently makes clear, the rower is a woman dressed in man's clothes. Smiling enigmatically at Casanova, she invites him to join her for the love scene at the French ambassador's villa. How is Casanova re-conceptualized via the suggestive reference to Böcklin's

Figure 5.4 *Fellini's Casanova*. A mysterious boat approaches the Isoletta di San Bartolo, DVD frame capture.

Isle of the Dead, a painting which distinctly figures the romantic idea of "the great solitary man," to use the words of Hans Henrik Brummer.[63]

Fellini's acquaintance with *The Isle of the Dead* is well established through archival and circumstantial evidence. The painting is reproduced in at least two books in his library. The first is *Histoire de la Peinture Surrealiste* by Marcel Jean (1959), where *The Isle of the Dead* illustrates a chapter on the precursors of surrealism. The second is volume 1 of the series *L'Arte Moderna* (1967), dedicated to Symbolist painting. It is worth noting that Böcklin's work was resurfacing in the public and critical attention during the 1970s, due to large exhibition projects. This change came in the wake of a long period where Böcklin was associated with the Nazi taste for kitsch.[64] The revival of interest in Böcklin would have been brought to Fellini's attention, if not directly then through the mediation of Fabrizio Clerici, whose *Labyrinth* paintings are discussed in chapter 4. In 1974 Clerici launched a series of paintings in which *The Isle of the Dead* was a central motif.[65] In this series, Clerici appropriates Böcklin's composition in its integrity, combining it into various compositions. In *Latitudine Böcklin* (*The Böcklin Latitude*, 1974; Figure 5.5), for

Figure 5.5 Fabrizio Clerici, *Latitudine Böcklin* (*Böcklin Latitude*), ca. 1979, oil on panel, 70 × 100 cm, courtesy Archivio Fabrizio Clerici, Rome.

example, *The Isle of the Dead* forms part of a hallucinatory scenery, while in *Le Presenze* (*The Presences*, 1974), two clusters of rocks and cypresses emerge from the floor of an otherwise empty room, while on the wall hangs the masterpiece by Böcklin.[66]

Notably, nine paintings of this series were completed during the summer of 1974,[67] thus coinciding with the initial stages of Fellini's work on *Casanova*. Given this circumstantial conjunction, it may be safely suggested that the image of Casanova ashore the Isoletta di San Bartolo, watching a mysterious boat approach from the distance, speaks to Böcklin's *Isle of the Dead* through the mediation of Clerici via the Böcklin series.

Fellini, however, significantly modifies the composition, transposing the standing figure from the boat onto the island and replacing the rock necropolis with an architectonic structure that looks like a small church, or place of worship. This architectonic addition forges a link with *The Seer* by de Chirico, discussed earlier, recalling the curtained temple in the background of this painting. To tangle the mesh of hyperlinks even further, the temple of Apollo in *The Enigma of the Oracle* may be recalled. The same painting has been pointed out earlier as pivotal to the alcove scene. The image of Casanova on the miniature island thus interweaves the veiled philosopher, or pagan priest, of de Chirico's *Enigma* with Böcklin's motionless silhouette. It seems that in this art-historically laden shot, de Chirico's mysterious temple meets Böcklin's enigmatic cypresses ashore Fellini's Isoletta di San Bartolo.

To take this reading a step further, the ambiguity of this scene in its representation of the individuated subject calls for attention. Does Casanova, having landed on Böcklin's "island of tombs" (Die Gräberinsel, as this painting was alternately titled), become the epitome of the postmodern subject? Or, in light of the art-historical layering just pointed out, which speaks to Symbolism and Metaphysical painting, does the uncanny island, with Casanova ashore and a mysterious boat approaching, rather tag Fellini's protagonist as an initiate of metaphysical revelation? The evident similarity between the image of Casanova ashore the island and the shrouded figure in Böcklin's *Odysseus and Calypso* hints that there is more to *Fellini's Casanova* than the failure of the subject as creative agent. Rather, a romantic quest is subtly implied, a quest for revival of the creative subject, a project long given up in postmodern art and thought. Ashore the island, positioned against the Böcklinesque cypresses and the Chiricoan temple, Fellini's Casanova re-establishes the romantic idea of the artist as seer and metaphysical explorer.

128   Federico Fellini

In *Fellini's Casanova*, the quest for revival is formulated as a hysterical pursuit of women. The very scene we are discussing marks the beginning of this quest. The mysterious emissary in the approaching boat is the one to involve Casanova in the first among countless sexual encounters featured in this film. While the compositional transposition of the upright figure from the boat to the island works to undermine easy recognition of the embedded intertext, Fellini visibly draws on the sense of metaphysical enigma which Böcklin's *Isle of the Dead* so powerfully conveys.

A Bridge over the Thames: *Fellini's Casanova* Meets Whistler's *Nocturnes*

At this point it clearly emerges that Fellini returns to nineteenth-century painting for its suggestion of metaphysical mystery and melancholy. Yet another scene is pertinent in this regard. On a bridge over the Thames, immersed in a foggy London atmosphere, a desperate Casanova is humiliatingly abandoned by his two lovers, a mother and her daughter. Alone with his luggage on a deserted London bridge, Casanova experiences a moment of *angst*. "Giacomo! May it be that your star faces its decline? ... Eros abandons you ... and in front of you rises the gloomy Thanatos," he exclaims.[68] Dressed in his best habit, the despairing Casanova descends into the grey waters of the Thames. A moment later his will to live will be reawakened by a mysterious giantess accompanied by two midgets. Resuming his obsessive pursuit of Woman, Casanova follows this archetypal female to the mysterious fairground, discussed earlier in this chapter.

Like the scenes reviewed earlier, the present scene is highly equivocal. The artificiality of Casanova's gesture and speech is emphasized to a point where his attempted suicide stands out as a markedly theatrical, hollow performance, rather than a meaningful human act. Fellini appears to have constructed a Casanova that is all appearances, an empty mask devoid of real humanity. This insight notwithstanding, one must admit that the haze that envelops the river elicits an almost tactile sensation of mystery, which I would like to think about in the terms offered by Merleau-Ponty, and Vivian Sobchack in his wake. And again, I wish to suggest, the embodied sensation of enigma is enabled primarily via recourse to painting. Intensely painting-like, the shots of the bridge and the river employ *effetto pitturato* in the blue mist that envelops them, much like the yellow haze in the car ride in *Toby Dammit*, which collapses cinematic space into an expressly flattened pictorial surface. Moreover, the atmospheric vagueness and grey mist of the Thames shots recall the characteristic haziness of Symbolist painting. In particular, analysis of these shots should look to the Thames sceneries by James McNeill Whistler as embedded art-historical links.

Notably, Fellini had at his disposal a reproduction of Whistler's *Nocturne in Blue and Gold: Old Battersea Bridge*, in volume 1 of *L'Arte Moderna*, lying on the shelves of his library.[69] The shot of Casanova, sunk up to his chest in the grey waters of the Thames, a huge column of the bridge dominating the composition, seems to reproduce the composition and colour scheme of Whistler's *Old Battersea Bridge*.

At first sight, Fellini's apparent recourse to Whistler as visual source for a scene that takes place on the Thames seems almost banal, recalling the prominence of the riverscape among Whistler's subjects. However, there is more to Fellini's evocation of Whistler than mere reconstruction of London's riverside views. Evoking the *Nocturnes*, Fellini is able to invest *Casanova* with what Frances Spalding, discussing Whistler, describes as "the sense that the visible world thinly veils the inexplicable."[70] Upon closer look, one realizes that the solitary and listless silhouette of Casanova, as he stands on the bridge wrapped in his heavy cloak, speaks to the veiled seer in Böcklin and de Chirico. Fellini seems insistent on reasserting the romantic idea of the visionary artist in this figure, notwithstanding the widely accepted reading of Casanova as the deflated simulacrum of an individuated subject.[71]

The choice of art-historical intertexts in this multilayered *lexia* sheds light on an essential trait of Fellini's cinematic idiom. As it clearly emerges from the reading of *Casanova* proposed in these pages, Fellini mobilizes potently suggestive paintings in order to fulfil an essentially romantic (and simultaneously modernist) project, in an age of acute disillusionment with the agency of the artist. Drawing on the evocative power of Symbolist and Metaphysical painting, heavily charged *lexiae*, such as the Chiricoan curtained alcove or the Böcklinesque island, alternate with the image of Casanova as a fragmented reflection in a hall of mirrors, or a shadow on the wall. In fact, Fellini's images bear an inner dialectic, as is the case with the mannequin, at once a lifeless humanoid and a poet or seer. The Golem, in turn, may be read at one and the same time as an inhuman "robot" or as the epitome of the human capacity for creation.

In the interview Fellini gave to Aldo Tassone, he remarked that *Casanova* was "a film on nothingness."[72] While this sort of remark seems to inform the general view of the film, past and present, it is irreconcilable with the conviction expressed by Fellini in the same interview, that "basically, cinema has ... its deep and indissoluble link with the romantic."[73] In *Casanova*, and in Fellini's middle period in general, painting constitutes the primary medium which enables film to realize this "deep and indissoluble link with the romantic." Gravitating toward the heightened embodied sensation that painting is able to arouse, the art-historical building blocks of *Casanova* give rise to an intense experience of mystery and of *angst*.

Conclusion

"A New Hypothesis of the Truth": Painting as Vehicle of the Real in Fellini's Films, 1960s–1970s

In the present study I set out to explore and elucidate the role of painting in Fellini's cinematic idiom. I opted to highlight the unique features of his art-historical references in their historical and cultural contexts. Particular attention has been given to the contribution of Fellini's art-historical hyperlinks, or *lexiae*, to the formation of a cinematic language approximating what Julia Kristeva has called *the sémiotique*. The role played by highly charged visual cues in Fellini's cinema was a pivotal concern of the four chapters dedicated to analysis of individual films.

A major issue addressed in these chapters was the particular function fulfilled by painting in constituting a dialectical play, alternately troubling and reaffirming the concept of the creative subject as the solid core of meaning in art. Embedded art-historical references, it was shown, maintain a delicate, if tense, balance between Fellini the modernist and Fellini the postmodernist.

As the present research has shown, Fellini's choice of art-historical intertexts distinctly privileges Symbolist painting. He makes recourse to the idealist-spiritual brand (Previati, Segantini, Sartorio, Whistler) as well as the Decadent vein (Klimt, Beardsley), and harks further back to predecessors of Symbolism such as the Pre-Raphaelites, Moreau, or Böcklin, and forward in art history, to the Metaphysical painting of de Chirico and Savinio. The paintings which serve as building blocks for Fellini's visual *lexiae* feature, alternately, a romantic quest for transcendence and intense psychological or mystical experiences. The intensity conveyed by these signifying units powerfully negates the vacuity of the hollow signifier in postmodern thinking. In *Casanova*, it has been argued, embedded reference to *The Enigma of the Oracle* by de Chirico and

Odysseus and Calypso and *Isle of the Dead* by Böcklin challenges widely accepted readings of the protagonist as the ultimate hollow simulacrum. Heavily charged hyperlinks, such as the curtained alcove evocative of de Chirico, or the Böcklinesque island, powerfully counter any reading of *Fellini's Casanova* as the story of a dehumanized automaton, a Baudrillardian *simulacrum*, a "dead Subject." Fellini's choice of art-historical intertexts reinstates the human subject, and moreover the creative individual, at the heart of a romantic quest for meaning. The artist is thus re-established as a potent agent, capable of retrieving and re-presenting real human experience.

The chapters that engage *Giulietta degli spiriti*, *Toby Dammit*, and *Fellini Satyricon* have in turn shown how brief shots packed with intertextual allusions potently communicate anxiety and depressiveness, and various other tensions. The shots discussed in these chapters evoke iconographical traditions which bear direct relevance to the protagonists' mental crises. Communicating a strongly felt psychological actuality, the visual *lexiae* embedded in these films indicate the existence of a subjective core of experience, a notion that is pivotal to Fellini's project.

Painting, it was argued, has a crucial role in constituting the *sémiotique*, a non-verbal mode of communication postulated by Julia Kristeva as articulating instinctual drives and primal sensations. Fellini privileges the *sémiotique* over the symbolic, or *symbolique*, as in Kristeva. In Fellini's middle period, painting is conceived as the one medium most capable of enabling access to the stratum of "raw meaning" referenced by the concept of *sémiotique*. Painting, in other words, is conceived as the vehicle of the *sémiotique* par excellence. Fellini's choice of art-historical intertexts makes this conviction manifest. Highly potent in their visual suggestiveness, the art-historical signifying units, or hyperlinks, embedded in the films discussed in this book, present a heightened affective immediacy.

Capable of evoking primary – or real – sensations independent of symbolic decipherment, Fellini's visual signs are thus essentially attributable to the Kristevan *sémiotique*, closely associated with drives and sensations rooted in early infancy. As formulated by Ann Marie Smith, the *sémiotique* constitutes a "transitional sensory space ... which is occupied by sensation, vocalics, and images,"[1] and which in turn bridges the gap between the imaginary and the symbolic.[2] It has been further asserted, and must be emphasized here, that Fellini's cinematic signs retain a suggestive potency regardless of whether their particular art-historical intertexts are recognized.

In his middle period Fellini seems to forge a cinematic idiom where notions of hollow signification are evoked only to be immediately countered. Painting emerges as bearing a fundamental role in the reconstitution of the real. Fellini's oeuvre, particularly during the period circumscribed here, assigns painting the role of origin, or core of "realness" whence the experience of meaning originates.

Notably, in the comprehensive interview on *Casanova* given to Aldo Tassone in 1978, quoted earlier, Fellini presents an expressed desire for a cinema that would "put an end to the ... anguishing representation of the 'negative,'" replacing it with "a new hypothesis of the truth," a cinema that would engage in a "euphoria of expressive liberation."[3] In my view, the foregoing remark epitomizes the conceptual premises fundamental to Fellini's middle period. "Euphoria" seems to denote an irruption of sensations, which openly articulates an unreserved celebration of artistic creation. Fellini's evocation of euphoria indicates an immanently romantic concept of art, which at the same time is essentially modernist in its assertion of the creative subject as the ultimate source of meaning. "Euphoria" thus reiterates the modernist view of artistic creation as an upsurge of psychic contents.

Fellini's employment of the term "liberation," in turn, points to a postmodern approach whose central concern is to liberate the text from the reins of linearity and monological unity. The notion of "liberation" connotes the complexity and plurality of a dialogic form. Whether thoroughly acquainted with poststructuralist concepts, or merely partaking of the epoch's heightened inclination toward complexity, Fellini distinctly privileges intertextuality and heteroglossia in his vision of a "euphoria of expressive liberation."

The essential heteroglossia that characterizes Fellini's cinematic text becomes manifest in the seamless interweaving of painting into the cinematic flux. It has been shown that Fellini avoids formal "quotation marks" and other bracketing devices through which cinema conventionally marks painting as Other, while his contemporaries tended to foreground dissonance and otherness. While they played the codes of cinema and painting against each other in evident commitment to the metadiscursive project, Fellini appears to have been less concerned with deconstructing discourse than with an essentially romantic reconstruction of art as a form of human expression.

As shown in chapter 1, dialogism, intertextuality, and heteroglossia are conceived in poststructuralist thinking as literary forms that bear a sociocultural function. A liberatory movement is thereby effected, away from the "multiple constraints – which are ultimately sociopolitical – [that] stop the signifying process," constraining it to "fixed, fragmentary, symbolic *matrices*, the tracings of various social constraints that obliterate the infinity of the process."[4] As I maintain in chapter 1, Fellini's implementation of these notions, whether fully intentional or only partly so, is rooted in his fundamental rejection of institutional authority, and his overt identification with the epoch's denunciation of hegemony, whether cultural or political. Fellini thus embraces quite readily the liberatory aspects of postmodern thought, and partakes of the fundamental shifts in the conception and construction of the text. He does not commit himself, however, to the loss of origin, or the vacuity of the simulacral signifier, so central to postmodern cultural theory.

As asserted in chapter 1, Fellini's idiom is incompatible with the existing body of theoretical writing on the subject of painting in film. This body of writing, I have argued, is predicated on the works of Pasolini, Godard, Greenaway, and a handful of other directors, and is hence unable to account for cinematic idioms which do not manifest the same degree of metadiscursive zeal. In the majority of critical works addressing this subject, the "end of representation" prevails. Painting is thus approached in the critical literature as a cultural signifier rather than a potent medium of aesthetic experience. The present study rejects the monopoly of the foregoing approaches, and opts to enlarge the scope of theoretical elaboration on the function of painting in, or on film. I have proposed to re-consider the function of painting as embedded vehicle of the real. Weaving a complex intertextual web, where painting is mobilized to unleash *the sémiotique*, Fellini undertakes a project of suturing the split between the artwork and the real. Eliciting intense affective experience via intertextual reference, he appears to be playing the formal tropes of postmodern discourse against the central ideas of this very same discourse. Painting is thus assigned a major role in an essentially romantic project, which Fellini never tired of pursuing in his films.

Notes

Preface

1 Federico Fellini, *Fare un film* (Turin: Einaudi, 1974), 107.
2 Ibid., 107.
3 Ibid, 14.
4 Ibid., 60.
5 Piero Tosi, interview with the author, Rome, 17 July 2005.
6 Fellini's private library has been preserved and catalogued by the Fondazione Federico Fellini in Rimini, Italy, and was opened to the public in November 2008 in an exhibition entitled *I libri di casa mia: La biblioteca di Federico Fellini*. For a full catalogue, see Oriana Maroni and Giuseppe Ricci, *I libri di casa mia: La biblioteca di Federico Fellini* (Rimini: Fondazione Federico Fellini, 2008). I was fortunate in being able to examine this library at a much earlier stage in September 1997. The results of this research constitute a major archival source for the present study.
7 Rinaldo Geleng, interview with the author, Rome, 21 March 2000. Fellini was probably familiar with Steinberg's work at an even earlier stage, during his work for the Florentine magazine *420*, one of the four leading humour magazines in 1930s and 1940s Italy.
8 Eventually, the "Steinberg shot" played a very marginal role in the final cut. The road workers wearing paper hoods appear in a brief shot and the hoods are barely visible. Thirty-seven years later, Piero Tosi still sounded quite exasperated about this.
9 This book is strongly committed to archival research, tracing the artist's visual sources, reading materials, and personal acquaintances. I believe that this approach, which owes a great deal to my training in the art-historical discipline, contributes to substantiating analyses of particular film images identified as embedded art-historical references.

10 For brief treatments of Fellini's reference to painting see Tullio Kezich, *Federico Fellini, la vita e i film* (Milan: Feltrinelli, 2002), 87, 251, 382; Peter Bondanella, *The Cinema of Federico Fellini* (Princeton: Princeton University Press, 1992), 134, 301, 303; John C. Stubbs, *Federico Fellini as Auteur: Seven Aspects of His Films* (Carbondale: Southern Illinois University Press, 2006), 25–7, 228–9; Roberto Campari, *Il fantasma del bello: Iconologia del cinema Italiano* (Venice: Marsilio, 1994), 83–94; Gianfranco Angelucci, "Fellini 15 e ½ e la poetica dell'onirico," in Angelucci and Betti, *Il Film "Amarcord" di Federico Fellini*, 28, 34; Alberto Moravia, "Dreaming up Petronius," in Bondanella, *Federico Fellini, Essays in Criticism*, 164; and Brunello Rondi, *Il cinema di Fellini* (Rome: Edizioni di Bianco e Nero, 1965), 19–20. Torunn Haaland's essay "Echoes of Scipione in Fellini's *Roma*," in *Fellini Amarcord* 2 (2005), 65–71, provides a comprehensive analysis of Fellini's *Roma* in association with the paintings of Scipione.
11 See W.J.T. Mitchell, *Picture Theory* (Chicago: University of Chicago Press, 1994).
12 Ibid., 15.
13 Ibid.

1. Fellini, Painting on Film

1 "What would I have wanted to do in this film [*Fellini's Casanova*]? Arrive once and for all at the ultimate essence of cinema, at that which for me is the total film. To succeed, that is, in turning a film into a painting." Valerio Riva, "Intervista à Fellini," *L'Espresso* (26 May 1976), quoted in Tullio Kezich, *Fellini* (Milan: Camunia, 1987), 463. Translations from Italian are mine unless otherwise indicated.
2 Chapter 2 also offers a comparative look at Pier Paolo Pasolini's use of the same painting in *Che cosa sono le nuvole* (1968), released about the same time as Fellini's *Toby Dammit*. When comparing the two films, essential differences come to light, enabling a more precise formulation of Fellini's mode of quotation.
3 Rondi, *Il cinema di Fellini*, 17.
4 Ibid., 19, emphasis mine.
5 Ibid.
6 See, for example, Oreste Del Buono, "Una vecchia coppia," in *I disegni di Fellini*, ed. Pier Marco de Santi (Florence: Laterza, 1981), 7–9; Bondanella, *Cinema of Federico Fellini*, 9–21; and Sasa Perugini, "The Aesthetics of Fellini's Art Seen through Its Ties with Popular Entertainment" (PhD diss., University of Michigan, 2002). This is not to imply that these scholars, and

many others, totally overlook certain art-historical echoes in Fellini's films. However, the associations they bring up are sporadic and lack systematic art-historical analysis.

7 Jill M. Ricketts, "Living Pictures: High Art Pastiche and the Cruising Gaze in Pasolini's *Decameron*," in *Visualizing Boccaccio: Studies on Illustrations of The Decameron, from Giotto to Pasolini* (Cambridge: Cambridge University Press, 1997), 118–64.

8 The main body of work on this subject includes Pascal Bonitzer, *Peinture et Cinéma: Décadrages* (Paris: Editions de l'Etoile, 1985); Jacques Aumont, *L'Oeil Interminable: Cinéma et Peinture* (1987; Paris: Séguier, 1995); Raymond Bellour, ed., *Cinéma et Peinture – Approches* (Paris: Presses Universitaires de France, 1990); François Jost, "Le picto-film," in Bellour, *Cinéma et Peinture*, 109–22; Antonio Costa, *Cinema e pittura* (Turin: Loescher, 1991); Campari, *Il fantasma del bello*; Brigitte Peucker, *Incorporating Images: Film and the Rival Arts* (Princeton, NJ: Princeton University Press, 1995); idem, *The Material Image: Art and the Real in Film* (Stanford: Stanford University Press, 2007); Angela Dalle Vacche, *Cinema and Painting: How Art Is Used in Film* (Austin: University of Texas Press, 1996); Susan Felleman, *Art in the Cinematic Imagination* (Austin: University of Texas Press, 2006); and Laura M. Sager Eidt, *Writing and Filming the Painting: Ekphrasis in Literature and Film* (Amsterdam: Rodopi, 2008). See also Angela Dalle Vacche, ed., *The Visual Turn: Classical Film Theory and Art History* (New Brunswick, NJ: Rutgers University Press, 2003).

9 Jost, "Le Picto-Film," 114–18.
10 Peucker, *Incorporating Images*, 6.
11 Fredric Jameson, *The Geopolitical Aesthetic: Cinema and Space in the World System* (Indianapolis: Bloomington University Press, 1992), 158–9.
12 Eidt, *Writing and Filming the Painting*, 23.
13 Ibid., 24.
14 Ibid.
15 Mitchell, *Picture Theory*, 163.
16 Peucker, *Material Image*, 30.
17 Mikhail Bakhtin, "Discourse in the Novel," in *The Dialogic Imagination: Four Essays by M.M. Bakhtin*, ed. Michael Holquist (Austin: University of Texas Press, 1981), 295.
18 Ibid., 303–4.
19 Franco Ricci, *Painting with Words, Writing with Pictures: Word and Image in the Work of Italo Calvino* (Toronto: University of Toronto Press, 2001), 273.
20 Mitchell, "Ekphrasis and the Other," in *Picture Theory*, 152.
21 Ibid., 154.

22 Ibid., 155.
23 Ibid., 156.
24 Ibid., 155.
25 Ibid., 173.
26 Julia Kristeva, "Intertextuality and Literary Interpretation," interview by Margaret Waller, in *Julia Kristeva Interviews*, ed. Ross Mitchell Guberman (New York: Columbia University Press, 1996), 189.
27 Julia Kristeva, *Desire in Language: A Semiotic Approach to Literature and Art* (New York: Columbia University Press, 1980), 66.
28 Julia Kristeva, *Revolution in Poetic Language* (New York: Columbia University Press, 1984), 60.
29 Kristeva, "Intertextuality and Literary Interpretation," 190.
30 Ibid. Kristeva's conception of the author as a fragmented "subject in process" whose plural identity emerges, revived, from the ruins of the earlier self, closely recalls the protagonist of Fellini's *Otto e mezzo* (1963). Speaking of "the challenge to this identity and even its reduction to zero, the moment of crisis, of emptiness, and then the reconstitution of a new, plural identity," Kristeva sounds as if she were reviewing *Otto e mezzo*, where a plethora of characters represent fragments of Guido's self and are finally integrated into the circle of dancers in white in the film's dramatic ending. "Intertextuality," 190. Was Fellini, in 1963, formulating a conception of the author similar to that of Kristeva? This is not, I believe, a question of precedence or influence, but rather of *zeitgeist*, reflecting the period's general preoccupation with the deconstruction of hegemonic unity and its replacement by the complex pluralities of the subject and the signifying system alike.
31 See Roland Barthes, "The Death of the Author," in *Image, Music, Text* (New York: Noonday Press, 1977), 142–8.
32 Megan Becker-Leckrone, *Julia Kristeva and Literary Theory* (New York: Palgrave Macmillan, 2005), 107.
33 My approach draws further support from American theories of intertextuality, which in the 1980s overtly opposed French definitions of intertextuality which privileged language, rather than the author, as focal to their speculation. As Susan Stanford-Friedman points out in her comprehensive review of theories of influence and intertextuality, American theory at large insists on a subject-centred theory. See Susan Stanford Friedman, "Weavings: Intertextuality and the (Re)Birth of the Author," in *Influence and Intertextuality in Literary Theory*, ed. Jay Clayton and Eric Rothstein (Madison: University of Wisconsin Press, 1991), 146–80; also Jay Clayton and Eric Rothstein, "Figures in the Corpus: Theories of

Influence and Intertextuality," in Clayton and Rothstein, *Influence and Intertextuality*, 3–36.
34 Clayton and Rothstein, *Influence and Intertextuality*, 30.
35 Kristeva, *Revolution in Poetic Language*, 25–7. To distinguish Kristeva's *le sémiotique* (the semiotic) from the general reference to semiotics, it will henceforth be referred to in italics, as the *sémiotique*.
36 Ann Marie Smith, *Julia Kristeva: Speaking the Unspeakable* (London: Pluto Press, 1998), 16.
37 Leon S. Roudiez, introduction to *Desire in Language*, by Kristeva, 18.
38 Vivian Sobchack, *Carnal Thoughts: Embodiment and Moving Image Culture* (Berkeley: University of California Press, 2004), 64.
39 Ibid., 64–5.
40 Ibid., 71.
41 Ibid., 84.
42 Vivian Sobchack, *The Address of the Eye: A Phenomenology of the Film Experience* (Princeton, NJ: Princeton University Press, 1992), 68.
43 Maurice Merleau-Ponty, "Eye and Mind," in *The Merleau-Ponty Aesthetics Reader: Philosophy and Painting*, ed. Galen A. Johnson and Michael B. Smith (Evanston, IL: Northwestern University Press, 1993), 123.
44 Ibid., 125.
45 Ibid., 126.
46 Merleau-Ponty, "Cézanne's Doubt," in *The Merleau-Ponty Aesthetics Reader: Philosophy and Painting*, ed. Galen A. Johnson and Michael B. Smith (Evanston, IL: Northwestern University Press, 1993), 65.
47 Merleau-Ponty, "Eye and Mind," 149.
48 Ibid., 142.
49 Christopher Sharrett, "*Toby Dammit*, Intertext, and the End of Humanism," in Burke and Waller, *Federico Fellini*, 124.
50 Roland Barthes, *S/Z* (New York: Hill and Wang, 1974), 13–14.
51 Ibid.
52 For a comprehensive discussion of this matter see George P. Landow, *Hypertext: The Convergence of Contemporary Critical Theory and Technology* (Baltimore: Johns Hopkins University Press, 1992), and idem, "What's a Critic to Do? Critical Theory in the Age of Hypertext," in Landow, *Hyper/Text/Theory*, 1–48.
53 Landow, "What's a Critic to Do?," 1.
54 *Hyperlinks*, as defined by Jacob Nielsen, are "pointers" that connect a node in the hypertextual web to other units of information. See Jacob Nielsen, *Multimedia and Hypertext: The Internet and Beyond* (London: Academic Press, 1995), 2.

55 George P. Landow and Paul Delany, "Hypertext, Hypermedia and Literary Studies: The State of the Art," in Delany and Landow, *Hypermedia and Literary Studies*, 10.
56 Ibid., 23–5.
57 Ibid., 2.
58 Roland Barthes, "The Third Meaning," *Image, Music, Text* (New York: Noonday Press, 1977), 66.
59 Ibid., 67.
60 Raymond Bellour, "The Film Stilled," *Camera Obscura, A Journal of Feminism and Film Theory* 24 (1991): 103.
61 While Brigitte Peucker has recently taken up Barthes as one among her theoretical premises in *The Material Image*, my reading of the linkage between painting and the real considerably differs from her engagement of the body as the core of real-ness. Peucker reads Barthes's "third meaning" in terms of a "residual uncodedness" or "natural dimension" to be traced in the photographic still, constituting a link between film and the material real. *Material Image*, 40. In the reading I will be proposing, however, the real is conceived not so much as the embodied trace of material experience as the unconscious trace of primal experience, or that which precedes the symbolic.
62 Eidt, *Writing and Filming the Painting*, 18.
63 Ibid., 45–7.
64 Mauro Aprile Zanetti, *La Natura Morta de La Dolce Vita; A Mysterious Morandi in the Matrix of Fellini's Vision* (New York: Italian Institute of Culture, 2008).
65 Graham Allen, *Intertextuality* (London: Routledge, 2000), 32.
66 Kristeva, *Desire in Language*, 69–70.
67 Alberto Farassino, "Extra Strong," in *Federico Fellini, disegni anni '30–'70*, ed. Gianfranco Miro Gori (Rimini: Giusti, 1994), 15.
68 Megan Becker-Leckrone, *Julia Kristeva and Literary Theory* (New York: Palgrave Macmillan, 2005), 91.
69 Fellini MSS, Lilly Library of Rare Books, Bloomington, Indiana, box 2, fol. 11, p. 7.
70 Fellini MSS, box 2, fol. 11, p. 13.
71 Quoted in Peter Bondanella, e-mail message to author, 22 September 2003.
72 Leckrone, *Julia Kristeva and Literary Theory*, 111.
73 Peter Bondanella, *Umberto Eco and the Open Text* (New York: Cambridge University Press, 1997), 193.
74 Ibid., 29.
75 Ibid.
76 Fellini MSS, box 2, fol. 11, pp. 16–17.

77 Ibid.
78 Bondanella, *Cinema of Federico Fellini*, 235.
79 Bondanella, e-mail message to author, 22 September 2003.
80 Barthes, "Death of the Author," 146.
81 Ibid.
82 Giovanni Grazzini, ed., *Comments on Film – Federico Fellini* (Fresno: California State University Press, 1988), 181.
83 Fellini MSS, box 2, fol. 11, p. 17.
84 Fellini is apparently inconsistent in allowing the dogmatic structuralist priest to bring up ideas of intertextuality in film. However, one should not look for consistency in a Fellinian figure (or film), since these are essentially complex and multivalent, lacking the expected consistency of a conventional film character. The lines of dialogue evoking cinematic intertextuality are thus to be read first and foremost as Fellini's own reflection on this issue, with little regard for the question of character consistency.
85 Kezich, *Federico Fellini, la vita e i film*, 219.
86 A full account of Fellini's relationship with Bernhard is given in Kezich, *Federico Fellini*, 215–21, and Bondanella, *Cinema of Federico Fellini*, 151–4.
87 Fellini's dream notebooks were made public by the Fondazione Federico Fellini in November 2007, and have been fully published, with English transcripts, in *Federico Fellini: The Book of Dreams*, ed. Tullio Kezich and Vittorio Boarini (New York: Rizzoli International, 2008).
88 Fellini's more or less official biography (Kezich, *Federico Fellini*) does not specify the date of Fellini's visit to the tower. However, I have first-hand information of such a visit having taken place during the summer of 1976. On that visit Fellini was received and shown through the place by Jung's grandson, Mr Jost Hoerni. Jost Hoerni, letter to author, 6 February 1998.
89 Niklaus Baumann in discussion with author, 15 July 1998.
90 See, for example, Bondanella, *Cinema of Federico Fellini*, 150–9.
91 John Freeman, introduction to *Man and His Symbols*, ed. Carl G. Jung (London: Aldus Books, 1964), 10–11. Fellini's copy bears a dedication, dated 1965, from the artist and filmmaker Hans Richter, with whom he maintained a close friendship. The two were introduced by the journalist and film critic Gideon Bachmann. Gideon Bachmann in discussion with author, 11 October 2003.
92 Notably, Jung's *Symbols of Transformation*, of which Fellini owned an Italian translation, *La libido – simboli e trasformazioni*, is similarly laden with art-historical references embedded in a rich scheme of illustration.
93 I am referring to a monograph on Bruegel, dedicated to Fellini in January 1954 by Ennio Flaiano, to mention but one example.

94 Julia Kristeva, "General Principles in Semiotics," interview by Pierre Oulet and Charles Bauer, in Guberman, *Julia Kristeva Interviews*, 181.
95 Keith Moxey, "Visual Studies and the Iconic Turn," *Journal of Visual Culture* 7 (2008): 140.
96 Ibid., 132.
97 Ibid.
98 Bellour, "Film Stilled," 103.

2. *Giulietta degli spiriti*: Symbolist Virgins Meet Decadent *Femmes Fatales* in Art Nouveau Interiors

1 Henceforth I will refer to the film as *Giulietta*.
2 Kezich, *Fellini*, 248. It should be noted that in 1961 Fellini filmed *The Temptations of Doctor Antonio* in colour; this was not an aesthetic choice but rather in compliance with the producers' demands. See Peter Bondanella, *Cinema of Federico Fellini*, 299.
3 Fellini, *Fare un film*, 94.
4 Ibid., 96.
5 Ibid., 95.
6 In this chapter, and the chapters to follow, I shall be making occasional use of the term *effetto dipinto*, coined by Antonio Costa in *Cinema e pittura*, and adopted by other critics addressing similar issues. By *effetto dipinto*, Costa refers to a wide range of cinematic evocations of painting, which he divides into two categories: *effeto pitturato* and *effetto quadro*. *Effetto pitturato*, the first of Costa's subcategories, indicates the effect produced by pronouncedly painted settings and backgrounds. An extreme example is Antonioni's repainting of whole outside locations, as in *The Red Desert* of 1964.

Costa's second category, *effetto quadro*, or the "picture effect," includes evocation of specific paintings, iconographic or compositional traits characteristic of a particular art-historical genre, and all manner by which a particular painting may be evoked in film. See Costa, *Cinema e pittura*, 155–7.

However, Costa has neglected to notice Fellini's frequent employment of *effetto quadro*, and has remarked solely upon the director's employment of visibly painted sets which qualify as *effetto pitturato*. The present study highlights Fellini's extensive use of *effetto quadro* in embedded art-historical hyperlinks.
7 Frank Burke, *Fellini's Films: From Postwar to Postmodern* (New York: Twayne, 1996), 162–3.
8 Peter Brunette, *The Films of Michelangelo Antonioni* (Cambridge: Cambridge University Press, 1998), 3.

9 Although it is not specified in the film or the script, the saint Giulietta is to impersonate is probably Santa Christina of Bolsena, who was burned at the stake by her father, a Roman officer, but was miraculously unharmed by the flames. The martyrdom of Santa Christina of Bolsena is recurrently depicted in early Renaissance Italian painting. See George Kaftal, *Saints in Italian Art* (Florence: Sansoni, 1952–85), 1:261–6.
10 Bondanella, *Cinema of Federico Fellini*, 304.
11 Bram Dijkstra, *Idols of Perversity: Fantasies of Feminine Evil in Fin-de-Siècle Culture* (New York: Oxford University Press, 1986), 13.
12 Ibid., 3.
13 Carolyn Geduld, "Juliet of the Spirits: Guido's Anima," in Bondanella, *Federico Fellini*, 142.
14 I would like to highlight a significant parallelism between the story of Santa Christina of Bolsena, whom Giulietta impersonates in the school play, and the story of Giulietta's own suffering at the hands of her fascist father. As specified in note 9, in the martyrdom of Santa Christina, the father, a Roman soldier, is the oppressor. I would like to suggest that, while the scenes that feature the fascist father in Fellini's script have not been included in the final cut of *Giulietta degli spiriti*, the sequence of the school play does indict Giulietta's fascist ancestry as responsible for her mental tribulations and, by implication, the suffering inflicted on Fellini's generation. For the relevant paragraphs in the script see Federico Fellini, "Giulietta degli spiriti," in *Quattro Film; Sceneggiature di Federico Fellini, Ennio Flaiano e Tulltio Pinelli* (Turin: Einaudi, 1975), 411–12.
15 Fellini, "Giulietta degli spiriti," 411.
16 Ibid., 412.
17 Naturally, this pun is effective in Italian only, where the phrase "barba rossa" graphically presents itself as *Barbarossa*, giving rise to the inevitable historical connotation.
18 Costa, *Cinema e pittura*, 155.
19 Fellini, *Quattro Film*, 428.
20 I am indebted to Milly Heyd for drawing my attention to this significant detail.
21 It should be noted that the penetration of primal, instinctual sensuality into Giulietta's virginal world is featured in more than one way in this film. This issue will be picked up at a later stage.
22 The books in question are *I grandi pittori dell'ottocento italiano*, a series of three volumes published in 1961, and *Pittura italiana dell'ottcento*, by Giuseppe de Logu, published in 1963. Both have been preserved in Fellini's private library.

23 Alberto Previati, *Gaetano Previati nelle memorie del figlio (1927)* (Ferrara: Liberty House, 1993), 71.
24 Aurora Scotti Tosini, "Divisionist Painters in Italy: Between Modern Chromatics and New Symbols," in *Lost Paradise: Symbolist Europe*, ed. Jean Clair and Pierre Theberge (Montreal: Montreal Museum of Fine Arts, 1995), 277.
25 A production still, reproduced in Tullio Kezich, *Giulietta degli spiriti di Federico Fellini* (Rome: Cappelli, 1965), fig. 83, indicates that the scene was indeed filmed. A brief shot appears toward the film's ending.
26 Fellini, *Quattro Film*, 477–80.
27 Federico Fellini, *Giulietta* (Genova: Il Melangolo, 1994), 113–14.
28 Rodolph Rapetti highlights the influence of contemporary psychiatric illustrations of Hysteria on the visual vocabulary of the Symbolists, particularly with regard to the image of Woman. See Rodolph Rapetti, *Symbolism* (Paris: Flammarion, 2005), 256–64.
29 Dijkstra, *Idols of Perversity*, 37.
30 Ibid., 42.
31 Geduld, "Juliet of the Spirits," 144.
32 I here disagree with Geduld, for whom Laura's drowning indicates an abortive attempt at accessing the unconscious.
33 Maria Vittoria Marini Clarelli, GNAM, Rome, letter to the author, 28 September 2004.
34 Notably, in 1865 Faruffini also painted *The Death of Ophelia*. In this painting, Ophelia is seen carried away by the current, though very much alive and still holding on to her bouquet of flowers.
35 Fellini, *Quattro Film*, 433.
36 I thank *EYE, Film Institute Netherlands* for providing me with a DVD copy of the film.
37 Notably, Ivo Blom in his discussion of Guazzoni's film associates the shot of the floating virgin with Millais's *Ophelia*. See Ivo Blom, "Quo Vadis? From Painting to Cinema and Everything in Between," in *La decima musa: Il cinema e le altre arti/The Tenth Muse: Cinema and Other Arts*, ed. Leonardo Quaresima and Laura Vichi (Udine: Forum, 2001), 286. In this film, then, the two intertextual strands we have been tracing seem to converge, the entire intertextual tangle woven into Fellini's overdetermined visual *lexia*.
38 The close resemblance between the shot of the drowned Laura in Fellini's film and the ending shot of *La Sposa del Nilo* begs the question of Fellini's acquaintance with Guazzoni's film. Given Fellini's expressed liking for early Italian cinema, and his recurrent reference to its central role in the formation of his imagery, it is highly probable that he was indeed familiar with *La Sposa del Nilo*. Whether he encountered Guazzoni's film as a child,

an adolescent, or a fully grown artist is difficult to ascertain. He may also have heard of *La Sposa del Nilo* in conjunction with Faruffini's painting, which was easily available for his observation at the GNAM.
39 Fellini, *Giulietta*, 91.
40 Burke, *Fellini's Films*, 162.
41 Ibid.
42 Carl Gustav Jung, *Collected Works* (London: Routledge and Kegan Paul, 1956), 9:ii, 422–3.
43 Ibid.
44 Fellini, *Quattro Film*, 439–40.
45 Jung, *Collected Works*, 5:293.
46 Fellini, *Giulietta*, 37–8.
47 Geduld, "Juliet of the Spirits," 145.
48 Bondanella, *Cinema of Federico Fellini*, 304.
49 Peter Bondanella, "Juliet of the Spirits," *Cinéaste* 27, no. 4 (2002): 48.
50 Geduld, "Juliet of the Spirits," 146.
51 Fellini, *Giulietta*, 86.
52 This has been confirmed to me by Vito Anzalone, who was in charge of furniture and interiors on the set of *Giulietta*, and worked closely with Fellini's set designer, Piero Gherardi, who was also Anzalone's first cousin. Vito Anzalone, e-mail to author, 20 August 2004.
53 *Stile Liberty* refers to the famous London store of exotic fabrics, associated with the art nouveau movement.
54 Richard A. Etlin, "Nationalism in Modern Italian Architecture, 1900–1940," in *Studies in the History of Art*, vol. 29, ed. Richard A. Etlin (Washington, DC: National Gallery of Art, 1991), 91–2.
55 Marla Suzan Stone, *The Patron State: Culture and Politics in Fascist Italy* (Princeton, NJ: Princeton University Press, 1998), 44.
56 Ibid., 177–9.
57 Ibid., 61–2.
58 The building, located in the EUR district, is now called *Palazzo della civiltà del lavoro*.
59 Vittorio Cini, *Esposizione Universale di Roma, 1942* (Rome, 1942), 50.
60 It is noteworthy that Rimini's Grand Hotel, one of Fellini's most cherished sites, and the locus of everything fantastic in his imagery, was built in 1908, when art nouveau was still dominant in Italy. To this day, the Grand Hotel preserves its *Liberty* grandeur. Given its role in Fellini's imagery, as the epitome of freedom from inhibition, the *Liberty* style of the Grand Hotel may have been more crucial to the formation of his visual idiom than has been hitherto recognized.

61 Fellini, *Quattro Film*, 437. The explicit reference to blasphemy ("a blasphemous via crucis") again indicates that "Suzy's place" is a site of defiance, directed against Church, political establishment, school, and family, the all-engulfing apparatus of psychic repression and social oppression.
62 This painting is actually part of a diptych that occupies the Veranda Sartorio at the GNAM, together with other Italian Symbolist works. The diptych consists of *La gorgona e gli eroi* and *Diana d'Efeso e gli schiavi* (*Diana of Ephesus and the Slaves*).
63 Aniela Jaffé, *C.G. Jung: Word and Image* (Princeton, NJ: Princeton University Press, 1979), 226.
64 Jung, *Collected Works*, 9:27. Carolyn Geduld notes that it is incongruent, from a Jungian point of view, to have an anima figure for a female protagonist. In this case an animus would be more in place than an anima. This fact, Geduld concludes, indicates the function of Giulietta as an alter ego for the male artist – Fellini. Geduld, "Juliet of the Spirits," 141.
65 Jung, *Collected Works*, 5:293.
66 Fellini, *Fare un film*, 158–9.
67 Erich Neumann, *The Great Mother* (Princeton, NJ: Princeton University Press, 1991), 148–9.
68 Vivian Sobchack, *Carnal Thoughts: Embodiment and Moving Image Culture* (Berkeley: University of California Press, 2004), 71.
69 Ibid., 84.
70 Jaffé, *C.G. Jung*, 228–9.
71 Ibid.
72 The information that Fellini discussed with the Jung family the possibility of producing a film on Jung was communicated to me by Jung's grandson, Mr Niklaus Baumann, on a visit to Jung's Tower on Lake Zurich (15 July 1998).
73 Gideon Bachmann, in discussion with the author, 11 October 2003.
74 A piquant anecdote recounted by Liliana Betti provides further indication of their close friendship. According to Betti, Fellini once sold two or three gold brooches and a medallion to a jeweller in Via del Tritone so as to be able to take Richter out to dinner. See Liliana Betti, *Fellini* (Boston: Little, Brown, 1979), 124.
75 The film consists of six separate episodes filmed respectively by Man Ray, Marcel Duchamp, Max Ernst, Fernand Léger, Alexander Calder, and Hans Richter himself.
76 Haim Finkelstein, *The Screen in Surrealist Art and Thought* (Aldershot: Ashgate, 2007), 133–4.
77 Ibid., 145.

78 Hal Foster, "Convulsive Identity," *October* 57 (1991): 37.
79 Finkelstein, *Screen in Surrealist Art and Thought*, 131.
80 Hal Foster, "Blinded Insights: On the Modernist Reception of the Art of the Mentally Ill," *October* 97 (2001): 22.

3. *Toby Dammit*: Rembrandt Meets Velázquez on Screen

1 The intertextual relations between Fellini's film and Poe's story are discussed in Bondanella, *Cinema of Federico Fellini*, 230–7. See also Stubbs, *Federico Fellini as Auteur*, 207–11.
2 The consequences of the film's production are discussed in detail in Kezich, *Fellini*, 258–69; Bondanella, *Cinema of Federico Fellini*, 227–9; and Burke, *Fellini's Films*, 15–17.
3 Bondanella, *Cinema of Federico Fellini*, 228.
4 Kezich, *Federico Fellini, la vita e I film*, 264.
5 Ibid., 268–73.
6 Bondanella, *Cinema of Federico Fellini*, 230.
7 Ibid., 229.
8 Burke, *Fellini's Films*, 15.
9 Ibid., 164.
10 To name but one example of this strain of critical approaches, I am in complete disagreement with Christopher Sharrett, who reads *Toby Dammit* as an accumulation of horror film clichés, an empty "piling up of signifiers," expressing the director's *ennui* in being the "willing contract employee" of the film industry. See Sharrett, "'Toby Dammit,'" 121–36.
11 Sharrett, "'Toby Dammit,'" 124.
12 This concept is discussed at some length in chapter 1.
13 Federico Fellini, "La sceneggiatura di 'Toby Dammit'," in *Tre passi nel delirio*, ed. Liliana Betti, Ornella Volta, and Bernardino Zapponi (Bologna: Cappelli, 1968), 75.
14 Sharrett, "'Toby Dammit,'" 132.
15 Fellini, "La sceneggiatura di 'Toby Dammit,'" 75–6.
16 Reading this sequence as a projection of Toby's tormented psyche, I naturally reject Sharrett's reductive interpretation of its imagery – including the butchered meat, in which he rightly identifies an echo of Bacon's painting – as "the cliché of this trope in the literature of the fantastic." Sharrett, "'Toby Dammit,'" 132. My point is that close visual analysis of the shot of butchered meat, supported by archival evidence and biographical data, shows that at that period Fellini was far too seriously committed to exploring the artist's psyche for Sharrett's reading to be sufficiently convincing.

17 Piero Tosi in discussion with the author, 25 September 2005. According to Tosi's testimony, he never touched the hashish Fellini gave him.
18 See Fellini, *Fare un film*, 93, and Kezich, *Fellini*, 249.
19 Fellini, "La sceneggiatura di 'Toby Dammit,'" 76.
20 Merleau-Ponty, "Eye and Mind," 123.
21 Avigdor W.G. Posèq, "The Hanging Carcass Motif and Jewish Artists," *Jewish Art* 16/17 (1990–91): 156.
22 Ibid.
23 Rondi, *Il cinema di Fellini*, 19.
24 The dates of publication for these two books are 1952 and 1955, respectively.
25 Avigdor W.G. Posèq, *Soutine: His Jewish Modality* (Sussex: Book Guild, 2001), 245.
26 Alfred Werner, *Chaim Soutine* (New York: Harry N. Abrams, 1977), 122.
27 Rinaldo Geleng in discussion with the author, December 2000. It should also be noted that, although Fellini's private library in its current state does not hold a Soutine catalogue or any other publication dedicated to this painter, some of Soutine's paintings, although not the "beef" series, are reproduced in Maurice Raynal's *Peinture Moderne* (1966), of which Fellini owned a copy.
28 It appears that issues related to Jewish culture did come up occasionally in the conversations Fellini had with Bernhard. It is known, for example, that they discussed the significance of Bernhard's Jewish name, *Haim Menachem*, which means "life and comfort." See Kezich, *Fellini*, 216. Although I have no proof that Fellini and Bernhard discussed Jewish artists, or Soutine in particular, I deem it quite possible that Jewish art would have come up in their conversations.
29 Mieke Bal, "Dead Flesh, or the Smell of Painting," in *Visual Culture: Images and Interpretation*, ed. Norman Bryson, Michael Ann Holly, and Keith Moxey (Hanover: Wesleyan University Press, 1994), 373.
30 Ibid.
31 Ibid.
32 Merleau-Ponty, "Eye and Mind," 126.
33 Margarita Cappock, "The Motif of Meat and Flesh," in Seipel, Steffen, and Vitali, *Francis Bacon and the Tradition of Art*, 311–14.
34 Ziva Amishai-Maisels, *Depiction and Interpretation: The Influence of the Holocaust on the Visual Arts* (Oxford: Pergamon Press, 1993), 190.
35 Cappock, "Motif of Meat and Flesh," 311.
36 Norman Bryson, "Bacon's Dialogue with the Past," in Seipel, Steffen, and Vitali, *Francis Bacon and the Tradition of Art*, 52.

37 Gianfranco Angelucci, e-mail to the author, 13 November 1997.
38 Cappock, "Motif of Meat and Flesh," 312, 359.
39 Wilfried Seipel, Barbara Steffen, and Christoph Vitali, eds., *Francis Bacon and the Tradition of Art* (Vienna: Kunsthistorisches Museum, 2004), 360.
40 Gilles Deleuze, *Francis Bacon: The Logic of Sensation*, trans. Daniel W. Smith (London: Continuum, 2003), 23.
41 Ibid., 35.
42 Ibid., 39.
43 Ibid., 21.
44 Ibid., 35.
45 Sobchack, *Address of the Eye*, 179.
46 Ibid., 173.
47 Ibid.
48 Bakhtin, "Discourse in the Novel," 303–4.
49 Patrick Rumble, *Allegories of Contamination: Pier Paolo Pasolini's* Trilogy of Life (Toronto: University of Toronto Press, 1996), 32.
50 Jost, "Le Picto-Film," 118.
51 Rumble, *Allegories of Contamination*, 48.
52 Deleuze, *Francis Bacon*, 21.
53 I am indebted to Gannit Ankori for drawing my attention to this detail.
54 Antonio Costa believes that it was Foucault's essay on *Las Meninas* that induced Pasolini's introduction of this painting into *Le Nuvole*. Costa, *Cinema e pittura*, 147.
55 The three paintings beside *Las Meninas* are: (1) *Don Diego de Acedo 'El Primo' (A Dwarf Holding a Tome on His Lap)*, ca. 1645, (2) *Prince Baltasar Carlos with a Dwarf*, 1631, and (3) *King Philip the IV of Spain*, 1644.
56 Antonino Repetto, *Invito al cinema di Pier Paolo Pasolini* (Milan: Mursia, 1998), 199.
57 Michel Foucault, "Las Meninas," in *The Order of Things* (New York: Vintage Books [Random House], 1994), 15.
58 Ibid., 12.
59 Ibid., 16.
60 Joel Snyder and Ted Cohen, "Reflexions on *Las Meninas*: Paradox Lost," *Critical Inquiry* 7, no. 2 (1980): 447.
61 Sobchack's approach to the phenomenology of film is discussed in some detail in chapter 1. For further reading see Sobchack, *Address of the Eye*.
62 Susan Grace Galassi, "Picasso in the Studio of Velázquez," in *Picasso and the Spanish Tradition*, ed. Jonathan Brown (New Haven: Yale University Press, 1996), 126–7.

63 Ibid., 160. The numerous portraits of the Infanta Margarita in Picasso's series are also pronouncedly split and dislocated.
64 Bondanella, *Cinema of Federico Fellini*, 134.
65 Ibid., 134.
66 Fellini, *Fare un film*, 86.
67 Ibid., 86.
68 The incorporation of Picasso into Fellini's conceptual and visual vocabulary may have been mediated by Jung's famous essay on Picasso, which Fellini had read, as noted in *Fare un film*. Fellini, *Fare un film*, 92.
  Beyond its Jungian analysis of the painter's work, Jung's essay includes a discussion of the role of automatic drawing in concretizing inaccessible unconscious materials. See C.G. Jung, "Picasso," in Jung, *The Spirit in Man, Art, and Literature* (Princeton, NJ: Princeton University Press, 1966), 136. This is probably what Fellini had in mind when he remarked that the Jungian essay opened "unknown vistas," and taught him ways of "recovering a lot of energies and materials, buried under a debris of fears, ignorance, and neglected injuries." Fellini, *Fare un film*, 92.
69 William S. Rubin, ed., *Picasso and Portraiture: Representation and Transformation* (New York: Museum of Modern Art, 1996), 419–20.
70 Fellini filmed *Toby Dammit* between October 1967 and January 1968, and post-production work was completed with the film's release in May 1968. Kezich, *Fellini*, 380–2.
71 This section of the chapter is based on my paper, "A Jungian Approach to Federico Fellini's Visual Imagery," *Harvest: Journal for Jungian Studies* 47, no. 2 (2001): 96–118.
72 It is noteworthy that in Luis Buñuel's 1965 film *Simon of the Desert* the devil is similarly incarnated in a blond girl, in this case playing with a hoop. However, Buñuel's blond devil is explicitly sexual. Exposing her breasts and gartered thighs, she conforms to the iconographical cliché of carnal temptation and sin in Western art. Fellini's *bambina-diavolo*, in turn, is distinctly asexual, and what it is exactly that she wants is much less obvious.
73 Verena Kast, *The Creative Leap: Psychological Transformation through Crisis* (Wilmette, IL: Chiron, 1990), 9–41.
74 Marie Louise Von Franz, "The Process of Individuation," in Jung, *Man and His Symbols*, 167.
75 Jung, ed., *Man and His Symbols*, 302.
76 Jung, *Collected Works*, 9:27.
77 Ibid., 5:293.
78 Von Franz, "Process of Individuation," 183.
79 Ibid., 178.
80 Jung, ed., *Man and His Symbols*, 302.

81 Von Franz, "Process of Individuation," 213.
82 Jaffé, *C.G. Jung*, 77.
83 Ibid.
84 Von Franz, "Process of Individuation," 247.
85 Bondanella, *Cinema of Federico Fellini*, 153.
86 William Van Watson, "Fellini and Lacan: The Hollow Phallus, the Male Womb, and the Retying of the Umbilical," in Burke and Waller, *Federico Fellini*, 85.
87 Van Watson proposes a view of Fellini's signifying system which is in some ways similar to mine. He elaborates on the "icon-archetype" as Fellini's privileged signifying unit. Unlike the symbolic signifier, no longer capable of relating to a real signified, the icon "at least partially embodies or overlaps its signified." In Fellini, Van Watson suggests, the icon and the Jungian archetype overlap, constituting "a semiotic correlative to the psychoanalytic archetype." See Van Watson, "Fellini and Lacan," 83–4. What Van Watson does not realize, however, is the major role of embedded art-historical *lexiae* in the formation of Fellini's "icon-archetypes."
88 Dorothy Kosinski, *Orpheus in Nineteenth-Century Symbolism* (Ann Arbor: Research Press, 1989), 20. The various versions of the Orpheus myth in antiquity, and the Symbolists' view of the myth and its implications, are comprehensively reviewed in Kosinski's book.
89 Ibid., 15. It is important to note that the Symbolists were the first since antiquity to employ the image of Orpheus's severed head as a central motif. See ibid., 190.
90 Notably, the portraits in both Redon and Fellini pronouncedly highlight the subject's right eye, while the left eye and the entire left half of the face remain in the dark. In Fellini, the one-eyed gaze binds together Toby and the *bambina-diavolo*, notwithstanding their different intertextual matrices.
91 The appeal of Redon for Fellini could have been augmented by Barilli's commentary, which emphasizes the Symbolist engagement with "'mystery', the infinite, and the indistinct." Renato Barilli, *Il Simbolismo: Parte I* (Milan: Fabbri, 1967), 5. (Original 1967 edition found in Fellini's private library) Barilli also describes the Symbolists' interest in mediumistic experiments, spiritualism, and the occult. Barilli, *Il Simbolismo*, 10. This detail may have found a responsive chord in Fellini, who was at the time exploring spiritualism and other occult phenomena.
92 Barbara Larson, *The Dark Side of Nature: Science, Society, and the Fantastic in the Work of Odilon Redon* (University Park: Pennsylvania State University Press, 2005), 114.
93 Sharrett, "'Toby Dammit,'" 122.
94 Van Watson, "Fellini and Lacan," 86.

4. *Fellini Satyricon*: Bruegel Meets Klimt in the Sewers of Imperial Rome

1 There has been wide scholarly consent about the predominance of the visual over the literary in *Fellini Satyricon*. Peter Bondanella asserts that this film constitutes a "nonliterary and completely visual narrative," simulating a dream. Bondanella, *Cinema of Federico Fellini*, 241. Bernard F. Dick, in his turn, maintains that "Fellini's compositions have the uncluttered look of Roman wall painting." Bernard F. Dick, "Adaptation as Archaeology: *Fellini Satyricon* (1969)," in Horton and Magretta, *Modern European Filmmakers and the Art of Adaptation*, 147.
2 Burke rightly notes that Encolpio is reborn through art, evolving into a painted figure at the film's ending. Burke, *Fellini's Films*, 179.
3 Close to the film's release, Italian writer Alberto Moravia expressed the extremely generalizing assertion that the film was "packed with cultural references ... ranging from surrealism to functional modernism, from cubism to abstract expressionism, from expressionism to pop. Without, of course, forgetting Pompeian art, Byzantine art, barbarian art, *l'art nègre*, and the archaics and primitives in general." Moravia, "Dreaming up Petronius," 164.

  The involvement of Fellini's new costume and set designer, Danilo Donati, should also be noted. Donati, who was educated at the Academy of Fine Arts in Florence, and hence well versed in the history of art, probably contributed to the film's wide-ranging art-historical intertextuality.

  Oreste del Buono, in turn, maintained that the film encompassed "all of painting, both antique and recent, authentic and false, plundered by the director." Quoted in Kezich, *Fellini*, 386. Dick asserts that in this film Fellini "is constantly quoting film, art, literature, and even himself" (Dick, "Adaptation as Archaeology," 150–1), while Roberto Campari, committed to reviewing the reverberations of painting in Italian cinema, finds in the shot of a graffiti-covered wall, which opens *Fellini Satyricon*, echoes of Cy Twombly and Novelli. Campari, *Il fantasma del bello*, 89.

  Philippe Jullian, who explored the legacy of late nineteenth-century Symbolist painting, was the most concrete in pointing out in *Fellini Satyricon* "a deliberate imitation of Beardsley and Klimt, and sequences which reproduce pictures by Böcklin, Rochegrosse, and Alma-Tadema." Philippe Jullian, *Dreamers of Decadence: Symbolist Painters of the 1890s* (London: Phaidon, 1971), 227.
4 Bondanella, *Cinema of Federico Fellini*, 250; Burke, *Fellini's Films*, 175.
5 Angelucci, "Fellini 15 e ½ e la poetica dell'onirico," 33.

6 Fellini apparently associated parental coercion with fascist oppression of the sort imposed by educational and other governmental authorities. This is made evident in the script of *Giulietta degli spiriti*, discussed in chapter 2, where the fascist father, the school headmaster, and Il Duce are amalgamated into one imposing figure. Fellini, *Quattro Film*, 411.
7 Federico Fellini, "*Amarcord*: The Fascism within Us; An Interview with Valerio Riva," in Bondanella, *Federico Fellini*, 21.
8 Ibid., 24.
9 Eileen Lanouette Hughes, *On the Set of Fellini Satyricon: A Behind-the-Scenes Diary* (New York: William Morrow, 1971), 27.
10 Fellini, *Fare un film*, 105.
11 Luciano Canfora, "Classicismo e fascismo," in *Matrici culturali del fascismo: Seminari promossi dal Consiglio Regionale Pugliese e dall'Ateneo Barese nel trentennale della Liberazione* (Bari: Università di Bari, 1977), 96–7.
12 Fellini, *Fare un film*, 101.
13 Federico Fellini, "Il trattamento," in Zanelli, *L'inferno immaginario di Federico Fellini*, 112–13.
14 Bernardino Zapponi regards this nexus between "butchers and senators" as meant to differentiate the two brands. Zapponi quoted in Haaland, "Echoes of Scipione in Fellini's *Roma*," 69. This reading, however, is reductive.
15 Emilio Gentile, "The Myth of National Regeneration in Italy," in *Fascist Visions: Art and Ideology in France and Italy*, ed. Matthew Affron and Mark Antliff (Princeton, NJ: Princeton University Press, 1997), 42.
16 Federico Fellini, "La Sceneggiatura," in *Fellini Satyricon*, ed. Dario Zanelli (Rocca San Casciano: Cappelli, 1969), 231–2, shots 767–89.
17 Ibid., shot 771.
18 Ibid., shots 775–6. Eileen Hughes reports that several corpses had indeed been prepared by Donati for this scene. In the final cut, however, the shot is very brief and hazy, and the images cannot be made out very clearly. For information from the filming set on this matter, see Hughes, *On the Set of Fellini Satyricon*, 224.
19 Fellini, "*Amarcord*," 22–3.
20 Angelucci, "Fellini 15 e ½ e la poetica dell'onirico," 28.
21 Fellini, "Sceneggiatura," 180, shot 339.
22 Walter S. Gibson, *Bruegel* (1977; London: Thames and Hudson, 1991), 178.
23 Fellini, *Fare un film*, 106.
24 Fellini, "Sceneggiatura," 165, shot 201.
25 Gibson, *Bruegel*, 96.

154 Notes to pages 92–97

26 Angelucci, "Fellini 15 e ½ e la poetica dell'onirico," 33.
27 Mario Praz, *The Romantic Agony* (Oxford: Oxford University Press, 1933), 322–3.
28 Fellini, "Sceneggiatura," 172, shot 272.
29 Bondanella, *Cinema of Federico Fellini*, 244–5.
30 Fellini, *Fare un film*, 107.
31 For a discussion of "richness" in Decadent art see also Edward Lucie-Smith, *Symbolist Art* (London: Thames and Hudson, 1972), 63, and Geneviève Lacambre, "Gustave Moreau and Exoticism," in Lacambre, *Gustave Moreau*, 18.
32 Praz, *Romantic Agony*, 322.
33 Moravia, "Dreaming up Petronius," 166.
34 Jullian, *Dreamers of Decadence*, 149.
35 Ibid., 91.
36 Maurice Bessy, *A Pictorial History of Magic and the Supernatural* (London: Spring Books, 1964), 147.
37 Jullian, *Dreamers of Decadence*, 227.
38 Is Jullian referring, for instance, to the 1874 painting by Alma-Tadema entitled *Picture Gallery*, as the template for the scene in which Encolpio and Eumolpo meet in an art gallery? This kind of analogy, which Jullian may have had in mind, although he does not say so explicitly, relies solely on the similarity of subject matter. While Alma-Tadema indeed portrays Roman figures clad in period *togas* contemplating antique art, the weakness of the foregoing association becomes evident upon closer analysis. Alma-Tadema's *Picture Gallery* is a genre scene concerned with period costume and atmosphere. The paintings are relegated to the obscure background, and obviously do not constitute the focus of interest, whereas in Fellini's shots of the gallery paintings dominate the foreground. In one significant shot, a fragment of a classical painting occupies over one third of the frame width. Moreover, in Fellini's art gallery painted figures occupy the larger part of the space, outweighing the living figures, who in their turn merge with the painted representations.
39 Hughes, *On the Set of Fellini Satyricon*, 34–5.
40 Rossana Bossaglia, "Un'altra modernità: La fortuna di Klimt in Italia," in *Gustav Klimt*, ed. Serge Sabarsky (Florence: Artificio, 1991), 35.
41 Fellini, "Sceneggiatura," 179, shots 324–5.
42 Ibid., 179, shot 325.
43 Ibid., 197, shot 498.
44 Ibid., 202, shot 543.
45 Ibid., 214.

46 Charles Bernheimer, *Decadent Subjects: The Idea of Decadence in Art, Literature, Philosophy, and Culture of the Fin de Siècle in Europe* (Baltimore: Johns Hopkins University Press, 2002), 104.
47 Fellini, "Sceneggiatura," 214.
48 Roberto Campari asserts that the image of Lica's head underwater derives from Symbolist painting. Campari, *Il fantasma del bello*, 90. Campari does not, however, indicate a specific source image. One may think, for example, of Arnold Böcklin as a viable association.
49 Hughes, *On the Set of Fellini Satyricon*, 99.
50 Daniela Hammer-Tugendhat, "Judith," in Natter and Frodl, *Klimt's Women*, 220–2.
51 Alessandra Comini, *Gustav Klimt* (New York: George Braziller, 1975), 22.
52 Hughes, *On the Set of Fellini Satyricon*, 151.
53 Fellini, "Sceneggiatura," 253–4, scene 53.
54 Hughes, *On the Set of Fellini Satyricon*, 149.
55 Rae Beth Gordon, "Aboli Bibelot? The Influence of the Decorative Arts on Stéphane Mallarmé and Gustave Moreau," *Art Journal* 45, no. 2 (1985): 107.
56 J.K. Huysmans, *Against the Grain* (New York: Albert and Charles Boni, 1930), 74–89.
57 Hughes, *On the Set of Fellini Satyricon*, 64.
58 Stephen Snyder has even made an attempt, which I regard as somewhat debatable, to trace a pattern of evolution and growth in the colour scheme of *Fellini Satyricon*. See Stephen Snyder, "Color, Growth, and Evolution in *Fellini Satyricon*," in Bondanella, *Federico Fellini*, 168–87.
59 Burke, *Fellini's Films*, 168–9.
60 Fellini, "Sceneggiatura," 247, shots 964–5.
61 Dick, "Adaptation as Archaeology," 151.
62 In *The Golden Ass*, a respectable merchant who arrives in town is implicated in a simulated murder. Believing that he had indeed murdered three young men, the horrified merchant awaits torture and death. When he finally learns of the cruel joke played on him, he resentfully accepts the explanation that it was all part of the festival of Risus. Robert Graves, *The Golden Ass of Apuleius* (New York: Pocket Books, 1954), 48–61. It may certainly be that Fellini was alluding to Apuleius in this scene, given that he owned a copy of *The Golden Ass*, now preserved in his private library. However, the two stories are so dissimilar that reading the Apuleius story cannot contribute much to understanding *Fellini Satyricon*.
63 Bondanella, *Cinema of Federico Fellini*, 246.
64 Ibid., 247; Burke, *Fellini's Films*, 169.

156 Notes to pages 102–3

65 As I have mentioned in previous chapters, *Man and His Symbols* had been presented to Fellini by the artist and film director Hans Richter. What is worth noting here is that Richter visited the set of *Fellini Satyricon* on the very day in which the Minotaur scene was being filmed. Hughes, *On the Set of Fellini Satyricon*, 170.
66 Joseph L. Henderson, "Ancient Myths and Modern Man," in Jung, *Man and His Symbols*, 125–6.
67 Ibid., 125.
68 In Jungian literature, it is worth noting, the hero's introspective mission often reaches its successful resolution in a harbour town, symbolizing psychic liberation and regained creativity. See Henderson, "Ancient Myths and Modern Man," 126. A noteworthy analogy may be drawn between Henderson's imagery and the ending of *Fellini Satyricon*, in which Encolpio's voyage ends by the sea, as he boards a ship ready to sail away toward new vistas.
69 Fellini, "Sceneggiatura," 249, shots 983–4. The script positions Arianna in the centre of the labyrinth, which is in the very heart of the unconscious. Fellini, "Sceneggiatura," 248, shot 969. In the film, however, the scene was realized differently, with Arianna sprawled on a pedestal outside the labyrinth.
70 Henderson, "Ancient Myths and Modern Man," 126. Henderson's version of the myth significantly differs from the accepted one, according to which it was Ariadne who helped Theseus survive the perilous voyage inside the labyrinth, only to be abandoned by the hero who broke his promise to marry her and take her back to Athens with him. Henderson's modification of the story clearly served his suggested reading of the myth. Henderson, "Ancient Myths and Modern Man," 125.
71 It is noteworthy that a Jungian psychoanalyst, Peter Ammann, was present on the set as consultant. Hughes, *On the Set of Fellini Satyricon*, 38.
72 De Chirico modelled his Ariadnes after a Roman sculpture from the Vatican Museums, which represents a dormant Ariadne. Given that the original sculpture is exhibited in Rome, Fellini may have had a first-hand acquaintance with it. See James Thrall Soby, *Giorgio De Chirico* (New York: Museum of Modern Art, 1955), 52.
73 Von Franz, "Process of Individuation," 171.
74 The Ariadnes in de Chirico derive from a Roman copy of a Hellenistic sculpture. Therefore, they are already thrice removed from what may be considered the original, in which case Fellini's Arianna is fourth in this intertextual sequence. Regardless of whether Fellini was aware of this, Arianna epitomizes the idea of intertextuality, which is all-pervasive in this film.

75 C.G. Jung, ed., *Man and His Symbols*, 147.
76 Hughes, *On the Set of Fellini Satyricon*, 225–6.
77 Pierre Daix, *Picasso* (London: Thames and Hudson, 1965), 150.
78 Ibid.
79 Kirk Varnedoe, "Picasso's Self Portraits," in *Picasso and Portraiture: Representation and Transformation*, ed. William S. Rubin (New York: The Museum of Modern Art, 1996), 153.
80 Ibid., 155.
81 Mary Mathews Gedo, *Picasso: Art as Autobiography* (Chicago: University of Chicago Press, 1980), 151.
82 Varnedoe, "Picasso's Self Portraits," 155.
83 Fellini would probably construe the young girl in the *Minotauromachy* in Jungian terms as an anima figure. A Jungian reading has in fact been applied to this figure by Curt G. Seckel, for whom the young girl, amalgamating the features of Picasso and Marie-Thérèse, represents "man's highest self." Seckel quoted in Gedo, *Picasso*, 162.
84 Maurizio Fagiolo, quoted in Ines Millesimi, "Catalogo," in Mantura, *Fabrizio Clerici*, 186.
85 Mario Quesada, "Cronologia," in Mantura, *Fabrizio Clerici*, 223–4.
86 GianfrancoAngelucci, e-mail message to author, 13 November 1997.
87 Kezich, *Federico Fellini, la vita e i film*, 275.
88 The drawing is reproduced in Bondanella, *Cinema of Federico Fellini*, 247.
89 Patrick Waldberg, *Fabrizio Clerici* (Bologna: Grafis, 1975), 46.
90 Ibid., 46.
91 Ibid., 32.
92 Millesimi, "Catalogo," 185.
93 Ibid., 191.
94 Ibid.,186.
95 Ibid., 187.
96 Waldberg, *Fabrizio Clerici*, 89.

5. *Fellini's Casanova*: Casanova Meets de Chirico on Böcklin's *Isle of the Dead*

1 The events of the film's production and its critical reception are discussed in detail in Kezich, *Federico Fellini, la vita e I film*, 306–17.
2 Federico Fellini, "*Casanova*: An Interview with Aldo Tassone," in Bondanella, *Federico Fellini*, 27.
3 Dale Bradley, "History to Hysteria: Fellini's Casanova Meets Baudrillard," in Bondanella and Degli-Esposti, *Perspectives on Federico Fellini*, 249–52.

4 More will be said about the mannequins in *Casanova* at a later stage.
5 Frank Burke mentions this scene in his discussion of the film's concern with copies and simulation. Burke, *Fellini's Films*, 233.
6 Kezich, *Federico Fellini, la vita e i film*, 310.
7 *midi/minuit Fantastique* (1962–71) was a French film magazine published by Eric Losfeld, publisher of the film magazine *Positif*. The magazine was dedicated to the cinema of the fantastic, as well as to horror and science-fiction films. At a later stage the magazine also offered discussions of more mainstream subject matter, and published, among others, a profile of Federico Fellini (http://en.wikipedia.org/wiki/Midi_Minuit_Fantastique). It is most probable therefore that Fellini was a more or less regular reader of this magazine. However, the aforementioned issue, no. 15–16, is the only one found in his private library to date.
8 In the Jewish mystic tradition the Golem is "a creature, particularly a human being, made in an artificial way by virtue of a magic act, through the use of holy names." The figure of the Golem originated in the legends of the Talmud, subsequently evolving into a recurrent motif in medieval legends and mystic rituals (*Encyclopaedia Judaica* 7, col. 753–4 [Jerusalem: Keter, 1971]).
9 Gustav Meyrinck, "Les apparitions du golem," *midi/minuit Fantastique* 15–16, (1966–7): 9.
10 Joseph Markulin, "Plot and Character in Fellini's *Casanova*: Beyond *Satyricon*," in Bondanella and Degli-Esposti, *Perspectives on Federico Fellini*, 141.
11 Meyrinck, "Les apparitions du golem," 11–12.
12 Gustav Meyrinck, *The Golem* (New York: Frederick Ungar, 1964), 17–23.
13 *Encyclopaedia Judaica* 7, col. 754.
14 Moshe Idel, *Golem: Jewish Magical and Mystical Traditions on the Artificial Anthropoid* (Albany: State University of New York Press, 1990), xxvii.
15 Ibid., xvi.
16 It may be worth noting that the French actress Magali Noël, who played the role of "Gradisca" in *Fellini Amarcord* (1973) precisely when Fellini was drawing the contract for *Casanova*, had a role in Kerchborn's *Le Golem* about six years earlier. I thus risk an assumption that she might have acted as the mediating agent who aroused Fellini's interest in *Le Golem*.
17 Burke, *Fellini's Films*, 223.
18 Costa, *Cinema e pittura*, 18.
19 Campari, *Il fantasma del bello*, 93.
20 Stubbs, *Federico Fellini as Auteur*, 228–9.
21 Quoted in Campari, *Il fantasma del bello*, 93.
22 Campari, *Il fantasma del bello*, 93.
23 Stubbs, *Federico Fellini as Auteur*, 228–9.

24 Ibid., 228.
25 To name but one example, Stubbs points out Hogarth's *Southwark Fair* (1733–4) as "inspiration for the London scenes." This assertion is not very persuasive, however. For example, Stubbs points to an image of a giant and two dwarfs, vaguely depicted on a showcloth in Hogarth's engraving, as source for the giantess and two midgets, featured in *Fellini's Casanova*. However, the image in Hogarth's engraving is very small and blurred by hatching to such an extent that it is hardly visible at all. I thus deem it highly improbable that this insignificant detail would be quoted at all in Fellini's film.
26 These shots feature drawings which were especially commissioned for this film from graphic artist Roland Topor, a close acquaintance of Fellini. Filmed with a frontal camera, the drawings are rendered completely parallel to the screen surface. As medium shots gradually give way to close-ups, the drawings fill the frame entirely, forcing the screen to overlap with the depthless graphic image. This is a rare instance where Fellini totally surrenders his privileged control of the screen and the cinematic frame to the graphic artist. The very conception of the director (or artist in general) as sole *auteur*, and the artwork as an individual utterance, is thus put in question by this overt statement of the film's intertextuality. However, such instances of overt quotation, unmediated by authorial intervention, are very rare and uncharacteristic of Fellini's oeuvre.
27 Fellini and Zapponi, "La sceneggiatura di 'Toby Dammit,'" 60.
28 Fellini, *My Rimini*, 33.
29 The scene I shall be discussing condenses scenes 9 and 11–16 in the script.
30 *The Enigma of the Oracle* is reproduced in *Il Surrealismo* by Enrico Crispolti (1967), of which Fellini owned a copy. De Chirico's painting is actually the first colour reproduction that appears in Crispolti's monograph on surrealism. It is thus conspicuous to any reader leafing through its pages. Evidently, Fellini had this particular image at his immediate disposal.
31 Paolo Baldacci, *De Chirico: The Metaphysical Period 1888–1919* (Boston: Little, Brown, 1997), 77.
32 Foster, "Convulsive Identity," 26.
33 Baldacci, *De Chirico*, 77.
34 Willard Bohn, "Giorgio de Chirico and the Solitude of the Sign," *Gazette des Beaux Arts* 6, vol. 117 (1991): 173.
35 The curtain undoubtedly evokes theatrical representation, given that de Chirico and his brother Savinio were involved in theatrical productions from the mid-1920s onward. See Marianne B. Martin, "On de Chirico's Theater," in Fagiolo dell'Arco and Rubin, *De Chirico*, 83–4.

Francesco Poli highlights the scenographic quality apparent in de Chirico's first Metaphysical paintings, noting the influence of contemporary theatre directors Adolphe Appia and Gordon Craig on the painter's compositions. Francesco Poli, *La Metafisica* (Rome: Laterza, 1989), 86. To the series of characters (Odysseus, Heraclitus, priest of Apollo) amalgamated in the mysterious figure of *The Enigma of the Oracle*, Poli adds Gordon Craig's *Hamlet*, which in turn epitomizes the artist who is able to gaze at the Beyond. See Poli, *La Metafisica*, 93–4.

36 Maria Vittoria Marini Clarelli (GNAM), letter to author, 28 September 2004.
37 Federico Fellini, "My Rimini," trans. Isable Quigley. In *Amarcord, a Film by Federico Fellini* (DVD booklet, Criterion Collection), 33.
38 Fellini and Zapponi, "La sceneggiatura di 'Toby Dammit,'" 28.
This remark has led Frank Burke to the conclusion, which in my view is erroneous, that Annamaria is an "art object intended for the male gaze," "a statue" serving the "macho validation" of an unconfident Casanova. See Burke, *Fellini's Films*, 228–9. Burke, however, appears to overlook the fact that Annamaria is not represented as just "a statue," but as Pygmalion's creation. The Pygmalion myth bears a specific significance in the present context, in that it asserts the mystery of artistic creation through the story of a statue which mystically comes to life.
39 The entire *Raphael and La Fronarina* series is reproduced in the exhibition catalogue: Dominique Dupuis-Labbé, "Raphael and *La Fornarina*," in *Picasso Érotique*, ed. Jean Clair (Munich: Prestel, 2001) 118–37, figs. 247–71.
40 David Sylvester, "End Game," in *Late Picasso: Paintings, Sculpture, Drawings, Prints, 1953–1972* (London: Tate Gallery, 1988), 137.
41 Dominique Dupuis-Labbé, "L'aréne, lieu de l'amour et du sang," in Clair, *Picasso*, 122–6.
42 Ibid., 124–6.
43 This drawing was shown to me by Rinaldo Geleng (Rome, 21 March 2000), and is discussed in my MA dissertation, "Fellini's Drawings – Their Sources and Significance" (2000). The analysis to follow derives from my paper "Jungian Visual Imagery in Fellini's Graphic and Cinematic Oeuvre," paper presented at *Felliniana*, University of Washington, Seattle, 2003.
44 Millicent Marcus, "Fellini's Casanova: Portrait of the Artist," *Quarterly Review of Film Studies* 5, no. 1 (1980): 29–30.
45 Bondanella, *Cinema of Federico Fellini*, 300.
46 Stubbs, *Federico Fellini as Auteur*, 57–64.
47 Jung, *Collected Works* 9:27–8.
48 Ibid., 27.

49 Jung, *Collected Works* 5:329–30.
50 Neumann, *Great Mother*, 35; Jung, *Collected Works* 5:330.
51 Fellini owned a 1965 Italian translation of this volume, titled *La Libido, simboli e trasformazioni*. The English edition is titled *Symbols of Transformation*.
52 Jung, *Collected Works* 5:293–4.
53 Neumann, *Great Mother*, 128.
54 Ibid., 32.
55 Ibid., 31.
56 Fellini and Zapponi, "La sceneggiatura di 'Toby Dammit,'" 26.
57 Ibid., 31.
58 Neumann, *Great Mother*, 33.
59 Willard Bohn, "Apollinaire and de Chirico: The Making of the Mannequins," in *Comparative Literature* 27, no. 2 (1975): 162–3.
60 Ibid., 164–5.
61 This image has not been recognized for its evocation of Böcklin, despite the obvious resemblance of central elements like the cypresses and the approaching boat. This failure may be attributed to the fact that scholars have been so intent on looking for eighteenth-century sources such as Longhi and Hogarth that they simply overlooked any other visual hint. It must also be noted that some video versions of *Fellini's Casanova* are so dark and murky that the details of the scene can hardly be made out. It is only in production stills and in new digitally mastered copies that the island and cypresses can be clearly discerned.
62 Fellini and Zapponi, "La sceneggiatura di 'Toby Dammit,'" 9.
63 Hans Henrik Brummer, "The Böcklin Case Revisited," in Ehrhardt and Reynolds, *Kingdom of the Soul*, 30–31.
64 Ibid., 41.
65 Clerici's *Labyrinth* series is discussed at length in chapter 3, in relation to *Fellini Satyricon*.
66 Notably, the floor is rendered in the sharp perspectival recession which is the signature of Giorgio de Chirico.
67 Waldberg, *Fabrizio Clerici*, 162.
68 Fellini and Zapponi, "La sceneggiatura di 'Toby Dammit,'" 69.
69 This is in fact the same volume which holds a reproduction of Böcklin's *Isle of the Dead*. The role of this particular volume as a mediating vehicle, and its participation in the generation of Fellini's intertextual network, is thus intriguing.
70 Frances Spalding, *Whistler* (Oxford: Phaidon, 1979), 50.
71 The ambivalence of this figure may best be demonstrated in the shots that feature Casanova in a boat on the dark lagoon. In half of these shots

dramatic backlighting is employed, while the other half employs intense frontal lighting. While the shots of the first category represent Casanova as a Romantic hero, struggling with the high-rising waves, the intense frontal lighting in the other shots exposes his expressly clownish makeup as well as the simulated plastic sea.
72 Fellini, "*Casanova*: An Interview with Aldo Tassone," 28.
73 Ibid., 31.

Conclusion

1 Smith, *Julia Kristeva*, 60.
2 William Van Watson indeed acknowledges Fellini's daring attempt to "leapfrog the Symbolic Order and make direct Imaginary contact with the Real." Van Watson fails, however, to recognize the central role which painting is assigned in this project. Van Watson, "Fellini and Lacan," 67.
3 Fellini, "*Casanova*: An Interview with Aldo Tassone," 34–5.
4 Kristeva, *Revolution in Poetic Language*, 88.

Bibliography

Fellini

Aldouby, Hava. "A Jungian Approach to Federico Fellini's Visual Imagery." *Harvest: Journal for Jungian Studies* 47, no. 2 (2001): 96–118.
———. "Jungian Visual Imagery in Fellini's Graphic and Cinematic Oeuvre." Paper presented at *Felliniana*, University of Washington, Seattle, October 2003.
Angelucci, Gianfranco. "Fellini 15 e ½ e la poetica dell'onirico." In *Il film "Amarcord" di Federico Fellini*, ed. Gianfranco Angelucci and Liliana Betti, 11–46. Bologna: Cappelli, 1974.
Angelucci, Gianfranco, and Liliana Betti, eds. *Il Casanova di Federico Fellini*. Bologna: Cappelli, 1977.
———. *Il film "Amarcord" di Federico Fellini*. Bologna: Cappelli, 1974.
Bertozzi, Marco, and Giuseppe Ricci, eds. *Il corpo, gli interni, la città, nell'opera grafica di Federico Fellini*. Rimini: Fondazione Federico Fellini, 2002.
Betti, Liliana. *Fellini*. Boston: Little, Brown, 1979.
Bondanella, Peter. *The Cinema of Federico Fellini*. Princeton, NJ: Princeton University Press, 1992.
———. "Juliet of the Spirits." *Cinéaste* 27, no. 4 (2002): 48–50.
Bondanella, Peter, ed. *Federico Fellini: Essays in Criticism*. New York: Oxford University Press, 1978.
Bondanella, Peter, and Christina Degli-Esposti, eds. *Perspectives on Federico Fellini*. New York: G.K. Hall, 1993.
Bradley, Dale. "History to Hysteria: Fellini's Casanova Meets Baudrillard." In *Perspectives on Federico Fellini*, ed. Peter Bondanella and Christina Degli-Esposti, 249–59. New York: G.K. Hall, 1993.
Burke, Frank. *Fellini's Films: From Postwar to Postmodern*. New York: Twayne, 1996.

Burke, Frank, and Marguerite R. Waller, eds. *Federico Fellini: Contemporary Perspectives*. Toronto: University of Toronto Press, 2002.
Costa, Antonio. "Figurazione caricaturale e messa in scena." In *Federico Fellini: Disegni anni '30–'70*, ed. Gianfranco Miro Gori, 20–3. Rimini: Giusti, 1994.
Costa, Fabienne. *Devenir corps: Passages de l'oeuvre de Fellini*. Paris: L'Harmattan, 2003.
De Santi, Pier Marco. *I disegni di Fellini*. Florence: Laterza, 1981.
Farassino, Alberto. "Extra Strong." In *Federico Fellini: Disegni anni '30–'70*, ed. Gianfranco Miro Gori, 15–19. Rimini: Giusti, 1994.
Fellini, Federico. "*Amarcord*: The Fascism within Us; An Interview with Valerio Riva." In *Federico Fellini: Essays in Criticism*, ed. Peter Bondanella, 20–6. New York: Oxford University Press, 1978.
———. "*Casanova*: An Interview with Aldo Tassone." In *Federico Fellini: Essays in Criticism*, ed. Peter Bondanella, 27–35. New York: Oxford University Press, 1978.
———. *Fare un film*. Turin: Einaudi, 1974.
———. *Giulietta*. Genova: Il Melangolo, 1994.
———. "Giulietta degli spiriti." In *Quattro Film; Sceneggiature di Federico Fellini, Ennio Flaiano e Tulltio Pinelli*, 379–493. Turin: Einaudi, 1975.
———. "My Rimini." Translated by Isable Quigley. In *Amarcord, a Film by Federico Fellini*, 19–59. DVD booklet, Criterion Collection.
———. "Premessa." In *Fellini Satyricon*, ed. Dario Zanelli, 107–10. Rocca San Casciano: Cappelli, 1969.
———. "La sceneggiatura." In *Fellini Satyricon*, ed. Dario Zanelli, 149–273. Rocca San Casciano: Cappelli, 1969.
———. "La sceneggiatura di 'Toby Dammit.'" In *Tre passi nel delirio*, ed. Liliana Betti, Ornella Volta, and Bernardino Zapponi. Bologna: Cappelli, 1968.
———. "Il trattamento." In *L'inferno immaginario di Federico Fellini*, ed. Dario Zanelli, 111–45. Rimini: Guaraldi, 1995.
Fellini, Federico, and Bernardino Zapponi. *Il Casanova di Fellini*. Turin: Einaudi, 1976.
Foreman, Walter C. "Fellini's Cinematic City: *Roma* and Myths of Foundation." In *Perspectives on Federico Fellini*, ed. Peter Bondanella and Christina Degli-Esposti, 151–65. New York: G.K. Hall, 1993.
Geduld, Carolyn. "Juliet of the Spirits: Guido's Anima." In *Federico Fellini: Essays in Criticism*, ed. Peter Bondanella, 137–51. New York: Oxford University Press, 1978.
Grazzini, Giovanni, ed. *Comments on Film – Federico Fellini*. Fresno: Press at California State University, 1988.
Haaland, Torunn. "Echoes of Scipione in Fellini's *Roma*." *Fellini Amarcord* 2 (2005): 65–71.

Hughes, Eileen Lanouette. *On the Set of Fellini Satyricon: A Behind-the-Scenes Diary*. New York: William Morrow, 1971.
Kezich, Tullio. *Federico Fellini, la vita e i film*. Milan: Feltrinelli, 2002.
———. *Fellini*. Milan: Camunia, 1987.
———. *Giulietta degli spiriti di Federico Fellini*. Rome: Cappelli, 1965.
Marcus, Millicent. "Fellini's Casanova: Portrait of the Artist." *Quarterly Review of Film Studies* 5, no. 1 (1980): 19–34.
Markulin, Joseph. "Plot and Character in Fellini's *Casanova*: Beyond *Satyricon*." In *Perspectives on Federico Fellini*, ed. Peter Bondanella and Christina Degli-Esposti, 139–50. New York: G.K. Hall, 1993.
Maroni, Oriana, and Giuseppe Ricci, eds. *I libri di casa mia: La biblioteca di Federico Fellini*. Rimini: Fondazione Federico Fellini, 2008.
Miro Gori, Gianfranco, ed. *Federico Fellini: Disegni anni '30–'70*. Rimini: Giusti, 1994.
Mollica, Vincenzo. *Fellini: Parole e disegni*. Turin: Einaudi, 2000.
Moravia, Alberto. "Dreaming Up Petronius." In *Federico Fellini: Essays in Criticism*, ed. Peter Bondanella, 161–8. New York: Oxford University Press, 1978.
Perugini, Sasa. "The Aesthetics of Fellini's Art Seen through Its Ties with Popular Entertainment." PhD dissertation, Ann Arbor, MI: UMI Dissertation Services, 2002.
Rondi, Brunello. *Il cinema di Fellini*. Rome: Edizioni di Bianco e Nero, 1965.
Sharrett, Christopher. "'Toby Dammit', Intertext, and the End of Humanism." In *Federico Fellini: Contemporary Perspectives*, ed. Frank Burke and Marguerite R. Waller, 121–36. Toronto: University of Toronto Press, 2002.
Snyder, Stephen. "Color, Growth, and Evolution in *Fellini Satyricon*." In *Federico Fellini; Essays in Criticism*, ed. Peter Bondanella, 168–87. New York: Oxford University Press, 1978.
Stubbs, John. *Federico Fellini as Auteur: Seven Aspects of His Films*. Carbondale: Southern Illinois University Press, 2006.
Van Watson, William. "Fellini and Lacan: The Hollow Phallus, the Male Womb, and the Retying of the Umbilical." In *Federico Fellini: Contemporary Perspectives*, ed. Frank Burke and Marguerite R. Waller, 65–91. Toronto: University of Toronto Press, 2002.
Zanelli, Dario. *L'inferno immaginario di Federico Fellini*. Rimini: Guaraldi, 1995.
———. *Nel mondo di Federico*. 2nd ed. Rome: Rai Radiotelevisione Italiana, 2001.
Zanetti, Mauro Aprile. *La Natura Morta de La Dolce Vita; A Mysterious Morandi in the Matrix of Fellini's Vision*. New York: Italian Institute of Culture, 2008.

Cinema and Painting

Aumont, Jacques. *L'Oeil Interminable: Cinéma et Peinture*. 1987; Paris: Séguier, 1995.
Bellour, Raymond, ed. *Cinéma et Peinture – Approches*. Paris: Presses Universitaires de France, 1990.
———. "The Film Stilled." *Camera Obscura, A Journal of Feminism and Film Theory* 24 (1991): 99–123.
Blom, Ivo. "Quo Vadis? From Painting to Cinema and Everything in Between." In *La decima musa: Il cinema e le altre arti/The Tenth Muse. Cinema and Other Arts*, ed. Leonardo Quaresima and Laura Vichi, 281–96. Udine: Forum, 2001.
Bonitzer, Pascal. *Peinture et Cinéma: Décadrages*. Paris: Editions de l'Etoile, 1985.
Campari, Roberto. *Il fantasma del bello: Iconologia del cinema italiano*. Venice: Marsilio, 1994.
Casetti, Francesco. *Theories of Cinema*. Austin: University of Texas Press, 1999.
Costa, Antonio. *Cinema e pittura*. Turin: Loescher, 1991.
Dalle Vacche, Angela. *Cinema and Painting: How Art Is Used in Film*. Austin: University of Texas Press, 1996.
Dalle Vacche, Angela, ed. *The Visual Turn: Classical Film Theory and Art History*. New Brunswick: NJ: Rutgers University Press, 2003.
Felleman, Susan. *Art in the Cinematic Imagination*. Austin: University of Texas Press, 2006.
Jameson, Fredric. *The Geopolitical Aesthetic: Cinema and Space in the World System*. Indianapolis, IN: Bloomington University Press, 1992.
Jost, François. "Le Picto-Film." In *Cinéma et Peinture – Approches*, ed. Raymond Bellour, 109–22. Paris: Presses Universitaires de France, 1990.
Peucker, Brigitte. *Incorporating Images: Film and the Rival Arts*. Princeton, NJ: Princeton University Press, 1995.

Intertextuality; Hypertext

Allen, Graham. *Intertextuality*. London: Routledge, 2000.
———. *Roland Barthes*. London: Routledge, 2003.
Bakhtin, Mikhail. "Discourse in the Novel." In *The Dialogic Imagination: Four Essays by M.M. Bakhtin*, ed. Michael Holquist, 259–422. Austin: University of Texas Press, 1981.
———. *Problems of Dostoevsky's Poetics*. Minneapolis: University of Minnesota Press, 1984.
Barthes, Roland. "The Death of the Author." In *Image, Music, Text*, 142–8. New York: Noonday Press, 1977.

———. *Elements of Semiology*. New York: Hill and Wang, 1968.
———. "From Work to Text." In *Image, Music, Text*, ed. Roland Barthes, 155–64. New York: Noonday Press, 1977.
———. *S/Z*. New York: Hill and Wang, 1974.
———. "The Third Meaning." In *Image, Music, Text*, ed. Roland Barthes, 52–68. New York: Noonday Press, 1977.
Becker-Leckrone, Megan. *Julia Kristeva and Literary Theory*. New York: Palgrave Macmillan, 2005.
Bondanella, Peter. *Umberto Eco and the Open Text*. New York: Cambridge University Press, 1997.
Clayton, Jay, and Eric Rothstein. "Figures in the Corpus: Theories of Influence and Intertextuality." In *Influence and Intertextuality in Literary Theory*, ed. Jay Clayton and Eric Rothstein, 3–36. Madison: University of Wisconsin Press, 1991.
Clayton, Jay, and Eric Rothstein, eds. *Influence and Intertextuality in Literary Theory*. Madison: University of Wisconsin Press, 1991.
Delany, Paul, and George P. Landow, eds. *Hypermedia and Literary Studies*. Cambridge, MA: MIT University Press, 1991.
Eco, Umberto. *La definizione dell'arte*. Milan: U. Mursia, 1972.
———. *The Role of the Reader: Explorations in the Semiotics of Texts*. Bloomington: Indiana University Press, 1979.
Harpold, Terence. "Threnody: Psychoanalytic Digressions on the Subject of Hypertexts." In *Hypermedia and Literary Studies*, ed. Paul Delany and George P. Landow, 171–81. Cambridge, MA: MIT University Press, 1991.
Kristeva, Julia. *Desire in Language: A Semiotic Approach to Literature and Art*. New York: Columbia University Press, 1980.
———. "General Principles in Semiotics." Interview by Pierre Oulet and Charles Bauer. In *Julia Kristeva Interviews*, ed. Ross Mitchell Guberman, 179–87. New York: Columbia University Press, 1996.
———. "Intertextuality and Literary Interpretation." Interview by Margaret Waller. In *Julia Kristeva Interviews*, ed. Ross Mitchell Guberman, 188–203. New York: Columbia University Press, 1996.
———. *Revolution in Poetic Language*. New York: Columbia University Press, 1984.
Landow, George P. *Hypertext: The Convergence of Contemporary Critical Theory and Technology*. Baltimore, MD: Johns Hopkins University Press, 1992.
———. "What's a Critic to Do? Critical Theory in the Age of Hypertext." In *Hyper/Text/Theory*, ed. George P. Landow, 1–48. Baltimore, MD: Johns Hopkins University Press, 1994.
Landow, George P., ed. *Hyper/Text/Theory*. Baltimore, MD: Johns Hopkins University Press, 1994.

Landow, George P., and Paul Delany. "Hypertext, Hypermedia and Literary Studies: The State of the Art." In *Hypermedia and Literary Studies*, ed. Paul Delany and George P. Landow, 3–50. Cambridge, MA: MIT University Press, 1991.
Moi, Toril, ed. *The Kristeva Reader*. New York: Columbia University Press, 1986.
Moriarty, Michael. *Roland Barthes*. Cambridge: Polity, 1991.
Nielsen, Jacob. *Multimedia and Hypertext: The Internet and Beyond*. London: Academic Press, 1995.
Roudiez, Leon S. "Introduction." In *Desire in Language: A Semiotic Approach to Literature and Art*, ed. Julia Kristeva, 1–20. New York: Columbia University Press, 1980.
Smith, Ann Marie. *Julia Kristeva: Speaking the Unspeakable*. London: Pluto Press, 1998.
Stanford Friedman, Susan. "Weavings: Intertextuality and the (Re)Birth of the Author." In *Influence and Intertextuality in Literary Theory*, ed. Jay Clayton and Eric Rothstein, 146–80. Madison: University of Wisconsin Press, 1991.

Art History and Film Studies

Amishai-Maisels, Ziva. *Depiction and Interpretation: The Influence of the Holocaust on the Visual Arts*. Oxford: Pergamon Press, 1993.
Arcangeli, Francesco. *L'opera completa di Segantini*. Milan: Rizzoli, 1973.
Arici, Laura. "Schwanengesang in Gold: 'Der Kuß' – eine Deutung." In *Gustav Klimt*, ed. Toni Stooss and Christoph Doswald, 43–51. Stuttgart: Verlag Gerd Hatje, 1992.
Bailey, Colin B., ed. *Gustav Klimt, Modernism in the Making*. New York: Harry N. Abrams, 2001.
Bal, Mieke. "Dead Flesh, or the Smell of Painting." In *Visual Culture: Images and Interpretation*, ed. Norman Bryson, Michael Ann Holly, and Keith Moxey, 365–83. Hanover: Wesleyan University Press, 1994.
Baldacci, Paolo. *Betraying the Muse: De Chirico and the Surrealists*. New York: Paolo Baldacci Gallery, 1994.
———. *De Chirico: The Metaphysical Period 1888–1919*. Boston: Little, Brown, 1997.
Barilli, Renato. *Il Simbolismo: Parte I*. Milan: Fabbri, 1967.
Barnes, Rachel. *The Pre-Raphaelites and Their World*. London: Tate Gallery, 1998.
Bellonzi, Fortunato. *Il Divisionismo nella pittura italiana*. Milan: Fabbri, 1967.
———. "Note sull'arte e sulla cultura di Sartorio." In *Giulio Aristide Sartorio (1860–1932)*, 13–18. Rome: De Luca, 1980.
Bernadac, Marie-Laure. "Picasso 1953–1972: Painting as Model." In *Late Picasso: Paintings, Sculpture, Drawings, Prints, 1953–1972*, 49–64. London: Tate Gallery, 1988.

Bernheimer, Charles. *Decadent Subjects: The Idea of Decadence in Art, Literature, Philosophy, and Culture of the Fin de Siècle in Europe.* Baltimore, MD: Johns Hopkins University Press, 2002.
Bessy, Maurice. *A Pictorial History of Magic and the Supernatural.* London: Spring Books, 1964.
Blandeau, Agnès. *Pasolini, Chaucer, and Boccaccio: Two Medieval Texts and Their Translation to Film.* Jefferson, NC: McFarland, 2006.
Bohn, Willard. "Apollinaire and de Chirico: The Making of the Mannequins." *Comparative Literature* 27, no. 2 (1975): 153–65.
———. "Giorgio de Chirico and the Solitude of the Sign." *Gazette des Beaux Arts* 6, no. 117 (1991): 169–87.
Bordini, Silvia. "Scienza, tecnica e creatività artistica negli scritti di Gaetano Previati." *Ricerche di Storia dell'arte* 51 (1993): 40–51.
Bossaglia, Rossana. "Un'altra modernità: La fortuna di Klimt in Italia." In *Gustav Klimt*, ed. Serge Sabarsky, 33–40. Florence: Artificio, 1991.
Bougault, Valérie. "Klimt ou l'insatiable recherche de la beauté." *Connaissance des Arts* 630 (2005): 46–54.
Brown, Jonathan, ed. *Picasso and the Spanish Tradition.* New Haven, CT: Yale University Press, 1996.
Brummer, Hans Henrik. "The Böcklin Case Revisited." In *Kingdom of the Soul: Symbolist Art in Germany 1870–1920*, ed. Ingrid Ehrhardt and Simon Reynolds, 29–41. Munich: Prestel, 2000.
Brunette, Peter. *The Films of Michelangelo Antonioni.* Cambridge: Cambridge University Press, 1998.
Bryson, Norman. "Bacon's Dialogue with the Past." In *Francis Bacon and the Tradition of Art*, ed. Wilfried Seipel, Barbara Steffen, and Christoph Vitali, 311–16. Vienna: Kunsthistorisches Museum, 2004.
Bullen, J.B. *The Pre-Raphaelite Body: Fear and Desire in Painting, Poetry, and Criticism.* Oxford: Clarendon, 1998.
Canfora, Luciano. "Classicismo e fascism." In *Matrici culturali del fascismo Seminari promossi dal Consiglio Regionale Pugliese e dall'Ateneo Barese nel trentennale della Liberazione*, 85–111. Bari: Università di Bari, 1977.
Cappock, Margarita. "'The Chemist's Laboratory': Francis Bacon's Studio." In *Francis Bacon and the Tradition of Art*, ed. Wilfried Seipel, Barbara Steffen, and Christoph Vitali, 85–103. Vienna: Kunsthistorisches Museum, 2004.
———. "The Motif of Meat and Flesh." In *Francis Bacon and the Tradition of Art*, ed. Wilfried Seipel, Barbara Steffen, and Christoph Vitali, 311–16. Vienna: Kunsthistorisches Museum, 2004.
Carr, Dawson W., ed. *Velázquez.* London: National Gallery, 2006.
Cini, Vittorio. *Esposizione Universale di Roma, 1942.* Rome, 1942.

Clair, Jean, ed. *Picasso: Sous le soleil de Mithra*. Martigny, Switzerland: Fondation Pierre Giannada, 2001.

———. "The Self beyond Recovery." In *Lost Paradise: Symbolist Europe*, ed. Jean Clair and Pierre Theberge, 125–36. Montreal: Montreal Museum of Fine Arts, 1995.

Comini, Alessandra. *Gustav Klimt*. New York: George Braziller, 1975.

Cowling, Elizabeth. *Picasso: Style and Meaning*. New York: Phaidon, 2002.

Craig, Kenneth M. "Rembrandt's Slaughtered Ox." *Journal of the Warburg and Courtauld Institutes* 46 (1983): 235–9.

Daix, Pierre. *Picasso*. London: Thames and Hudson, 1965.

Daly, Nicholas. "The Woman in White: Whistler, Hiffernan, Courbet, Du Maurier." *Modernism/Modernity* 12, no. 1 (2005): 1–25.

Davies, Hugh, and Sally Yard. *Bacon*. New York: Abbeville Press, 1986.

Deleuze, Gilles. *Francis Bacon: The Logic of Sensation*. Translated by Daniel W. Smith. London: Continuum, 2003.

Delevoy, Robert. *Symbolists and Symbolism*. New York: Rizzoli, 1982.

Dick, Bernard F. "Adaptation as Archaeology: *Fellini Satyricon* (1969)." In *Modern European Filmmakers and the Art of Adaptation*, ed. Andrew Horton and Joan Magretta, 145–57. New York: Frederick Ungar, 1981.

Dijkstra, Bram. *Idols of Perversity: Fantasies of Feminine Evil in Fin-de-Siècle Culture*. New York: Oxford University Press, 1986.

Dorment, Richard. "Nocturnes." In *James McNeill Whistler*, ed. Richard Dorment and Margaret F. Macdonald, 120–2. London: Tate Gallery, 1994.

Dorment, Richard, and Margaret F. Macdonald, eds. *James McNeill Whistler*. London: Tate Gallery, 1994.

Druick, Douglas W. "Moreau's Symbolist Ideal." In *Gustave Moreau: Between Epic and Dream*, ed. Geneviève Lacambre, 33–9. Chicago: Art Institute of Chicago, 1999.

Druick, Douglas W., and Peter Kort Zegers. "Taking Wing, 1870–1878." In *Odilon Redon: Prince of Dreams 1840–1916*, ed. Douglas W. Druick, 74–117. New York: Harry N. Abrams, 1994.

Duncan, Alastair. *Art Nouveau*. London: Thames and Hudson, 1994.

Dupuis-Labbé, Dominique. "L'aréne, lieu de l'amour et du sang." In *Picasso: Sous le soleil de Mithra*, ed. Jean Clair, 29–32. Martigny, Switzerland: Fondation Pierre Giannada, 2001.

———. "Raphael and *La Fornarina*." In *Picasso Érotique*, ed. Jean Clair, 118–37. Munich: Prestel, 2001.

Ehrhardt, Ingrid, and Simon Reynolds, eds. *Kingdom of the Soul: Symbolist Art in Germany 1870–1920*. Munich: Prestel, 2000.

Eidt, Laura M. Sager. *Writing and Filming the Painting: Ekphrasis in Literature and Film*. Amsterdam: Rodopi, 2008.

Eisenman, Stephen. *Nineteenth Century Art: A Critical History*. New York: Thames and Hudson, 2002.
Escritt, Stephen. *Art Nouveau*. London: Phaidon, 2000.
Etlin, Richard A. "Nationalism in Modern Italian Architecture, 1900–1940." In *Studies in the History of Art*, vol. 29, ed. Richard A. Etilin, 89–109. Washington, DC: National Gallery of Art, 1991.
Fagiolo dell'Arco, Maurizio. "'Giuda bifronte', Giulio Aristide Sartorio tra 'critici d'arte, affaristi, preraffaeliti, donne senza sesso, uomini magniloquenti.'" In *Giulio Aristide Sartorio (1860–1932)*, 25–30. Rome: De Luca, 1980.
Fagiolo dell'Arco, Maurizio, and William Rubin, eds. *De Chirico: Essays*. New York: Museum of Modern Art, 1982.
Faxon, Alicia Craig. *Dante Gabriel Rosetti*. 1989; New York: Abbeville Press, 1994.
Finkelstein, Haim. *The Screen in Surrealist Art and Thought*. Aldershot: Ashgate, 2007.
Fliedl, Gottfried. *Gustav Klimt 1862–1918: The World in Female Form*. Cologne: Benedikt Taschen, 1991.
Foster, Hal. "Blinded Insights: On the Modernist Reception of the Art of the Mentally Ill." *October* 97 (2001): 3–30.
———. "Convulsive Identity." *October* 57 (1991): 19–54.
Foucault, Michel. "Las Meninas." In *The Order of Things*, ed. Michel Foucault, 3–16. New York: Vintage Books [Random House], 1994.
Galassi, Susan Grace. "Picasso in the Studio of Velázquez." In *Picasso and the Spanish Tradition*, ed. Jonathan Brown, 119–61. New Haven, CT: Yale University Press, 1996.
Gedo, Mary Mathews. *Picasso: Art as Autobiography*. Chicago: University of Chicago Press, 1980.
Gentile, Emilio. "The Myth of National Regeneration in Italy." In *Fascist Visions: Art and Ideology in France and Italy*, ed. Matthew Affron and Mark Antliff, 25–45. Princeton, NJ: Princeton University Press, 1997.
Gibson, Walter S. *Bruegel*. 1977; London: Thames and Hudson, 1991.
Gordon, Rae Beth. "Aboli Bibelot? The Influence of the Decorative Arts on Stéphane Mallarmé and Gustave Moreau." *Art Journal* 45, no. 2 (1985): 105–12.
Graves, Robert. *The Golden Ass of Apuleius*. New York: Pocket Books, 1954.
Greene, Naomi. *Pier Paolo Pasolini: Cinema as Heresy*. Princeton, NJ: Princeton University Press, 1990.
Hammer-Tugendhat, Daniela. "Judith." In *Klimt's Women*, ed. Tobias G. Natter and Gerbert Frodl, 220–4. Cologne: Dumont Buchverlag, 2000.
Heyd, Milly. *Aubrey Beardsley: Symbol, Mask and Self-Irony*. New York: Peter Lang, 1986.

Horton, Andrew, and Joan Magretta, eds. *Modern European Filmmakers and the Art of Adaptation*. New York: Frederick Ungar, 1981.
Huysmans, J.K. *Against the Grain*. New York: Albert and Charles Boni, 1930.
Jameson, Fredric. "High-Tech Collectives in Late Godard." In *Geopolitical Aesthetic: Cinema and Space in the World System*, ed. Fredric Jameson, 158–85. Indianapolis, IN: Bloomington University Press, 1992.
Jullian, Philippe. *Dreamers of Decadence: Symbolist Painters of the 1890s*. London: Phaidon, 1971.
Kaftal, George. *Saints in Italian Art*. Florence: Sansoni, 1952–85.
Kosinski, Dorothy M. "Gustave Moreau's 'La Vie de l'Humanité': Orpheus in the Context of Religious Syncretism, Universal Histories, and Occultism." *Art Journal* 46 (1987): 9–14.
———. *Orpheus in Nineteenth-Century Symbolism*. Ann Arbor, MI: Research Press, 1989.
Koval, Anne. *Whistler in His Time*. London: Tate Gallery, 1994.
Krauss, Rosalind. "The Master's Bedroom." *Representations* 28 (1989): 55–76.
Lacambre, Geneviève. "Catalogue." In *Gustave Moreau: Between Epic and Dream*, ed. Geneviève Lacambre, 42–274. Chicago: Art Institute of Chicago, 1999.
———. "Gustave Moreau and Exoticism." In *Gustave Moreau: Between Epic and Dream*, ed. Geneviève Lacambre, 15–20. Chicago: Art Institute of Chicago, 1999.
Lacambre, Geneviève, ed. *Gustave Moreau: Between Epic and Dream*. Chicago: Art Institute of Chicago, 1999.
Landini, Enrica Torelli. "Federico Faruffini tra l'esigenza realista e il rinnovamento della pittura di storia nel quadro dell'ottocento italiano." *Bollettino d'arte* 71 (1986): 124–31.
Larson, Barbara. *The Dark Side of Nature: Science, Society, and the Fantastic in the Work of Odilon Redon*. University Park: Pennsylvania State University Press, 2005.
Lawton, Ben. "The Storyteller's Art: Pasolini's *Decameron* (1971)." In *Modern European Filmmakers and the Art of Adaptation*, ed. Andrew Horton and Joan Magretta, 203–21. New York: Frederick Ungar, 1981.
Leutrat, Jean-Louis. "Godard's Tricolor." In *Jean-Luc Godard's* Pierrot le fou, ed. David Wills, 64–80. Cambridge: Cambridge University Press, 2000.
———. "Qu'est que c'est que cette histoire?" In *Cinéma et Peinture – Approches*, ed. Raymond Bellour, 123–35. Paris: Presses Universitaires de France, 1990.
Lucie-Smith, Edward. *Symbolist Art*. London: Thames and Hudson, 1972.
MacBean, James Roy. "Filming the Inside of His Own Head: Godard's Cerebral Passion." *Film Quarterly* 38, no. 1 (1984): 16–24.

Mantura, Bruno, ed. *Fabrizio Clerici*. Rome: De Luca Edizioni d'Arte, 1990.
———. "Pittura 'in distanza.'" In *Fabrizio Clerici*, ed. Bruno Mantura, 11–12. Rome: De Luca Edizioni d'Arte, 1990.
Marcus, Millicent. "Screening *The Decameron.*" *Studi sul Boccaccio* 20 (1991–2): 345–53.
Martin, Marianne B. "On de Chirico's Theater." In *De Chirico: Essays*, ed. Maurizio Fagiolo dell'Arco and William Rubin, 81–100. New York: Museum of Modern Art, 1982.
Martineau, Jane, and Andrew Robison, eds. *The Glory of Venice: Art in the Eighteenth Century*. New Haven, CT: Yale University Press, 1994.
Masden, S. Tschudi. *Art Nouveau*. London: Weidenfeld and Nicholson, 1967.
Mathews, Patricia. *Passionate Discontent: Creativity, Gender, and French Symbolist Art*. Chicago: University of Chicago Press, 1999.
Mazzocca, Fernando. "Visionario Divisionista: Previati a Milano." *Art e Dossier* 144 (1999): 21–6.
Meeks, Carroll L.V. "The Real *Liberty* of Italy – The *Stile Floreale.*" *The Art Bulletin* 43 (1961): 113–30.
Meighan, Judith. "In Praise of Motherhood: The Promise and Failure of Painting for Social Reform in Late-Nineteenth-Century Italy." *Nineteenth Century Art Worldwide* (Spring 2002): n.p.
Merleau-Ponty, Maurice. "Cézanne's Doubt." In *The Merleau-Ponty Aesthetics Reader: Philosophy and Painting*, ed. Galen A. Johnson and Michael B. Smith. Evanston, IL: Northwestern University Press, 1993.
———. "Eye and Mind." In *The Merleau-Ponty Aesthetics Reader: Philosophy and Painting*, ed. Galen A. Johnson and Michael B. Smith. Evanston, IL: Northwestern University Press, 1993.
Messina, Maria Grazia. "L'egida di Atena: La suggestione dell'arcaismo nell'opera di Klimt." In *Gustav Klimt*, ed. Serge Sabarsky, 45–54. Florence: Artificio, 1991.
Millesimi, Ines. "Catalogo." In *Fabrizio Clerici*, ed. Bruno Mantura, 185–217. Rome: De Luca Edizioni d'Arte, 1990.
Miracco, Renato. "From the Conquest of Light to Its Decomposition: Brief Notes on Italian Divisionism." In *Painting Light: Italian Divisionism 1885–1910*, ed. Renato Miracco, 11–14. Milan: Mazzotta, 2003.
Monferini, Augusta. "Prefazione." In *Fabrizio Clerici*, ed. Bruno Mantura, 9–10. Rome: De Luca Edizioni d'Arte, 1990.
Moxey, Keith. "Visual Studies and the Iconic Turn." *Journal of Visual Culture* 7 (2008): 131–46.
Natter, Tobias G., and Gerbert Frodl, eds. *Klimt's Women*. Cologne: Dumont Buchverlag, 2000.

Ofield, Simon. "Wrestling with Francis Bacon." *Oxford Art Journal* 24, no. 1 (2001): 113–30.
Ollinger-Zinque, Gisèle. "Belgium at the Turn of the Century: A Very International Nationalism." In *Lost Paradise: Symbolist Europe*, ed. Jean Clair and Pierre Theberge, 264–73. Montreal: Montreal Museum of Fine Arts, 1995.
Ornstein, Nadine M., ed. *Pieter Bruegel the Elder: Drawings and Prints*. New York: Metropolitan Museum of Art, 2001.
Paladilhe, Jean, and José Pierre. *Gustave Moreau*. New York: Praeger, 1972.
Pedrocco, Filippo. "Artists of Religion and Genre." In *Glory of Venice: Art in the Eighteenth Century*, ed. Jane Martineau and Andrew Robison, 267–84. New Haven, CT: Yale University Press, 1994.
Pepall, Rosalind. "*Cette Enchanteresse Matière*: Symbolism and the Decorative Arts." In *Lost Paradise: Symbolist Europe*, ed. Jean Clair and Pierre Theberge, 406–16. Montreal: Montreal Museum of Fine Arts, 1995.
Peucker, Brigitte. *The Material Image: Art and the Real in Film*. Stanford, CA: Stanford University Press, 2007.
Poli, Francesco. *La Metafisica*. Rome: Laterza, 1989.
Pollock, Griselda. "Woman as Sign in Pre-Raphaelite Literature." In *Vision and Difference: Femininity, Feminism, and Histories of Art*, ed. Griselda Pollock, 91–114. London: Routledge, 1988.
Portús, Javier. "Nudes and Knights: A Context for Venus." In *Velázquez*, ed. Dawson W. Carr, 56–67. London: National Gallery, 2006.
Posèq, Avigdor W.G. "The Hanging Carcass Motif and Jewish Artists." *Jewish Art* 16/17 (1990–91) 139–56.
———. *Soutine: His Jewish Modality*. Sussex: Book Guild, 2001.
Prater, Andreas. *Venus at Her Mirror: Velázquez and the Art of Nude Painting*. Munich: Prestel, 2002.
Praz, Mario. *The Romantic Agony*. Oxford: Oxford University Press, 1933.
Prettejohn, Elizabeth. "Beautiful Women with Floral Adjuncts: Rossetti's New Style." In *Dante Gabriel Rossetti*, ed. Julian Trueherz, Elizabeth Prettejohn, and Edwin Becker, 51–109. London: Thames and Hudson, 2004.
Previati, Alberto. *Gaetano Previati nelle memorie del figlio (1927)*. Ferrara: Liberty House, 1993.
Quesada, Mario. "Cronologia." In *Fabrizio Clerici*, ed. Bruno Mantura, 219–44. Rome: De Luca Edizioni d'Arte, 1990.
Rapetti, Rodolphe. *Symbolism*. Paris: Flammarion, 2005.
Repetto, Antonino. *Invito al cinema di Pier Paolo Pasolini*. Milan: Mursia, 1998.
Ricci, Franco. *Painting with Words, Writing with Pictures: Word and Image in the Work of Italo Calvino*. Toronto: University of Toronto Press, 2001.

Ricketts, Jill M. *Visualizing Boccaccio: Studies on illustrations of* The Decameron, *from Giotto to Pasolini*. Cambridge: Cambridge University Press, 1997.
Rowe, Kathleen K. "Romanticism, Sexuality, and the Canon." *Journal of Film and Video* 42, no. 1 (1990): 49–65.
Rubin, William S. *Dada and Surrealist Art*. New York: Harry N. Abrams, 1969.
Rubin, William S., ed. *Pablo Picasso: A Retrospective*. New York: Museum of Modern Art, 1980.
———. *Picasso and Portraiture: Representation and Transformation*. New York: Museum of Modern Art, 1996.
Rumble, Patrick. *Allegories of Contamination: Pier Paolo Pasolini's* Trilogy of Life. Toronto: University of Toronto Press, 1996.
Sabarsky, Serge, ed. *Gustav Klimt*. Florence: Artificio, 1992.
Schmitter, Amy M. "Picturing Power: Representation and *Las Meninas*." *Journal of Aesthetics and Art Criticism* 54 (1996): 255–68.
Schorske, Carl E. *Fin-de-Siècle Vienna: Politics and Culture*. 1961; Cambridge: Cambridge University Press, 1981.
Scotti Tosini, Aurora. "Divisionist Painters in Italy: Between Modern Chromatics and New Symbols." In *Lost Paradise: Symbolist Europe*, ed. Jean Clair and Pierre Theberge, 274–82. Montreal: Montreal Museum of Fine Arts, 1995.
Seidel, M., and R.H. Marijnissen. *Bruegel*. New York: G.P. Putnam's Sons, 1971.
Seipel, Wilfried, ed. *Pieter Bruegel the Elder at the Kunsthistorisches Museum in Vienna*. Milan: Skira, 1998.
Seipel, Wilfried, Barbara Steffen, and Christoph Vitali, eds. *Francis Bacon and the Tradition of Art*. Vienna: Kunsthistorisches Museum, 2004.
Sellink, Manfred. "The Very Lively and Whimsical Peter Bruegel: Thoughts on His Iconography and Context." In *Pieter Bruegel the Elder: Drawings and Prints*, ed. Nadine M. Ornstein, 57–65. New York: Metropolitan Museum of Art, 2001.
Silverman, Kaja, and Harun Farocki. *Speaking about Godard*. New York: New York University Press, 1998.
Snodgrass, Chris. *Aubrey Beardsley, Dandy of the Grotesque*. New York: Oxford University Press, 1995.
Snyder, Joel, and Ted Cohen. "Reflexions on *Las Meninas*: Paradox Lost." *Critical Inquiry* 7, no. 2 (1980): 429–47.
Sobchack, Vivian. *The Address of the Eye: A Phenomenology of the Film Experience*. Princeton, NJ: Princeton University Press, 1992.
———. *Carnal Thoughts: Embodiment and Moving Image Culture*. Berkeley: University of California Press, 2004.
Soby, James Thrall. *Giorgio de Chirico*. New York: Museum of Modern Art, 1955.

Spalding, Frances. *Whistler*. Oxford: Phaidon, 1979.
Staley, Allen. "Whistler and His World." In *From Realism to Symbolism: Whistler and His World*, 11–22. Philadelphia, PA: Philadelphia Museum of Art, 1971.
Steffen, Barbara. "The Representation of the Body: Velászquez – Bacon." In *Francis Bacon and the Tradition of Art*, ed. Wilfried Seipel, Barbara Steffen, and Christoph Vitali, 205–7. Vienna: Kunsthistorisches Museum, 2004.
Steinberg, Michael P. "*Die Walküre* and Modern Memory." *University of Toronto Quarterly* 74, no. 2 (2005): 704–13.
Stone, Marla Suzan. *The Patron State: Culture and Politics in Fascist Italy*. Princeton, NJ: Princeton University Press, 1998.
Stott, Rebecca. *The Fabrication of the Late Victorian Femme-Fatale: The Kiss of Death*. Houndmills, UK: Macmillan, 1992.
Stratton-Pruitt, Suzanne L., ed. *Velázquez's Las Meninas*. Cambridge: Cambridge University Press, 2003.
Sutton, Denys. *Nocturne: The Art of James McNeill Whistler*. Philadelphia: J.B. Lippincott, 1964.
Sylvester, David. "End Game." In *Late Picasso: Paintings, Sculpture, Drawings, Prints, 1953–1972*, 136–47. London: Tate Gallery, 1988.
———. *Looking Back at Francis Bacon*. London: Thames and Hudson, 2000.
Taylor, Hilary. *James McNeill Whistler*. New York: G.P. Putnam's Sons, 1978.
Thomas, Hugh. *Goya: The Third of May 1808*. London: Penguin, 1972.
Torjusen, Bente. *Words and Images of Edvard Munch*. Chelsea, VT: Chelsea Green, 1986.
Trueherz, Julian, Elizabeth Prettejohn, and Edwin Becker, eds. *Dante Gabriel Rossetti*. London: Thames and Hudson, 2004.
Ulivi, Ferruccio, "Sartorio scrittore." In *Giulio Aristide Sartorio (1860–1932)*, 19–23. Rome: De Luca, 1980.
Uno sguardo ad oriente. Istanbul: Istituto italiano di cultura, 1996.
Van Alphen, Ernst. *Francis Bacon and the Loss of Self*. London: Reaktion Books, 1992.
Varnedoe, Kirk. "Picasso's Self Portraits." In *Picasso and Portraiture: Representation and Transformation*, ed. William S. Rubin, 111–79. New York: Museum of Modern Art, 1996.
Vaughan, William. "Spiritual Landscapes." In *Kingdom of the Soul: Symbolist Art in Germany 1870–1920*, ed. Ingrid Ehrhardt and Simon Reynolds, 79–88. Munich: Prestel, 2000.
Vergo, Peter. "Between Modernism and Tradition: The Importance of Klimt's Murals and Figure Paintings." In *Gustav Klimt, Modernism in the Making*, ed. Colin B. Bailey, 19–39. New York: Harry N. Abrams, 2001.

Vigorelli, Valerio. "Previati e l'arte cristiana moderna." *Arte Cristiana* 87, no. 793 (1999): 313–16.
Visser, Romke. "Fascist Doctrine and the Cult of the *Romanità*." *Journal of Contemporary History* 27, no. 1 (1992): 5–22.
Waldberg, Patrick. *Fabrizio Clerici*. Bologna: Grafis, 1975.
Werner, Alfred. *Chaim Soutine*. New York: Harry N. Abrams, 1977.
Wildman, Stephen, and John Christian, eds. *Edward Burne-Jones: Victorian Artist-Dreamer*. New York: Metropolitan Museum of Art, 1998.
Wills, David, ed. *Jean-Luc Godard's* Pierrot le fou. Cambridge: Cambridge University Press, 2000.
Zatlin, Linda Gertner. *Aubrey Beardsley and Victorian Sexual Politics*. Oxford: Clarendon, 1990.

Jung

Henderson, Joseph L. "Ancient Myths and Modern Man." In *Man and His Symbols*, ed. C.G. Jung, 95–156. London: Aldus Books, 1964.
Jaffé, Aniela. ed. *C.G. Jung: Word and Image*. Princeton, NJ: Princeton University Press, 1979.
Jung, Carl Gustav. *Collected Works*. Vols. 5 and 9. London: Routledge and Kegan Paul, 1956.
———. "Picasso." In *The Spirit in Man, Art, and Literature*, ed. Carl Gustav Jung, 135–41. Princeton, NJ: Princeton University Press, 1966.
Jung, Carl Gustav, ed. *Man and His Symbols*. London: Aldus Books, 1964.
Kast, Verena. *The Creative Leap: Psychological Transformation through Crisis*. Wilmette, IL: Chiron, 1990.
Neumann, Erich. *The Great Mother*. Princeton, NJ: Princeton University Press, 1991.
Von Franz, Marie Louise. "The Process of Individuation." In *Man and His Symbols*, ed. Carl Gustav Jung, 160–229. London: Aldus Books, 1964.

The *Golem*

Idel, Moshe. *Golem: Jewish Magical and Mystical Traditions on the Artificial Anthropoid*. Albany: State University of New York Press, 1990.
Meyrinck, Gustav. "Les apparitions du golem." *midi/minuit Fantastique* 15–16 (1966–7): 6–14.
———. *The Golem*. New York: Frederick Ungar, 1964.

Index

Alma-Tadema, Lawrence, 94; *Apodyterium* by, 95; *Picture Gallery* by, 154n38; *The Tepidarium* by, 95
Angelucci, Gianfranco, 86
Anzalone, Vito, 145n52
Apuleius (*The Golden Ass*), 102, 155n62
L'Arte Moderna, 126
art history: *bambina diavolo* in, 70; butchered animal motif in, 58; Fellini referencing, xv, 20–1, 131–2; *Fellini Satyricon* references to, xv, 85, 94–5; *Fellini's Casanova's* references to, 115–17; *Giulietta degli spiriti* as turning point with, 15; *Giulietta degli spiriti* referencing, 4, 22–3, 41–2
art nouveau: fascism and, 40–1; *Giulietta degli spiriti's femmes fatales* and influence of, 38–46; ornamentation in, 40
auteur theory, intertextuality and, 159n26

Bachmann, Gideon, xv, 48
Bacon, Francis: butchered animal motif in work of, 61–2; Deleuze on, 63; Fellini referencing, 62–3, 69–70; *Figure with Meat* by, 61; *Painting 1946* by, 61, 65; presence in work of, 63–4; *Teorema* using work of, 65–6; *Three Studies for a Crucifixion* by, 61–3, 65, 69–70; *Two Figures* by, 65; *Two Figures in the Grass* by, 65
Bakhtin, Mikhail, 7, 9
Bal, Mieke, 60–1
Baldacci, Paolo, 118–19
bambina diavolo (devil-girl): in art history, 70; gaze of, 74–8; Jung and, 77–80; *Las Meninas* and, 71–5; psychic force of, 77; in *Simon of the Desert*, 150n72; in *Toby Dammit*, 70–80
Barthes, Roland, 9–10, 13, 83, 140n61; film still understanding of, 14; *Toby Dammit* referencing, 18
Beardsley, Aubrey, 43, 44
Bellour, Raymond, 14, 21
Bernhard, Ernst, 19–20, 33, 60, 148n28
Bessy, Maurice, 94
Betti, Liliana, 146n74
Blake, William, 78

Block-notes di un regista (*Fellini: A Director's Note-books*), 87–8
Blom, Ivo, 144n37
Böcklin, Arnold, 118, 132; Clerici referencing, 126–7; *Fellini's Casanova* referencing, 125–8, 161n61; *The Isle of the Dead* by, 125–8, 132, 161n69; *Odysseus and Calypso* by, 118, 127, 132; revival of interest in, 126
Bohn, Willard, 118–19, 124
Bondanella, Peter, 17, 18, 23, 53, 70, 76, 79, 93, 102, 122, 152n1
Bonitzer, Pascal, 5
Bruegel, Pieter: *Big Fish Eat Little Fish* by, 90; Fellini influenced by, 89–92; *Fellini Satyricon* referencing, 90–3; *Gluttony* by, 90–1; *Land of Cockaigne* by, 89, 91; *Lust* by, 89; *Parable of the Blind* by, 90; slit-bellied creatures in work of, 90–1; *Tower of Babel* by, 89, 91–3, 107
Bryson, Norman, 62
Buñuel, Luis, 150n72
Burke, Frank, 22, 38, 53–4, 85, 114, 160n38
butchered animal motif: in art history, 58; Bacon's use of, 61–2; in *Fellini's Roma*, 68–70; painting representations of death and, 60–1; in *Toby Dammit* deviating from script, 55–7, 60, 147n16
Byzantium, 94–101

Campari, Roberto, 115, 155n48
carnivalism, 9, 111–12
Casanova, Giacomo, 111
Ceruti, Giacomo, 116; *Portrait of a Young Nun* by, 115; *Women at Work* by, 115
Che Cosa sono le nuvole?, 72–3, 136n2

cinema. *See* film
circus, 4
Clerici, Fabrizio, 106; *Afternoon in Knossos* by, 107–8; *Latitudine Böcklin* by, 126–7; *The Minotaur Accuses His Old Mother* by, 109; *The Minotaur Publicly Accuses His Mother* by, 109; *Il Sonno Romano* (*Roman Slumber*) by, 110; *La Stanza* (*The Room*) by, 109–10
colour: Fellini on use of, 22; in *Fellini's Roma*, 69; *femmes fatales* and, 42, 43; *Giulietta degli spiriti*'s use of, 22, 25; in *La Ricotta*, 67; *Toby Dammit*'s use of, 55
comic strips, Fellini influenced by, 4, 20
Costa, Antonio, 115, 142n6, 149n54

Decadent aesthetics, 93–4, 100
Il Decameron, 91
de Chirico, Giorgio, 48; *Anxioius Journey* by, 103; *The Enigma of an Autumn Afternoon* by, 118; *The Enigma of the Oracle* by, 118–20, 124, 131–2, 159n30; Ernst influenced by, 50; *Fellini's Casanova* referencing, 117–24; mannequins in work of, 123–4; mythology in work of, 103; Roman sculpture in work of, 156n72; *The Seer* by, 123–4
De Laurentiis, Dino, 52, 111
Deleuze, Gilles, 63, 68, 149n40
Delville, Jean, *Orpheus* by, 82
De Santi, Pier Marco, 115
devil-girl. *See bambina diavolo*
dialogism, 7, 9, 64
Dijkstra, Bram, 23–4, 32
La dolce vita, 51; Jungian influence in, 78; painting featured in, 15

Donati, Danilo, 104, 152n3
dreams: Fellini's focus on, 20, 78–9; *femmes fatales* and, 45; Pre-Raphaelites interest in, 33
Dreams That Money Can Buy, 48–9
Dupuis-Labbé, Dominique, 121

Eco, Umberto, 17–18
To Edgar Poe, 81
effetto dipinto, 33, 69, 142n6
effetto pitturato: in *Fellini's Casanova*, 128–9; in *Fellini's Roma*, 69; in *Giulietta degli spiriti*, 22, 25–6; in *Toby Dammit*, 56–7
effetto quadro, 56, 69, 142n6
Eger, Raymond, 53
Eidt, Laura Sager, 5–6
ekphrastic fear, 8–9
ekphrastic hope, 8–9
ekphrastic indifference, 8
embodied aesthetic experience: in film, 10–11; in painting, 11–12
Ernst, Max: de Chirico's influence on, 50; "Desire" short film, in *Dreams The Money Can Buy*, 49; Fellini referencing, 48–9; *Giulietta degli spiriti*'s similarities to short film of, 49; *The Master's Bedroom* and perspective of, 50; *Two Children Are Menaced by a Nightingale* by, 49
"Eye and Mind" (Merleau-Ponty), 10–12

Falkenberg, Georg, 32
Farassino, Alberto, 16
Fare un film (Fellini), xv, 22, 76, 86–7
Faruffini, Federico, *La vergine al Nilo (Sacrifice of a Virgin to the Nile)* by, 33–6, 144n38

fascism: architecture and art inspired by, 41; art nouveau and, 40–1; Colosseum and, 92–3; Fellini's view of, 86; in *Giulietta degli spiriti*, 24–5, 86; parental coercion and, 153n6; and *Romanità*, 86–7
Fellini, Federico: adaptation views of, 53; art history references of, xv, 20–1, 131–2; Bacon referencing of, 62–3, 69–70; Bruegel referencing of, 89–92; carnivalism in work of, 9; character consistency with, 141n84; Colosseum opinion of, 92; on colour's meaning, 22; comic strips influencing, 4, 20; dreams focus on, 20, 78–9; Eco's influence on, 17–18; on 18th century painting, 117; Ernst referencing, 48–9; euphoria and liberation in work of, 133; fascism view of, 86; hyperlinks embedded by, 19; intertextuality of, 9–10, 12–13, 16, 132; Jungian influence on, 19–20, 33, 39, 146n72; magic and, 21; middle-period in work of, 15–16, 19, 133; occult, interest in, 94, 114; painting as conceived by, 7, 64, 131–5; Pasolini's joint influence with, 73–4; Pasolini's use of painting and film compared to, 68, 91; periodization of study on, 14–15; perspectival distortion used by, 50–1, 57; phallus and paintbrush in work of, 121–2; Picasso interest in, 76; Saul Steinberg's inspiration and friendship for, xvi, 135n7; Soutine's interest in, 60; on structuralism, 18; Symbolist painting approach of, 30–1, 83; tableau vivant and, 64; transmedialization and, 7–8;

Ulysses identification with, 120; Velázquez referencing of, 71; visual arts engagement of, xvi–xvii, 3–5; *The Voyage of G. Mastorna*'s 'economic problems for, 52–3

Fellini: A Director's Note-books. See *Block-notes di un regista*

Fellini Amarcord, 24

Fellini Satyricon, 15; art history references in, xv, 85, 94–5; *Block-notes di un regista* on making of, 87–8; Bruegel and *Romanità* in, 90–3; Byzantium and, 94–101; Decadent aesthetics in, 93–4, 100; female inorganic and dehumanized nature in, 97–101; *femmes fatales* in, 97; inertia represented in, 93; intertextuality in, 85, 110, 156n74; Jung and, 103–4; Klimt, referencing of, 95–6, 98–101, 152n3; labyrinth representation in, 109–10; military heroism deflated in, 88–9; Minotaur in, 101–10; occult and, 96–7; *Romanità* represented in, 85–93; sarcasm in, 92; visual over literal in, 152n1

Fellini's Casanova, 15; art history references in, 115–17; artist as pensive figure in, 119–20; basis of, 111; Böcklin, referencing of, 125–8, 161n61; carnivalism in, 111–12; Casanova as Golem in, 112–17; de Chirico, referencing of, 117–24; *effetto pitturato* in, 128–9; mannequins in, 123–4; mystical epiphany in, 120; romantic mysticism of, 115, 123, 127–8; sexual performance anxiety in, 122; Sutherland's facial features altered for, 112–13; Whistler, referencing of, 128–30

Fellini's Roma: butchered animal motif in, 68–70; colour in, 69; *effetto pitturato* in, 69; *Toby Dammit* compared to, 68–70

femmes fatales: colour and, 42, 43; dreams and, 45; in *Fellini Satyricon*, 97; *Giulietta degli spiriti*'s art nouveau influence with, 38–46; Jung and, 45; serpents and, 44–5

film: Barthes' understanding of stills in, 14; embodied experience in, 10–11; as engagement, 63–4; painting transformation of, 3. See also painting and film

"The Film Stilled" (Bellour), 14

film studies: units within, 14; visual arts in, xvii

fin-de-siècle painting, 93–4, 99

Foster, Hal, 51, 118

Foucault, Michel, 72–4

Francis Bacon: The Logic of Sensation (Deleuze), 63

Galassi, Susan, 75

Galleria nazionale d'arte moderna e contemporanea (GNAM), 27–8, 33

Gedo, Mary Mathews, 104

Geduld, Carolyn, 33–4, 47, 146n64

Geleng, Rinaldo, xv, 60, 121, 148n27, 160n43

Gentile, Emilio, 88

Giulietta degli spiriti (*Juliet of the Spirits*): art history references in, 4, 22–3, 41–2; Beardsley's work and, 43, 44; cinematic signifiers in, 45–6; colour use in, 22, 25; demons confronted in climax of, 46–7; *effetto pitturato* in, 22, 25–6; Ernst's short film similarities to, 49; fascism in, 24–5, 86; female insanity

representation in, 32; *femmes fatales* and colour in, 42, 43; *femmes fatales* in art nouveau interiors in, 38–46; Franz Von Stuck's visual signifiers in, 44–5; *I funerali di una vergine* referenced in, 27–30; intertextuality of, 29; Jung and Shadow archetype in, 47–8; Liberty style (*Stile Liberty*) in, 41; mysticism in, 30–1 36–37; Ophelia motif in, 32–7; perspectival distortion in, 50–1; race representations in, 38–9; Santa Christina of Bolsena and, 143n14; *La Sposa del Nilo*'s influence on, 36–7; Symbolist painting in childhood scenes in, 23–37; as turning point in referencing of art history, 15; *La vergine al Nilo* influence on, 34–6; water motif in, 39
GNAM. *See Galleria nazionale d'arte moderna e contemporanea*
Godard, Jean-Luc, 6–7
The Golden Ass (Apuleius), 102, 155n62
Golem, *Fellini's Casanova* and, 112–17
Le Golem, 113, 158n16
Grand Hotel, 145n60
The Great Mother (Neumann), 122–3
Grimaldi, Alberto, 52, 111
Guazzoni, Enrico, 33, 36–7, 144n38

Hébert, Ernest, 32
Henderson, Joseph L., 102, 156n70
heteroglossia, 7, 9, 64, 133
Histoire de la Peinture Surréaliste (Jean), 33, 126
Hogarth, William, 116, 161n61; *Southwark Fair* by, 159n25
Hughes, Eileen, 104

hyperlinks, 13; definition of, 139n54; in *Fellini's Casanova*, 128–30; Fellini's use of, 19; of Rembrandt's *Slaughtered Ox* in *Toby Dammit*, 57–60
hypertext, 13

icon-archetype, 151n87
Idel, Moshe, 114
intertextuality: American compared to French definitions of, 138n33; auteur theory and, 159n26; of Fellini, 9–10, 12–13, 16, 132; in *Fellini Satyricon*, 85, 110, 156n74; in *Giulietta degli spiriti*, 29; Kristeva's view of, 16; *lexia* of, 13; post-structuralist theory and, 15–16; in *Toby Dammit*, 54, 83; in *Toby Dammit* with Symbolist painting, 80–3

Jean, Marcel, 33, 126
Jewish mysticism, 114, 158n8
Joyce, James, 16–19
Juliet of the Spirits. See Giulietta degli spiriti
Jullian, Philippe, 94–5, 152n3
Jung, C. G., 102, 141n91, 146n64, 156n65, 156n68; anima archetype and, 78; *bambina diavolo* and, 77–80; *La dolce vita*, influence of, 78; Fellini influenced by, 19–20, 33, 39, 146n72; *Fellini Satyricon* and, 103–4; female aspect of male psyche in, 122; *femmes fatales* and, 45; *Giulietta degli spiriti* and Shadow archetype of, 47–8; *mandalas* and, 79; Minotaur and, 157n83; on Picasso, 150n68; *Toby Dammit*, influence of, 77–80

Kerchbron, Jean, 113
Kezich, Tullio, xv
Khnopff, Fernand, 31–2; *Of Animality* by, 95
Klimt, Gustav, 95–6, 101, 152n3; *Judith I* by, 98–9; *Medicine* by, 99; *Water Serpents I* by, 100
Kristeva, Julia, 9–10, 68, 131; author concept of, 138n30; intertextuality view of, 16

Landow, George, 13
lexia, 13
Longhi, Pietro, 115

magic, 21
magic circles (*mandalas*), 79
Man and His Symbols (Jung), 20, 48, 77–9, 102, 104–5, 141n91, 156n65
mandalas (magic circles), 79
The Material Image (Peucker), 140n61
Las Meninas, 3–4; gaze in, 74–6; Pasolini using, 72–3; Picasso's version of, 75–7; *Toby Dammit*'s use of *bambina diavolo* and, 71–5
Merleau-Ponty, Maurice, 10–12, 57
Meyrinck, Gustave, 113–14
La mia Rimini (Fellini), 120
midi/minuit Fantastique, 113–14, 158n7
Millais, John Everett, 33; *Ophelia* by, 32, 34, 144n37
Minotaur: Clerici's series on, 106–10; in *Fellini Satyricon*, 101–10; hero myth and, 102, 105; Jungian reading of, 157n83; in Picasso's work, 104–6, 109; Shadow archetype and, 105; surrealist conception of, 108–9
Mitchell, W. J. T., xvii, 8
Moravia, Alberto, 152n3

Moreau, Gustave: *The Apparition* by, 100; *Salomé Dancing before Herod* by, 100
Moxey, Keith, 21
Munch, Edvard, *Vampire* by, 43

Neumann, Erich, 45, 122–3
Never Bet the Devil Your Head (Poe), 52
The New World (Steinberg), xvi

occult, 94, 96–7, 114
Opera aperta (Eco), 17
Ophelia motif, in *Giulietta degli spiriti*, 32–7
Orpheus decapitation, 80–3
Otto e mezzo, 15, 138n30

painted effect. See *effetto pitturato*
painting: butchered animal motif for representations of death with, 60–1; in *La dolce vita*, 15; *effetto pitturato*, 22, 25–6; embodied experience in, 11–12; Fellini on 18th century, 117; Fellini's concept of, 7, 64, 131–5; film transformation into, 3; *fin-de-siècle*, 93–4, 99; Pasolini using, 65–7; phallus and paintbrush in, 121–2; "realness" and, 13; in *La Ricotta*, 67–8; *sémiotique* and, 131–2; in *Toby Dammit*, 66; for visual communication, xvii. See also Symbolist painting
painting and film: Fellini's compared to Pasolini's use of, 68, 91; filmmakers commonly discussed with, 6–7; function of, 134, 162n2; power-relation systems in, 5–6; suspension of movement in, 67; tableau vivant in, 6–7
painting-like shot (*plan-tableau*), 5

Pasolini, Pier Paolo, 6–7, 136n2; Fellini's joint influence with, 73–4; Fellini's use of painting and film compared to, 68, 91; *Las Meninas* used by, 72–3; painting in work of, 65–7
Peucker, Brigitte, 140n61
Picasso, Pablo, 75–7; art and eroticism in work of, 121; Fellini's interest in, 76; Jung on, 150n68; *Las Meninas, after Velázquez* and, 75–7; *Minotauomachy* by, 104, 109, 157n83; Minotaur in work of, 104–6, 109; *Raphael and La Fornarina* by, 121
A Pictorial History of Magic and the Supernatural (Bessy), 94
"pictorial turn," xvii
Picture Theory (Mitchell), xvii
plan-tableau (painting-like shot), 5
Poe, Edgar Allan, 52–3
Poséq, Avigdor, 58–60
Positif, 158n7
post-structuralist theory, intertextuality and, 15–16
Praz, Mario, 93
Pre-Raphaelites, 31, 33
Previati, Gaetano: *Assunzione* by, 28; female types of, 28–9; *I funerali di una vergine* by, 27–30; *Maternità* by, 27; religious art interests of, 28, 30
Pygmalion myth, 121, 160n38

race, in *Giulietta degli spiriti*, 38–9
Rapetti, Rudolph, 144n28
Raynal, Maurice, 148n27
Red Book (Jung), 47
Redon, Odilon, 81–2, 151n90
Rembrandt, *Slaughtered Ox* by, 57–60
representational hybridity. See tableau vivant

Richter, Hans, 48, 156n65
La Ricotta: colour in, 67; painting in, 67–8; tableau vivant used in, 66
Riva, Valerio, 136n1
The Role of the Reader (Eco), 17
Romanità: Colosseum as emblem of, 92; fascism myth of, 86–7; *Fellini Satyricon* representing, 85–93; *Fellini Satyricon* with Bruegel referencing of, 90–3; military heroism and, 88–9; resentment and, 86
Rondi, Brunello, 4, 59
Rops, Félicien, 97
Rossetti, Dante Gabriel, 31–2

Santa Christina of Bolsena, 143n14
Sartorio, Giulio Aristide, *La Gorgone e gli eroi* (*The Gorgon and the Heroes*) by, 43
Savinio, Alberto, *The Oracle* by, 118
Segantini, Giovanni, *Vanità* (*Vanity*) by, 43
sémiotique, 10, 83–4, 131–2
serpents, *femmes fatales* and, 44–5
severed head symbolism, 80–3
Shadow archetype: Jung and, 47–8; Minotaur and, 105
Sharrett, Christopher, 54, 84, 147n10, 147n16
Simon of the Desert, 150n72
Smith, Ann Marie, 132
Snyder, Joel, 74
Sobchack, Vivian, 11, 63–4
Soutine, Chaim, 57, 59–60, 148n27
La Sposa del Nilo (*The Spouse of the Nile*), 36–7
The Spouse of the Nile. See *La Sposa del Nilo*
Stamp, Terence, 65
Steinberg, Saul, xvi, 135n7
Stile Floreale. See art nouveau

Stile Liberty. *See* art nouveau
structuralism, 18–19
Stubbs, John, 116
Il Surrealismo, 159n30
surrealists, 33
Sutherland, Donald, 112–13
Sylvester, David, 121
Symbolist painting: Fellini's approach to, 30–1, 83; female types of, 26–9; in *Giulietta degli spiriti*'s childhood scenes, 23–37; of Khnopff, 31–2; mysticism in, 30–1; Orpheus decapitation and, 80–3; Pre-Raphaelites influencing, 31; *Toby Dammit*'s intertextuality with, 80–3

tableau vivant (representational hybridity): Fellini and, 64; in film, 6–7; in *La Ricotta*, 66
Tassone, Aldo, 130, 133
Teorema: Bacon's work in, 65–6; *Toby Dammit* compared to, 65–6, 68
Toby Dammit, xvi; adaptation of, 52–3; *bambina diavolo* in, 70–80; Barthes' influence on, 18; butchered animal motif shot deviating from script in, 55–7, 60, 147n16; colour's use in, 55; crucifixion referenced in, 59; *effetto pitturato* in, 56–7; *Fellini's Roma* compared to, 68–70; intertextuality of, 54, 83; Joyce's *Ulysses* in, 16–19; Jungian influence on, 77–80; mandalas in, 79; *Las Meninas, after Velázquez* and, 75–7; *Las Meninas* and, 71–5; omitted scene in, 17; Orpheus decapitation and, 80–3; painting in, 66; perspectival distortion in, 57; Redon's influence in, 81–2, 151n90; Rembrandt's *Slaughtered Ox* hyperlink to, 57–60; structuralism commentary in, 18–19; Symbolist painting intertextuality in, 80–3; *Teorema* compared to, 65–6, 68; white ball image in, 77–9
Topor, Roland, 159n26
Tosi, Piero, xv–xvi, 56
transmedialization, 5–8

Ulysses (Joyce), 16–19
Une Semaine de Bonté, 49

Van Watson, William, 84, 151n87, 162n2
Velázquez, Diego, 3–4; *Las Meninas* by, 71–7; mirror imagery in work of, 74–5
visual arts: Fellini's engagement with, xvi–xvii, 3–5; film studies with, xvii; *Man and His Symbols* focus on, 20. *See also* film; painting
Von Stuck, Franz: *Sensuality* by, 44–5; *Sin* by, 44–5
The Voyage of G. Mastorna, 52–3

Waldberg, Patrick, 108–9
Welles, Orson, 66–7
Whistler, James McNeill, 128, 130; *Nocturne in Blue and Gold: Old Battersea Bridge* by, 129
Writing and Filming the Painting: Ekphrasis in Literature and Film (Eidt), 5–6

Zapponi, Bernardino, 53, 116–17

www.ingramcontent.com/pod-product-compliance
Lightning Source LLC
Chambersburg PA
CBHW030320080526
44584CB00012B/641